30974572

mL

**Books are to be ret    ed on or**
**the last da      low.**

The Great Rebuildings of Tudor and Stuart England

# The Great Rebuildings of Tudor and Stuart England

## Revolutions in architectural taste

Colin Platt

*University of Southampton*

UCL

PRESS

© Colin Platt, 1994

First published in 1994 by UCL Press

UCL Press Limited
University College London
Gower Street
London WC1E 6BT

The name of University College London (UCL) is a registered trade mark used by
UCL Press with the consent of the owner.

ISBN:
1-85728-315-5  HB
1-85728-316-3  PB

**British Library Cataloguing-in-Publication Data**
A catalogue record for this book is available from the British Library.

**Library of Congress Cataloging-in-Publication Data**

Platt, Colin.
   The great rebuildings of Tudor and Stuart England : revolutions in
architectural taste / Colin Platt.
      p.   cm.
   Includes bibliographical references and index.
   ISBN 1-85728-315-5 (HB) : $65.00. — ISBN 1-85728-316-3 (PB)
$21.95
      1. Architecture, Domestic—England.  2. Architecture. Renaissance—
England.  3. Architecture, Modern—17th, 18th centuries—England.
I. Title.
NA965.P83   1994
728'.0942'09081—dc20                                          94-32050
                                                                CIP

Typeset in Bembo.
Printed and bound by
Butler & Tanner Ltd., Frome, England.

# Contents

# Preface

The Great Rebuilding of Tudor and Stuart England, as Professor Hoskins first described it, has not survived the test of later criticism. And it has long been clear that a one-off Great Rebuilding, however generously defined, never happened. Even the term "Great Rebuilding" can be seriously misleading, for it focuses too much attention on a capriciously surviving housing stock, to the loss of other evidence of changing tastes. Yet the fact remains that the disposable wealth of English property-holders of every known degree – from the gentry and nobility of Lawrence Stone's well-known books to the more modest yeomen farmers of Hoskins's seminal article – was rising very rapidly during Elizabeth's reign, and that the quality of their housing rose with it. Hoskins used a broad brush. But those widespread contemporary improvements to which his study drew attention – the flooring-over of medieval open halls, the insertion of stairs and chimneys, the glazing of windows and the accumulation of household goods – all commonly happened when he said they did, between 1570 and 1640. "If something *looks* like a duck and *sounds* like a duck", common sense dictates, "it probably *is* a duck." By that measure at least, Professor Hoskins's original Great Rebuilding is still persuasive.

Hoskins never wrote about a second Great Rebuilding. Instead, he stopped his own Rebuilding when the Civil War began, and clearly viewed that costly struggle as a watershed. So indeed it proved to be for the many formerly prosperous landowning families who had built before the war, but who found themselves impoverished by the conflict.

Those were the post-war rebuilders, unable to afford better, who turned most readily to new-style "compact boxes" as a remedy. Even so, it was less the Civil War which promoted such developments than the re-opening of continental Europe to English travellers. "He that will know much out of this great Book, the World, must read much in it", wrote Richard Lassels, author of a popular *Voyage of Italy* (1670). The urban terrace, the compact villa and the double-pile house – each the direct ancestor of houses we build today – were all learnt abroad by Grand Tour travellers.

Travel abroad would certainly have meant less, had it not been for changing attitudes in the homeland. Traditional hospitality, already on the wane in late-medieval England, continued its decline throughout this period. The once extended English family became nuclear. But while social historians have long debated these changes, very few have looked to architecture as a source. Their neglect is my opportunity. To quote Lassels again: "Well; if others have written upon this subject, why may not I? They did the best they could, I believe: but they drew not up the Ladder after them."

It was Roger North who once said that "he that hath no relish of the grandure and joy of building is a stupid ox". On change, he was equally direct. "Here ended the antique order of housing", said North of his youth, writing of the reign of Charles II. It was a half-truth only, restricted to gentry-builders such as himself. And the *new* order of housing, which North announced, took its time trickling downwards through the classes. Nevertheless, the way we live now has more in common with the life-style of Roger North's generation than he himself admitted sharing with his father. It was the second Great Rebuilding, far more than the first, which departed from the past and broke new ground.

I also break new ground in giving special prominence to that Rebuilding in my book. But I owe an obvious debt to earlier writers on this subject, not least to Professor Hoskins who began it all. Another debt is to John Harris, whose collected contemporary views of English country houses, in *The artist and the country house* (1985), taught me more about the expectations of Restoration gentry-builders than any written source save Roger North. My third debt is to Claire Donovan, who gave me Harris's book – with so much else.

Southampton 1994

## CHAPTER 1

# The First Great Rebuilding

*"Then down with old houses and new set in their places"*

When W. G. Hoskins, back in 1953, identified a revolution in housing in late Tudor and Stuart England, calling it the "Great Rebuilding", he found general support for his thesis. Indeed, the material evidence of an improved housing stock from the reign of Elizabeth I is still there for everybody to see. But like many of the most significant historical insights – R. H. Tawney's precisely contemporary "rise of the gentry" was another[1] – the Hoskins model drew criticism by its very simplicity. Tawney had put dates on the gentry's rise, between 1558 (the accession of Elizabeth) and 1640 (the Civil War). And it was Hoskins's similarly narrow dating of the Great Rebuilding to 1570–1640 which then attracted the most agonizing debate. While aware of regional differences, including the relative backwardness of the north-west, Hoskins had chosen to make little of them. "Elsewhere in England", he had observed, "from Cornwall up to Lancashire, and from Herefordshire across to Suffolk, the evidence for the Great Rebuilding between 1570 and 1640 is abundant and inescapable".[2] And that, with reservations, remains the case.

Most of those reservations concern individual localities, where major rebuildings occurred both earlier and later than Hoskins's model. In parts of rural Wales, for example, substantial late-medieval farmhouses required little remodelling until the mid-seventeenth century at the earliest.[3] There was a fifteenth-century Great Rebuilding in West Kent and the Sussex Weald; another in the Halifax area of the Yorkshire Pennines; a third (less well marked but anticipating many of the characteristics of later sixteenth-century modernizations) in rural Devonshire.[4] More commonly, the terminal date of Hoskins's Rebuilding has been extended throughout the seventeenth century and even into the next, while the seductive clarity of his original proposition has been challenged and obscured by many later candidates for "Great Rebuildings". Certainly, there were central counties, Oxfordshire among them, where a general rebuilding came only towards the end of Hoskins's housing boom, in the four decades from 1600 to 1640.[5] In Gloucestershire, surviving evidence of dated buildings suggests that the major regional rebuilding took place through six decades, between 1630 and 1690, interrupted only in the 1640s by civil war.[6] Comprehensive recent inventories of the early-modern housing stock of West Yorkshire and Glamorgan have shown, in each case, a moving frontier of modernization, dictated by relative wealth. Here improvements came first to the prosperous regions – to the clothier communities of Upper Calderdale, next to Halifax, and to the arable farmers of South Glamorgan – peaking in the seventeenth century. They came last to the more remote Yorkshire Dales and to the Gower Peninsula, where the pastoralists of the one and the smallholders of the other had little surplus wealth for rebuildings of any consequence before the mid-eighteenth century or later.[7]

Plainly, an accumulated surplus on the land was what enabled remodellings to take place. But that was never the only reason for new building. Indeed, so individual were the circumstances of even major rebuildings, occurring at so many different periods, that one of the most effective critics of the single Great Rebuilding thesis has counselled its abandonment altogether. "Instead of a thesis of a Great Rebuilding at some specific period", Machin wrote in 1977, "we require a theory of building history which will explain (with regional variations in timing) the medieval preference for impermanent building, the emergence of permanent vernacular building in the fifteenth century, its extension and the successive rebuildings of vernacular houses from the late sixteenth to the early eighteenth century, and the replacement of vernacular by 'polite' or 'pattern-book' architecture from the mid-eighteenth century."[8] No such general theory has since emerged. And if it ever does, it will have to take account of the capricious tastes and irrational purchasing preferences of real people. "Then began costly apparel", wrote an anonymous critic of Southampton society in 1582, after a brief trading boom. "Then down with old houses, and new set in their places:

ed 1576, this substantial merchant's house in Mermaid Street (Rye) is typical of many Elizabethan
ings in towns all over the country, "for the houses where the fathers dwelt could not content their
".

for the houses where the fathers dwelt could not content their children. Then must every man of good calling be furnished with change of plate, with great store fine linen, rich tapestry, and all other things which might make show of bravery. And who then but Hampton for fine diet and great cheer."[9] No solid achievement nor lasting worth promoted the rebuilding of Elizabethan Southampton, as insubstantial as a paradise of fools.

Five years earlier, in 1577, William Harrison had first published the *Description of England* which has since been used as a primary source by all historians of the Tudor Rebuilding.[10] Harrison, rector of Radwinter (Essex) from 1559 until his death in 1593, wrote – as would his contemporary, the Southampton burgess – about the social changes he had personally witnessed. But he was not the first observer, even of his own generation, of "excessive" building at his time and in his region. In Essex again, Sir Thomas Smith (d.1577) spent many years improving his two houses at Theydon Mount. And it was Smith, soon an obsessive builder in his own right, who had already noticed "our buildings that we have here in England of late days, far more excessive than at any time heretofore". Smith wrote in the context of a major monetary crisis in the mid-century. And he defended building in his *Discourse of the commonweal of this realm of England* (1549) as the provider of employment and new wealth in the locality, "for all the expense of buildings for the most part is spent among ourselves and among our neighbours and countrymen as among carpenters, masons, and labourers". However, what he had liked less well was the contemporary passion (as he saw it) for imported "trifles" of all kinds, fuelling inflationary pressures:

> Of the which sort I mean glasses as well looking as drinking as to glass windows, dials, tables, cards, balls, puppets, penhorns, inkhorns, toothpicks, gloves, knives, daggers, owches [buckles], brooches, aglets [pendants], buttons of silk and silver, earthen pots, pins, points, hawks' bells, paper both white and brown, and a thousand like things that might either be clean spared or else made within the realm sufficient for us. . . . [For] there is no man can be contented now with any gloves than is made in France or in Spain; nor kersey, but it must be made of Flanders dye; nor cloth, but French or frizado; nor owche, brooch, nor aglet, but of Venice making or Milan; nor dagger, sword, nor girdle, or knife,

but of Spanish making or some outward country; no not as much as a spur, but that is fetched [bought] at the Milaners [milliners].[11]

Sir Thomas Smith, for all his impatience with modern ways, was a leading intellectual: some said, the cleverest man of his day. William Harrison, while similarly inclined to look with favour on the past, was a shrewd observer of the contemporary scene and no mere *laudator temporis acti*. In such company, the Southampton critic carries more weight. As nostalgic as the others for a hardier era – "when this town chiefly flourished . . . maintained by Gallies, Argosies and other Strangers' Shipping" – he very likely had the present rightly measured.

Certainly, he would have agreed with Harrison's judgement that "if ever curious [fanciful and expensive] building did flourish in England, it is in these our years". And although Harrison was then describing the houses of the nobility, he makes it clear that he saw the same obsessions spreading downwards. Of furnishings, he observes:

The furniture of our houses also exceedeth and is grown in manner even to passing delicacy; and herein I do not speak of the nobility and gentry only but likewise of the lowest sort in most places of our South Country that have anything at all to take to. Certes [assuredly] in noblemen's houses it is not rare to see abundance of arras, rich hangings of tapestry, silver vessel, and so much other plate as may furnish sundry cupboards, to the sum oftentimes of £1,000 or £2,000 at the least, whereby the value of this and the rest of their stuff doth grow to be almost inestimable. Likewise in the houses of knights, gentlemen, merchantmen, and some other wealthy citizens, it is not geason [uncommon] to behold generally their great provision of tapestry, Turkey work [carpets and tapestries], pewter, brass, fine linen, and thereto costly cupboards of plate, worth £500 or £600 or £1,000 . . . But as herein all these sorts do far exceed their elders and predecessors, and in neatness and curiosity the merchant all other, so in time past the costly furniture stayed there, whereas now it is descended yet lower, even unto the inferior artificers and many farmers, who . . . have for the most part learned also to garnish their cupboards with plate, their joint [carpentered] beds with tapestry and silk hangings, and their tables with carpets and fine napery.[12]

*2  Among "the multitude of chimneys lately erected  .  .  .
within their sound remembrance", the old men of Radwinter
(Essex) would certainly have been thinking of this late
sixteenth-century chimneystack (the shafts are modern) at
Grange Farm, just south of their village.*

When Harrison wrote, population everywhere was on the increase.
But this had led, in his own Essex parish, to the "enhancing of rents"
and to the "daily oppression [by fines] of [landless] copyholders". Alongside these, the freeholding yeoman and the secure tenant farmer had
never had it so good. It had all happened in less than a generation:

There are old men yet dwelling in the village [Radwinter] where I
remain which have noted three things to be marvellously altered in
England within their sound remembrance . . . One is the multitude of chimneys lately erected, whereas in their young days there
were not above two or three, if so many, in most uplandish towns
of the realm (the religious houses and manor places of their lords
always excepted, and peradventure some great personages), but

each one made his fire against a reredos in the hall, where he dined and dressed his meat. The second is the great (although not general) amendment of lodging, for (said they) our fathers, yea, and we ourselves also, have lien full oft upon straw pallets, on rough mats covered only with a sheet, under coverlets made of dagswain or hap-harlots (I use their own terms), and a good round log under their heads instead of a bolster or pillow. If it were so that our fathers or the goodman of the house had within seven years after his marriage purchased a mattress or flock-bed, and thereto a sack of chaff to rest his head upon, he thought himself to be as well lodged as the lord of the town, that peradventure lay seldom in a bed of down or whole feathers, so well were they contented and with such base kind of furniture . . . Pillows (said they) were thought meet only for women in childbed. . . . The third thing they tell of is the exchange of vessel, as of treen [wooden] platters into pewter, and wooden spoons into silver or tin. For so common were all

*3 This fourteenth-century farmhouse at Barrington (Cambridgeshire) was almost completely rebuilt in the early seventeenth century, when the original open hall (at the centre) was floored-over and new brick chimneys were inserted both in the hall and its cross-wings.*

sorts of treen stuff in old time that a man should hardly find four pieces of pewter (of which one was peradventure a salt) in a good farmer's house.[13]

In the 1570s, the new comforts identified by the old men of Radwinter had yet to reach every part of the nation. Harrison himself observed the fact, commenting that furniture was "not very much amended as yet in some parts of Bedfordshire [the next-but-one county] and elsewhere further off from our southern parts". But Harrison's qualification – his "not as yet" – is crucial evidence of the rising curve of expectations. The English had long lived well by any standards less exacting than their own. Aristocrats, in particular, had developed nice personal habits in the Late Middle Ages.[14] But so also, according to their degree, had the merchantmen, the farmers and the "inferior artificers" – better lodged than they had ever been before.[15] It was a visiting Dutch

*4 Gullege, near East Grinstead (Sussex), is among the more lavish of the early seventeenth-century rebuildings, where a late-medieval timber-framed hall-house has been provided with brick chimneystacks and with a costly stone show-front in the new fashion.*

physician, Levinus Lemnius, who said it all. He came from the house-proud Netherlands, and this certainly influenced his judgement. But, as a doctor, he was concerned to explain the good health of the English – how they "be so freshe and cleane coloured". One reason, he surmised, was their diet – their "exquisite meat". Another was their lodging, "in so holesome and healthfull ayre", for:

> The neate cleanlines, the exquisite finenesse, the pleasaunte and delightfull furniture in every poynt for household, wonderfully rejoysed mee; their chambers and parlours strawed over with sweete herbes refreshed mee; their nosegayes finely entermingled wyth sundry sortes of fragraunte floures in their bedchambers and privy roomes, with comfortable smell cheered mee up and entire-lye delyghted all my sences.[16]

Levinus Lemnius, when he visited England in 1560, found its fresh-faced citizens in good health. But in 1557–59, just before he came, there had been a major mortality crisis. The cause and nature of that crisis have been disputed, and estimates of the death-rate vary widely. Some place it as low as five per cent; others as high as twenty. However, no one now doubts the severity of a country-wide epidemic more de-structive than any other in "Tawney's Century".[17] Such mortalities are a reminder that Tudor England was still catastrophe-prone. But they were exceptional at the time, and have remained so ever since. Furthermore, they interrupted a period of slow but sustained growth which saw the doubling of population between 1538 (when the parish registers begin) and 1656 (the start of three decades of decline).[18] Steady growth of this kind, although nothing out of the ordinary today, furnished the context in Elizabethan England for an entirely new level of entrepreneurial activity, encouraged by deliberate state protectionism. Before the end of the sixteenth century, in response to both demand and public policy, many of those "trifles" still imported in Sir Thomas Smith's day – from vessel and window glass to knitted stockings, from ribbons and buttons to linen and lace – were being manufactured and traded in the home country. And there was another generation of such activity still to come, before the economic disruption of the Civil War.[19]

Some of these commodities – among them window glass and linen – feature prominently in probate inventories from the 1580s. They are most in evidence, of course, in the grander households: those of the aristocracy, the gentry and the richer merchants. But they can also occur quite commonly by this time in the surviving record of comparatively modest estates, confirming the development of a consumer society and the descent of "costly furniture . . . yet lower". Consumption, moreover, was kept artificially high by a web of inherited conventions. "There is no day", wrote Harrison of the English nobility, "wherein they have not only beef, mutton, veal, lamb, kid, pork, cony, capon, pig, or so many of these as the season yieldeth, but also some portion of the red or fallow deer, beside great variety of fish and wild fowl".[20] It was the good "country custom", so the rural squire, Vincent, explained to the doubting Londoner, Valentine, "to bid every man welcome . . . keeping our gates open for all men, and feeding many tall fellows to attend upon us: also relieving all beggars, that ask at our gates, with money, meat, or both".[21] Valentine saw less merit in such promiscuous hospitality: "for my part, I had rather have a little with quiet, than a great deal with such confusion". Yet even in 1579, when this popular dialogue was first published, more would have joined Vincent in defending rural values than could have applauded the urban sophistries of his opponent. The "worship of a Gentleman", from time out of mind, had required a "whole Army or Camp" of serving-men. Better that, by far, than that "being out of service, they [the jobless rustics] should fall into offence of law . . . for well you know, it were great pity to see a tall fellow to climb a gibbet".[22]

A country gentleman such as Vincent could afford such liberality because the economy marched entirely in his favour. True, not everybody ate as well as Vincent and his kind,[23] and even the landed squire had his anxieties. "I pray you tell me", Vincent mused, touching the fate of his younger sons, "how many ways a man, without land, may gain his living Gentlemanlike". "There are three ways to do it", came Valentine's reply. "There is Art [Learning and the Law], Industry [Adventure], and Service".[24] But none of these paths kept the family intact at home, and Vincent took persuading of their utility. No problem was more widely acknowledged by his class. As Thomas Wilson put it:

I cannot speak of the number of younger brothers, albeit I be one of the number myself, but for their estate there is no man hath better cause to know it, nor less cause to praise it; their state is of all stations for gentlemen most miserable . . . [for] such a fever hectic hath custom [primogeniture] brought in and inured amongst fathers, and such fond desire they have to leave a great show of the stock of their house, though the branches be withered, that they will not do it [give land to their younger children], but my elder brother forsooth must be my master. He must have all, and all the rest that which the cat left on the malt heap.[25]

Thomas, one of "the rest", got what the cat left. His brother, the "young Master", took all. And while there were other cadets of noble families who were treated more generously – among them Sir Francis Hastings, politician, estate manager, brother of Henry, Earl of Huntingdon (d. 1595), and builder of the great house at North Cadbury [26] – the advantage was almost always with the main stem.

5 *Francis Hastings, a younger son, was yet able to build this "fair beautiful house" at North Cadbury (Somerset), which he embellished with the heraldic glass of his father and brother, Earls of Huntingdon. He sold the house to a friend in 1596.*

That advantage could be huge. The strong influence of agricultural improvement and technological revolution on Elizabethan England can no longer be taken for granted.[27] But there is no doubting the growing wealth of the propertied classes, whether landowners, lawyers or merchants. Squire Vincent exemplifies the first of these; Thomas Wilson, scholar and civil lawyer, the second; John Isham, a London mercer, the

11

third. Each saw landed wealth as the most socially acceptable of riches, for "to meddle with any Mechanical manner of living" (Valentine again) is "a thing utterly unfit for Gentlemen". [28] Additionally, in taking the long view of family honour by the acre, they also bought security and decent profits. John Isham, the mercer, purchased the manor of Lamport, in his native Northamptonshire, while still making his way in the City. And though it was the future of his heirs that chiefly motivated that purchase, he nevertheless ran Lamport as a business. Ten years later, in 1570, Isham launched the first of his many enclosures. Like other landowners, he "pull[ed] down houses and destroy[ed] towns, leaving only the church to pen his sheep in".[29] But dedication to profit and to his books of account cost Isham little in the esteem of his neighbours. After 1577, he returned to Lamport for good, and "would nott by any meanes be drawne agayn to dwell at London; . . . heer he continued till his dyinge day, havinge as great good frendship of gentelmen in this his cuntry, as he had before of Cytesens".[30]

Such friendships grew, in Midland England, on the gentry's community of interests. Isham was a successful encloser. And most notorious of Tudor enclosers were the Spencers of Althorp, another Northamptonshire family. It was Robert, first Lord Spencer (d.1627), who was "reputed to have by him the most money of any person in the kingdom". And while this was certainly an exaggeration – as was any talk of large-scale depopulations as the necessary price of this wealth – it was overflowing Spencer surpluses which built the first Althorp House and that packed Great Brington Church with Spencer monuments. Neither service at Court nor the profits of war contributed to Spencer riches. Instead, they made their fortunes on the land. Living comparatively modestly, they reinvested their profits in new enclosures and further purchases, meeting the needs even of their younger sons by buying them manors of their own.[31]

It was "ideal conditions" for landowning graziers in Tudor England that allowed this durable family of gentlemen farmers to rise into the greater nobility. By the time those conditions altered for the worse, the Spencers were seriously rich. Simultaneously, the older established Treshams of Rushton suffered comparative impoverishment. But buffeted by Fortune though this third Northamptonshire family proved to be, it nevertheless showed considerable resilience. The Treshams had prospered especially in the fifteenth century, serving monarchs "under whom they were dignified with many noble offices and advancements and lived in high prosperity, and at whose feet and in whose service sundry of them (even hundreds of years since) have faithfully ended their lives with honour in the field".[32] It was the quiet-living squire, John Tresham (d.1521), who built the greater part of Rushton Hall. Then John's only son, Thomas (d.1559), was again a royal servant, well placed to take advantage of the suppression of the religious houses to extend and consolidate his estates. Thomas was succeeded by his grandson, another Thomas. And it was in Thomas II's time, from 1559 to 1605, that the winds began to blow chill. As Catholic gentry, resolute preservers of a suspect faith, the Treshams aligned themselves with the losers. Sir Thomas paid large fines, causing him to sell family land, for his recusancy. He was damaged in other ways by his conservatism. Whereas it was acceptable enough in the *parvenu* Lord Spencer that he should "make a carefull frugality the fuell of his continuall hospitality", it remained the pride of the Treshams, as "heirs of ancient wealth", to bid all comers welcome without stint – "to the number of twenty, forty, yea sometimes an hundred". Then there were Sir Thomas's building enterprises, replete with Catholic symbolism and especially dear to his heart, at Rushton (the Triangular Lodge) and in the New Building at Lyveden; there was the reckless and profligate life-style of the "young master" and next heir, Francis; and there were portions to be found for another eight Tresham children, of whom Margaret (married to a nobleman) would receive almost £4000 – "a portion seldom or never heard of for a knight, having no small number of children . . . to give in marriage with a baron's son and heir". If Sir Thomas survived these trials still in reasonable shape, it was because he also (like his neighbours) became a grazier. It was at Rushton, especially, that he enclosed arable for pasture, doubling the size of an already large flock during the final two decades of the century.[33]

Enclosure was no panacea even for the Treshams. It was neither as complete in Tudor England as some contemporaries were persuaded, nor as harmful to the interests of poor commoners.[34] What was never in serious doubt was its profitability. In the next century – the "golden age" of enclosure – productivity gains per acre enclosed would rank "somewhere between substantial and formidable".[35] And although the more "formidable" of those gains, doubling receipts on the land, were probably rare before the seventeenth century, successful enclosures had

*6  The Triangular Lodge at Rushton (Northamptonshire) was built in 1594–97 by the recusant landown
Sir Thomas Tresham, as an emblem of the Trinity and a defiant memorial to the old religion.*

long since shown the way to future profit. With prices firm and receipts rising faster than costs, it was a good time for landowners of all conditions. That young rakehell Roger Manners, Earl of Rutland (1588–1612), could compete in "absurdly conspicuous expenditure" with his friend Henry Wriothesley, Earl of Southampton (1581–1624), because their land was growing in value all the time. When Earl Roger spent £60 on the gold embroidery of a single suit, and when Earl Henry lost 18,000 crowns on a few games of tennis, they knew that (in the long run) they could afford it.[36]

Not all their expenditure was irresponsible. Both Earl Roger and Earl Henry (under Roger's influence) were ironmasters, investing considerable sums in new equipment. Later, after only limited success with iron, Henry would find the capital also for a tin mill.[37] In neither case did the returns from these ventures ever remotely compare with the earls' more conventional landed receipts. But they showed another, less familiar side of Tudor England: the world of the entrepreneur and the "projector". Iron-founding, on which other great landed families – the Sidneys, the Sackvilles and the Pelhams – were likewise contemporaneously engaged, was only one of a large number of similar enterprises, filling the void in domestic production that Sir Thomas Smith had only lately deplored.[38] It was by profitably combining sheep-farming and lead-mining that the Derbyshire Eyres of Hassop built a comfortable fortune from their estates. Among those who bought the Eyres' wool were the Huguenot weavers of fashionable "new draperies". Rowland Eyre's lead furnished the raw material for the pewterers, the glaziers and the roofers of rural England, all riding on the crest of the Great Rebuilding.[39]

Ultimately, what supported these industries was growing consumer demand. But new invention was also a spur. Cast iron was an innovation of the already busy iron industry, at once in demand for cannon founding. In the fashion trade, the lighter and more colourful "new draperies" – the serges and perpetuanas, bays and says, camlets, callimancoes and "Norwich stuffs" – swiftly captured their own large sector of the market. Both industries had benefited from the skills of immigrant craftsmen, fleeing from religious persecution on the Continent. And in window-glass also, the key to the Rebuilding, it was largely imported expertise which attained that rarest and most welcome of all commercial ends – more products of higher quality, at lower cost.[40]

7 *Imported glass technology, which simultaneously cut the cost of window-glass and improved its qual* *enabled the builder of this big Jacobean farmhouse at Glemsford (Suffolk) to make a window of every wall.*

One of the more important advances in glass-making – the conversion to coal as fuel – had yet to be made. It was pioneered in the 1610s at such coalfields-based glassworks as Wollaton, near Nottingham, where it was Sir Percival Willoughby's ambition, whether in this way or another, to restore the family fortune recently squandered on the building of Wollaton Hall.[41] But many-windowed Wollaton, built for Sir Francis Willoughby in the 1580s, was already a splendid show-case for the new industry. That industry, even in Sir Percival's day, was barely a generation old. Thomas Charnock's lament that "as for glassmakers, they be scant in the land" was still the literal truth in 1557.[42] Ten years later, Jean Carré was granted his glass-making patent, and it was he who first attracted Lorrainer and other master glass-makers to settle permanently in England. From the 1570s, as more Lorrainers arrived, furnaces were built in scattered parts of the country, and prices – kept high in the past by transport costs – began to fall almost at once.[43] At Sir John Thynne's Longleat in the 1570s, as at Sir Francis Willoughby's Wollaton in the

*ollaton Hall (near Nottingham) was built in the 1580s for the wealthy coal-owner, Sir Francis oughby; but at such huge cost that it almost ruined his heirs. In this painting of 1697 by Jan Sibe-, prominence is given to Wollaton's fine new formal gardens, made in the French style for Sir Thomas.*

–following decade, prodigies of glazing were now possible. The market responded with enthusiasm.

Demand for the product was already firm. Huge painted windows, almost always of expensive imported glass, had attracted wealthy patrons since the Late Middle Ages. Accordingly, when Sir Thomas Lucy placed an order for heraldic glass at Charlecote (Warwickshire) in 1558, there was nothing exceptional in his decision. What was more unusual was his source. Lucy was the patron, and became the friend, of Nicholas Eyffeler, once of Osnabrück in Westphalia, who "did leave his native Countrey, and made a free Denizen in England, inhabited here within this Borough of Warwick, where using the mistery of Glazier painfully, and walking in his vocation uprightly, God so blessed the increase of his goods and good name, that he was preferred to be one of the principall Burgesses of this Borough".[44] Some panels of Eyffeler's glass – painted arms of Queen Elizabeth and of the Acton and Lucy families – survive at Charlecote Park. They compare in quality with the still near-complete heraldic display of the Fairfax Chamber at Gilling Castle.[45]

Nicholas Eyffeler, rich and ripe in years, died on 14 January 1592. He was survived another five years by his widow, Katherine, his long-term partner in pious works. Jointly, they had already provided, before Eyffeler's death, for the building of an almshouse for four "oulde maydens of Warwicke that by reason of age or impotencie are not able to get their livinge". It was this foundation, known as Eyffeler's Charity, which led to the preservation of an archive. Among the papers kept by the Charity's trustees – along with particulars of sale, with building accounts, with funeral expenses, leases, schedules of fittings and much else – was a complete inventory of Eyffeler's goods and furnishings, compiled on 25 January 1592. In his old age, this successful immigrant glazier had lived very comfortably, with much pewter on his buffet, with "change of plate" in his chest, and with "great store fine linen" in his presses. Eyffeler's bed alone, in the private parlour by the hall, was valued at a lordly £7.[46] But such attention to personal comfort was only to be expected of a "man of good calling" in the 1590s. And the more particular interest of Eyffeler's inventory is the record it preserves of his glass. Eyffeler had some vessel-glass in stock in 1592, including "drinkinge glasses, urynalls & glasse bottels", kept in "the little Glasse Howse at home" and valued at an estimated £5. But glass-manufacture was not Eyffeler's trade, and the principal items in his "Store Howse of

Glasse" were cases of plain glass, ready for his brush, and the lead for creating his "story" panels. The old man was probably still working near the day of his death, for there were "storyes, bookes, armes, quarryes, boxes, bordes, paynes of glass and implements" listed in his "workinge howse" and "drawinge clositt".[47]

Eyffeler's premises evidently doubled as his showroom. In 1621, when the house was leased for a second time, a new schedule was compiled of its fittings. There were still many examples of the master's work: in the hall, six "armes" in the street-side window and another three against the yard, "whereof twoe paines of Mr Eyffelers armes and all the paines painted"; in the parlour, "fyve story peeces of Jacob, fower paines of glasse in another windowe there & fower drawne peeces in yt"; in the chamber reserved for Sir Thomas Lucy (builder of Charlecote) and his heirs, "foure stories, one paine of Sir Thomas Lucy his armes, twoe other paines all wrought, one the late Quenes armes"; in "Mr Wrytes Chamber" (probably Christopher Wright of Hopsford, another patron), "fyve storyes of tyme, one paine of Mr Writes armes, one paine of glass behinde the chymney, one paine against the dore with an armes in yt"; in "Mr Clarkes chamber", "fower paines of glasse there whereof one Mr Actons armes".[48]

Already, 30 years earlier, even the Eyffelers' smallest family chamber had been glazed. The "nyne little paines of glasse" of the "Maydes Chaumber" may have been part of Eyffeler's stock-in-trade in 1592, for there was also a "chest to carrye quarryes of glasse in". However, the function of the "glass windoew & casementes" of the "Chamber over the Parlour", appraised separately at 13s 4d, is obvious enough. And the same must apply to the "foure paynes of glasse & a casemente" included with the only furnishings – two "little bedsteades with joyned heades" and their bedding – of the "little Chaumber over the Halle".[49] There was no mention of glass in the Eyffelers' kitchen and other service rooms in 1592. But full glazing throughout the house, if it was not installed already, must have followed soon afterwards. In "the Kitchin & Kitchin Entry", in 1621, there were:

Eleaven paines of glasse in the entry, eleaven paines of glasse & one iron casement in the kytchin, fyve paines of glasse in the well howse, fiftene paines of glasse in the longe howse, fower paines of glasse in the milke howse, fower paines of glasse in the next howse to yt, twoe paines of glasse with armes on the steares and on the same steares in all six paines of glasse.

Up under the roof, there were "twoe paines of glasse over the topp of the steares . . . twentye fyve paines of glasse in the chamber over Mr Writes chamber and one casement of wood; eleaven paines of glasse and twoe woodden casements in the cock lofte [attic]".[50]

The Eyffelers' Warwick townhouse, spectacularly glazed from the ground floor up, had few immediate parallels in Elizabethan England. But others of their class and affluence, able to take advantage of falling prices, were beginning to substitute glass for the old-style lattice, cloth and shutters ("window leaves") of at any rate their principal apartments. Already in 1577, William Harrison had seen the future and found it good:

Of old time our country houses [farmhouses] instead of glass did use much lattice, and that made either of wicker or rifts of oak in checkerwise. I read also that some of the better sort in and before the times of the Saxons . . . did make panels of horn instead of glass and fix them in wooden calms. But as horn in windows is now quite laid down in every place, so our lattices are also grown in to less use, because glass is come to be so plentiful and within a very little so good cheap, if not better than the other. . . . only the clearest glass is most esteemed; for we have diverse sorts, some brought out of Burgundy, some out of Normandy, much out of Flanders, beside that which is made in England, which would be so good as the best if we were diligent and careful to bestow more cost upon it, and yet as it is each one that may will have it for his building.[51]

One who might and had was William Wilcox, a Worcester cloth-worker, who died that very same year. Wilcox's probate inventory, taken on 16 July 1577, recorded "3 foote of glas and a frame to it" in his hall, valued together at two shillings.[52] Yet glazing of this kind was still exceptional outside the towns, and far from usual even within them. Of only 11 Oxfordshire inventories that record window-glass before 1590, none was earlier than the 1580s and just one was the inventory of a country-man. Moreover, glazing remained partial in every case. Thomas Smith (d.1587), an Oxford blacksmith, had "glasse in the windors" of his hall and of no fewer than three other chambers – the "middle Chamber", the "litle Chamber" and the "higher Chamber". More typical were the two Banbury small-town households, inventoried in 1588, where there was glass only in the hall and private chamber. Here Henry Pilkington, a rich haberdasher of Banbury, had "wenscot & Glase" in his hall and "glase in the tow wyndoes" of his "Chamber over the shope". John Addams, a miller, had "glasse in the wyndowes" of his hall and of his parlour.[53]

The fashion in Oxfordshire, even so, was ahead of other regions. Early in the next century, the only Staffordshire households to have glass in their windows were those of the more prosperous citizens of Lichfield.[54] There was much "glasse in the windowes" of Richard Sweete's house in Exeter, inventoried in 1591:

> Inprimis in the fore Chamber a windowe of nyne lightes glased, in the parlor one windowe glased of vj lightes transide [transomed], in the halle one windowe of vj lightes glased, in the gallery one windowe of one lighte glased, in the chamber over the parlor a transide windowe of vj lights glased, in the kitchen a windowe of vij lights halfe glased, in the forechamber over the kitchinge a windowe of vij lights, in the studie a window of iiij lightes glased, in the highest forechamber a windowe of iiij lightes, in the butterie a windowe of one lighte glazed, all of which glasse amounteth unto Clviij foote. 52s 8d.[55]

But outside the city, in Devonshire as a whole, glass was barely known before the 1640s.[56]

Glass windows, novel and appealing, track the course and speed of the Rebuilding. But they disappear from the inventories as glass becomes more common. Nor are they always a reliable witness to the growing affluence of this period, touching all but the truly disadvantaged. "Glass-houses [furnaces] are in plenty here", observed a German traveller to England in 1598, noting the phenomenon in his journal.[57] But, when he wrote, the glass-makers had yet to reach many parts of the realm, which were nevertheless advancing in other ways. If Thomas Blampin, of Gittisham (Devon), had "window leaves" – but was still without glass – in his hall and chamber in 1623, he was not on that account a poor man. There was much pewter in Blampin's hall, on his death in January that year, valued at £3 16s, with "2 dozen of Napkyns 6 bord clothes [tablecloths] 8 paire of Sheetts & 4 pair of Pilloties [pillow cases]", worth £6. Blampin had 20 silver spoons, valued at £6 13s 4d; his clothes alone – "the Apparrell of his body" – were worth £10, more than many individual estates.[58]

Blampin may be compared with another Devon yeoman, Thomas Spicer, who died just four months later. Spicer's goods and chattels, appraised at £376 on 20 May 1623, were worth only about a third of Blampin's assets. Yet he had spent as much or more, in later life, on luxuries of the same sort, allotting them an even higher proportion of his wealth. Along with the great bed and other furnishings of Spicer's "Chamber over the Hall" were "seven Coverlettes six payre of Blanckettes, three Carpettes & seaven Cushions £4 8s; his wearinge apparell £13 14s 8d; one White bole of silver and one dosen of silver spoones, one Carrick Cupp [mazer?] tipt with silver £5; six payre of sheets eight borde Clothes, three dosen of table napkins, five payre of pillowties ten Towells, & one side bordcloth £5 7s 4d". The pewter in Spicer's hall, valued at £3 10s, included "two dosen & one Platter of tynn three basins seven Porringers, one Dosen of Tynnen dishes, one dosen & ten saucers, one pottle [half-gallon measure] one quart pott, fower pottes, two saltes three Candlestickes, one funell, all of tynne", with a similarly large quantity of domestic brassware.[59]

Spicer and Blampin were both prosperous yeoman farmers. They came from the same county and were direct contemporaries. They shared a common hunger for plate and linen. But there direct comparisons must end. The valuation of goods has never been an exact science. Then, as now, it could often be wide of the mark. There is an account of 1597, among the Eyffeler papers at Warwick, of the prices subsequently fetched by the glazier's goods. Nicholas Eyffeler's executor asked allowance in that year "for some certaine household stoofe sold under the pryces sett down in the inventory [of 1592]". Most of the differences recorded were trivial enough, beginning with: "Item solde to Mr Leay one bucket rope & cheane preased as 6s 8d & sold for vjs, I ask alowance viijd". However, they included also some quite serious miscalculations, from the "sixe candlestickes weaing 15 poundes and sayd by the inventory to weay 40 pounds praysed at 20s" (sold subsequently to William Fox for 11 shillings) to the "one hundred of lead that was over reckoned in weaing of the same lead and sett downe in the inventory for 13c. & 7 poundes & it was in truth but 12c. & 2 poundes & so according to the rate I aske alowance viij*s* vj*d*".[60]

Such miscalculations add to the difficulty of making true comparisons between inventories.[61] Appraisers were seldom expert. The dead are always unique. Nevertheless, there are two broad trends which unquestionably stand out in the many inventory series now in print. One is towards the increase, through the period as a whole, in the number and specialized use of family rooms. The other establishes a growing personal accumulation of household goods, showing both in the *amount* of those furnishings listed on a death and – less universally – in the *proportion* of the testator's wealth given over to them. William Harrison is most often quoted on the second of these trends, but had something to say also on the first. There was a clear separation, Harrison noted in his *Description* of 1577, in the farmsteads of Essex, where:

> The mansion houses of our country towns and villages are builded in such sort generally as they have neither dairy, stable, nor brewhouse annexed unto them under the same roof (as in many places beyond the sea and some of the north parts of our country) but all separate from the first and one of them from another.[62]

It was a separation which had begun well before his time, even within the "mansion house" itself, to be recorded in some of the very earliest probate inventories. At Worcester, for example, it is these first generation inventories, starting in the 1530s, which confirm that the city's houses were already "as large before 1550 as Derby and Coventry houses were to become after the [Great] Rebuilding. Cellars and attics were as common in Worcester in the mid-Elizabethan period as they were to be in other towns a century later, while the single-storey medieval house had virtually disappeared by 1570".[63] In the next generation, when William Wilcox died, his Worcester inventory of 1577 explains his pioneering interest in window-glazing (p. 20). There is a special significance, in a Worcester context, in William's given occupation as a "walker". High quality Worcester broadcloth – the "finest cloth in the worlde", boasted one of its makers in 1576 – was still being "walked" (fulled) by foot in William's time.[64] And William himself was among those Worcester tradesmen who profitably combined the crafts (distinct at other centres) of walker, weaver and clothier. Small wonder that William was better off than most, having pewter in his hall and fine linen in the "best chamber", where he slept. He had banished the bed from the ground-floor parlour, where others still kept it, having two further bedchambers besides his own.[65]

There was no cause for complete rebuilding in every case. When Nicholas Hill, baker of Witney (Oxfordshire), partitioned his town-house in the 1580s, he had an over-large hall to divide. Glazing the hall and furnishing it with a chimney, he floored the apartment over, creating two new bedchambers above. On the ground floor, part of the hall was retained for cooking and eating. The remainder was partitioned, for Nicholas's inventory of 1590 records "twoo Joyned particions (the over-parte of eache of them Lattised) which make the Buttrye that is in the same Haule with the Settles and shelves in the same Buttrye". Nicholas kept his pewter in the buttery and his "naperye" (linen) in a well-furnished parlour – still with its great bed – also partitioned off "within the haule". Over the brewhouse, a fourth big chamber was furnished with two canopied beds and held "all his wearing apparell".[66]

The bed in the parlour of Nicholas Hill's house was in no way out of place in 1590. Two decades later, in the big and comfortable townhouse of Hugh Robinson, a Worcester brewer, the parlour was still being used in just that fashion. Yet Robinson, in that brief time, had begun to look like a conservative. James Hill – "of the parishe of Saynte Clemmentes within the citie of Worcester, tanner" – had predeceased Robinson by six years. But Hill's house, in 1602, already had three purpose-built bed-chambers (above his hall, parlour and kitchen). And the Worcester tanner, although sufficiently affluent by the standards of his day, was only about a third as wealthy as the brewer.[67] If change was most likely in the go-ahead communities, it was not just the rich who led the way. In Late Elizabethan Ipswich, as was still the case elsewhere, there were beds in many parlours; but not in all. William Eyreman, who was without a bed in his parlour when he died in 1589, was a poor tailor of Ipswich, appraised at little more than £5. The "Chamber over the Hall" was probably his own, and he had two other upper chambers also furnished with beds (but nothing else).[68]

In striking contrast to the tailor's austere furnishings were the house-hold effects of Widow Goodeere, who was worth almost £700 on her death in 1628, and whose favourite colour was green. Ann Goodere, also of Ipswich, was again one of those, ever more frequent in her time, who had furnished her "best parlour" exclusively as a sitting room, with two tables (one square and one long), a livery cupboard, "five greene frindged high stooles, one great greene frindged chaire, twoe greene chaires frindged, three greene Cushions frindged silke and three greene Cushions frindged Cruell [with crewel, a worsted yarn]". She had slept in the "parlour chamber" ("one great posted bedstead . . . one greene Rugg . . . one high greene chaire and twoe lowe greene frindged stooles"), and had a second bedroom also in the "litle parlour chamber", with "posted beddstead", chest and chair, and with "a paire of Say [serge] greene curteins". She and her late husband, Michael Goodeere "deceased", had placed their wealth on show in other ways. Ann Goodeere's plate was worth, "in a generall estimate", £32 8s. Her chest of pewter, appraised at only £3, was comparatively empty. But "all the Linnen in the Chest" came to another £10. And the largest composite entry in the widow's 1628 inventory covered "all her wearing apparrell, linnen and wollen, together with all her Jewells", valued at £42 12s.[69]

It is a remarkable fact that between a third and a half of Ann Goodeere's listed assets were counted on her death as "household stuff". But that high proportion, unthinkable today, was far from exceptional in her period. Consumer demand had been rising for some decades. Take the case of Thomas Gyll, of Wardington (near Banbury), a representative yeoman farmer of Late Tudor England, warmed by the "good gigantic smile o' the brown old earth". Gyll was comfortably off in 1587, but not wealthy. Yet almost half his inventoried possessions, when he died that year, were held neither as farm stock nor in loans or "readie monie", but in some of the least essential of household goods. Appraised at barely a tenth of Widow Goodeere's worth, Gyll had nevertheless found the means to purchase "Eyght & twentye peces of pewter, fowre candlestickes two saltes & A basen, fyve sylver sponnes" (for his hall); "six brasse potes, Two brasse pannes & two kettles" (for his kitchen); and "Thirtene pare of sheetes & A halfe . . . fowre Table clothes three towels & one dosen of table napkins with all other Aprye ware [aprilware, napery]" (for his parlour and chamber), and much else.[70]

"That is a poor peasant", said one German visitor about the English in 1585, "who has no silver-gilt salt-cellars, silver cups, and spoons".[71] In 1598, "their beds are covered with tapestry, even those of farmers", remarked another.[72] Both descriptions fit Thomas Gyll, but would not have suited Edward Kempsale, Gyll's near-neighbour at Great Bourton, who in every other way was Gyll's equivalent. Kempsale, like Gyll, was a yeoman farmer. "They both", it has been claimed, "had almost the same numbers of livestock and farm equipment, and although their crop acreages are not recorded (because both inventories were taken in the winter) these appear to have been about the same also."[73] What divided them was the space of 30 summers, coinciding with some of the best harvests of the century. Much, in that interval, had changed. In 1560, Kempsale's hall was his kitchen, and he had just one other chamber, where he slept. But Gyll had a kitchen distinct from the hall, and a parlour as well as a chamber. Where Gyll had "Thirtene pare of sheetes & A halfe", Kempsale had only three. There were no "table napkins" in Kempsale's house and no silver spoons. Gyll had 28 pewter platters; Kempsale just eight. The treen vessels ("6 dysshes 6 trenchers and a ladle") of Kempsale's hall in 1560, had been removed to Gyll's kitchen

*9  By the early seventeenth century, Oxfordshire's more prosperous yeomen farmers commonly lived in comfortable well-finished houses like this one at Hornton, north of Banbury. Here an old-style central hall survives, with the farmer's private parlour in its customary position at one end (right). But the farmhouse now has an integral kitchen (left of the front door), and there are three good-sized bedchambers, two of which have fireplaces, on the first floor.*

before 1587, or were no longer considered worth recording.[74]

Overall, not only had Thomas Gyll amassed more than three times the personal estate of Edward Kempsale – £67 16s 8d against Kempsale's £19 8s 2d – but he had invested twice as much of it in household goods. His farmhouse had expanded to four rooms. The same pattern was repeated throughout that fertile Oxfordshire territory to which both farmers belonged. By the 1590s, Banbury's yeomen were already the richest element (after the gentry) in their rural communities, and their share of personal wealth was still growing.[75] Along with Thomas Gyll, they spent their surplus profits on rebuilding their farmhouses, usually (from the mid-sixteenth century) in costly stone. For the first time – the earliest known example is a datestone of 1579 – even the lesser houses of the Banbury region carried a date of construction.[76] They were signed with the joined initials of the farming couples who built them, and made the kinds of statement about dynastic continuity which had hitherto been reserved to the nobility. "Wise men", warns the Forty-Ninth Psalm ("O hear ye this, all ye people") in the Book of Common Prayer, "also die, and perish together: as well as the ignorant and foolish, and leave their riches for other. And yet they think that their houses shall continue for ever: and that their dwelling-places shall endure from one generation to another; and call the lands after their own names. Nevertheless, man will not abide in honour: seeing he may be compared unto the beasts that perish; this is the way of them. . . . They lie in the hell like [their] sheep."

## CHAPTER 2

# Of building

"I can shew you a man's character in his house", said Roger North. "If he hath bin given to parsimony or profusion, to judge rightly or superficially, to deal in great matters or small, high or low, his edifices shall be tincted accordingly, and the justness or imperfections of his mind will appear in them."[1] Quite so. But what a man wanted of his house, by the time Roger North "cast anchor in Norfolk" in 1691, was not the same as it had been just 50 years earlier, even if few could shed the past absolutely. "Really there is scarce an old house", North observes in *Of building* (1698), "but alter it as you will, shall leave some staine of obsolete antiquity upon the model, either by low floors, beams appearing, or walls patch't"; accordingly, "all new is best". Yet North himself, in his rebuilding of Rougham Hall, had begun with no *tabula rasa*. After almost a decade of works at Rougham, which he thought at one time he might never finish, North addressed his *Cursory notes of building* to like-minded addicts, explaining his particular circumstances as "the Repair, or rather Metamorfosis, of an old house in The Country". Others, in North's direct experience, had contrived no less remarkable transformations. And it was probably of his Suffolk neighbour, Henry Lord Arlington – "given to no expensive vice but building"[2] – that North was thinking when he concluded: "the greatest statesmen, and favorites of fortune, after proof of all the envyed grandure upon earth, have chosen, either upon disgrace or voluntary retiredment, to imploy their time in designing fabricks and executing them. I shall add, that designing and executing is not onely a lawfull, but a very great pleasure . . . more lofty

10 *A near-contemporary view (attributed to John Wyck) of the demolished Euston Hall (Suffolk), as re* *and hugely extended by Henry Lord Arlington (d.1685), with his still-surviving parish church in the* *ground.*

and aspiring than any other injoyment upon earth, and savours of crea- tion, the knowne act of an almighty power . . . he that hath no relish of the grandure and joy of building, is a stupid ox".[3]

Every architectural writer, Roger North included, has had some- thing to say about prospect. In 1698, North advises:

Scituation. Let it be due south if possible. I mean so as the best rooms, which are usually the front, have that prospect. The reason is obvious: there is less venom, and hurt in those winds than the opposite. And fear not heat, (which is in truth more troublesome than winds where it is extream), for the sun falls not early in the morning nor is late in the evening in the sumer time upon that scituation, and when it comes on it is high, and shines not much into the room, especially when at the warmest pitch, noon. But in an east or west scituation the sumer sun every shining morning and evening makes the chambers furnace-hot.[4]

These were sensible observations, still relevant today. But the received wisdom had once – and until lately – been very different. The Henrician Andrew Boorde (d.1549) was a professional physician, trained (he tells us with characteristic rodomontade) at "all the unyversyties and scoles approbated and beynge within the precinct of chrystendome". Boorde wrote his *Dyetary of helth* (1542) at Montpelier ("well-hed of

30

Physycke") after lengthy resort to the "many egregyous Doctours" of
that place. On that authority, the best available at his time: "Ordre &
edyfy the howse", Boorde advised, "so that the pryncypall and chefe
prospectes may be Eest and weest, specyally North-eest, Sowth-eest,
and South-weest, for the merydyal wynde, of al wyndes is the moste
worst, for the South wynde doth corrupt and doth make evyl vapours.
The Eest wynde is temperate, fryske, and fragraunt. The weest wynde is
mutable. The North wynde purgeth yll vapours; wherfore, better it is,
of the two worst, that the wyndowes do open playne North than playne
Sowth".[5]

"In my judgment", wrote Robert Burton in the *Anatomy of melancholy* (1621), "the best sites for chamber windows are north, east, south,
and which is the worst, west." Quoting Levinus Lemnius: "A clear air
cheers up the spirits, exhilarates the mind; a thick, black, misty, tempes-
tuous, contracts, overthrows". Accordingly (Burton again): "Great heed
is to be taken at what times we walk, how we place our windows, lights,
and houses, how we let in or exclude this ambient air".[6] Sir Henry
Wotton, three years later, was still claiming to be "but a gatherer and
disposer of other mens stuffe", naming Vitruvius as his "principall Master". But it was the "Logicall" rather than the "Historical" way that
Wotton chose in *The elements of architecture* (1624). And it is typical of
Wotton's method that his guiding principle in the placing of any chamber was that it must "always [have] regard to the use". Thus:

> Let all the principall chambers of Delight, all Studies and Libraries,
> be towards the East: for the Morning is a friend to the Muses. All
> Offices that require heat, as Kitchins, Stillatories, Stoves, roomes
> for Baking, Brewing, Washing, or the like, would be Meridionall
> [South]. All that need a coole and fresh temper, as Cellers, Pan-
> tries, Butteries, Granaries, to the North. To the same side likewise,
> all that are appointed for gentle Motion, as Galleries, especially in
> warme Climes, or that otherwise require a steadie and unvariable
> light . . . which at any other Quarter, where the course of the
> Sunne doth diversifie the Shadowes, would loose much of their
> grace.[7]

In the final event, as Wotton acknowledges, it is the "nature of the
Region" which must count for most, "every Nation being tyed above

all Rules whatsoever, to a discretion of providing against their own Inconveniences: And therefore a good Parler in Egypt would perchance make a good Celler in England".[8]

That clear vision again, whether for health or other reasons, was being applied in Wotton's time to the "seating" of the house; for the eventual choice of a site was "a kinde of Marriage to a Place", in which "Builders should be as circumspect as Wooers".[9] Andrew Boorde had once counselled any builder wishing "to lengthen his lyfe" to make sure that "there be not aboute the howse or mansion no stynkynge dyches, gutters, nor canelles". But it was the noxious stagnant pond, not the clean-running moat, of which Boorde warned in 1542. And he remained eloquent on the merits of woods and water.[10] Such considerations continued to weigh heavily with northern builders. When Burton wrote in 1621, it was still the custom of the English gentry to build "in bottoms or near woods". "Some discommend moated houses as unwholesome", Burton reported, "but I am of opinion that these inconveniences will be mitigated, or easily corrected by good fires". While foreigners "build on high hills, in hot countries, for more air . . . We [English] build in bottoms for warmth". [11]

Very soon, such traditional practices were past history. "It was the usage in ancient times to build low, and neer water", observed Roger North only two generations later, "but that is [now] found or thought unwholesome, and the next course is to take the other extream and build, as our age doth, upon the summit of hills, where they are intollerably exposed to weather." North himself favoured a compromise: "The mean is best, the side of an hill, a little rising, but not farr from the bottom".[12] And that was the advice, too, of Sir Roger Pratt (1620–84), England's first architectural knight:

Let the house be placed if not in a park, yet at the least in some large pasture, with grounds of that nature round about, for so the surface of the earth being always green, will accordingly be pleasant, whereas arable is never so, but whilst the corn is upon it.

Let it stand at the least a furlong distant from the common way out of which you turn up to it, the ground gently rising all along and the level of it both on the one hand, and on the other if not equal, yet at least not remarkably otherwise; the height of the situation will not only render it very pleasant when you come towards it and are afterwards at it, but will likewise occasion it to stand dry, by the fall of all wet from it, and also give you a great convenience for to drain all sinks and the like from it.[13]

Shun extremes and "fly th' inhospitable Hills and Wilds", sang Sir John Clerk (1676–1755) – Edinburgh Scot, landscape gardener and poetaster – rather than attempt "a British Edifice to raise/On lofty grounds and thereby emulate/Palladio's manner in a warmer clime".[14]

Nobody came to know better the deficiencies of a site than Francis Bacon, who spelled them out in one of his last *Essays* (1625):

Want of water; want of wood, shade, and shelter; want of fruitful-ness, and mixture of grounds of several natures; want of prospect; want of level grounds; want of places at some near distance for sports of hunting, hawking, and races; too near the sea, too remote; having the commodity of navigable rivers, or the discom-modity of their overflowing; too far from great cities, which may hinder business, or too near them . . . ill ways, ill markets, and ill neighbours.[15]

But nothing had ever stopped the lord chancellor building obsessively for himself. And he shared with Robert Burton an appreciation of the Roman general Lucullus who, when challenged on the suitability of his grand summer palace for winter living, replied that "he had other houses furnished and built for that purpose, all out as commodious as this", for "the lord of the house had wit like a crane, that changeth her country with the season".[16]

"Houses are built to live in, and not to look on", Bacon began *Of building*, as if launching a plain man's guide. "Leave the goodly fabrics of houses, for beauty only, to the enchanted palaces of the poets; who build them with small cost." However, what he then chose to describe was no bourgeois dwelling but "a princely palace". While neither a Vati-can nor an Escorial – "huge buildings", he sniffs, "yet scarce a very fair room in them" – Bacon's ideal vision matched the grandest English models: Theobalds or Burghley, Hatfield, Ham House or Audley End. In long years of public office, Bacon had come to know them all, not least as political monuments. Back in 1594, when still a rising lawyer, he had provided the text for a Christmas revel at Gray's Inn, presided over

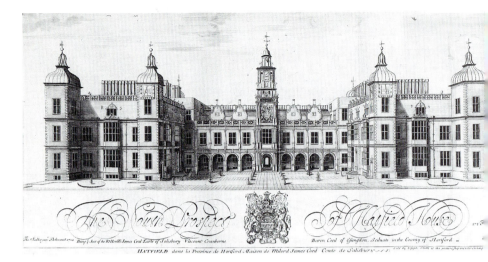

11 Hatfield House (Hertfordshire), built for Robert Cecil, Earl of Salisbury (d.1612), was one Jacobean "prodigy" houses well known to Francis Bacon. Although still traditional in plan, its new f included Cecil's parade of tall brick chimneys, his Italianate central loggia with Long Gallery above, grand open-well stair.

by the "Prince of Purpoole". The Prince addressed his counsellors, requiring them to advise him in turn concerning "the scope and end whereunto you think it most for our honour and the happiness of our state that our government should be rightly bent and directed". The first learned counsellor advised "the Exercise of War"; the second "the Study of Philosophy"; the third argued forcefully, in what is clearly Bacon's voice, that the only "plain and approved way, that is safe and yet proportionable to the greatness of a monarch, to present himself to posterity, is not rumour and hearsay, but the visible memory of himself in the magnificence of goodly and royal buildings and foundations . . . for the fame of great actions is like to a landflood which hath no certain head or spring; but the memory and fame of buildings and foundations hath, as it were, a fountain in an hill, which continually feedeth and refresheth the other waters".[17]

Bacon's dream-house, like the "enchanted palaces" of his poets, was never built. It belonged to a world almost lost. "You cannot have a perfect palace", wrote Bacon in old age, "except you have two several sides: a side for the banquet . . . and a side for the household; the one for feasts and triumphs, and the other for dwelling. I understand both these sides to be not only returns [wings], but parts of the front, and to be uniform without, though severally partitioned within; and to be on both sides of a great and stately tower in the midst of the front, that, as it were, joineth them together on either hand".[18] The obligatory symmetry of Bacon's show facade ("uniform without") was something new. But it disguised an older world of groaning boards and generous halls ("of good state and bigness"), to which the stranger, once admitted, was bid welcome. Bacon wrote *Of building* shortly before his death in 1626, when medieval conventions of hospitality were in full retreat.[19] Seventy years earlier, in 1556, George Rainsford's *Portrait of England* might just as well have been describing the Middle Ages:

> The English take no pleasure in rich tapestries, or in garments of velvet or silk, but their pleasure is to have a number of good horses in the stable, to see a hundred or so suits of armour hanging in the great hall, and to have at their service some forty, one hundred, or even two hundred (more or less, depending on their means) brave young men always in their livery, and to have them eat and sleep in their house in addition to the stipend which they give them, which is honourable. They invite one another continually to feast, and it is astonishing how much meat is consumed in a year in one of these houses. All the vessels used at the table are made of silver. . . . Whoever wishes to come will always find an abundance of meat at their tables, and will not need an invitation. To entertain men gladly at their tables is held among them to be the highest humanity.[20]

And that was still the case in the 1570s, when William Harrison continued to find unstinting hospitality meritorious in the nobility, "for sith they have daily much resort unto their tables (and many times unlooked for), and thereto retain great numbers of servants, it is very requisite and expedient for them to be somewhat plentiful in this behalf".[21] But then William Cornwallis, in just the next generation, could write in a very different vein: "I am readie . . . to entertaine all: but to keepe open house untill I shall be compelled to shut up my doores, must be pardoned me. I have a purse and a life, and all that I am for some fewe; but they are indeed but a fewe".[22]

In Cornwallis's *Of entertainment*, published in 1600, a seismic shift of values has occurred. It is not that the old beliefs and practices had entirely gone away. Well into the nineteenth century, conspicuous waste remained the "mark of the *generosus*, the man of old, and distinguished, birth".[23] But modern good-housekeeping and traditional open handedness were now at odds. The symbol of the new age was the private "dining room", distinct from the hall but also separate from the family's "little parlour". Francis Farrar's Harrold Hall, begun in 1608 and demolished in 1961, has been well described as a "medium-sized house, spare of ornament but symmetrical and well-proportioned, the sort of house being built at the turn of the century not by the very rich who preferred more ostentation but by the moderately well off, ambitious for a new house but content with a building traditional in form and detail". At Harrold, the big first-floor chamber, over the hall and "little parlour", was in use as a "dining room" before 1690, and very likely had that function from the start.[24]

Harrold Hall, in Bedfordshire, was under London's spell. However, even the remoter gentry, on polite society's northern rim, were adopting the new fashions by the 1660s. At Bierley Hall (Yorkshire), what was described in Richard Richardson's inventory of 1656 as the "best Parlor next the hall" would plainly change its role inside a decade. When William Richardson died in 1667, another inventory was taken of Bierley's contents. The great bed had gone from the best parlour, renamed the "Dineng Roome". The big "drawe table" was still there, but where Richard (the father) had been content with "five chaires & nine stooles great & small", valued at just over £1, his son must have "one Dozen of Rushy leather chaires [and] two great chaires, of the same work", worth nearly five times as much.[25] The "Little Dyninge Roome" at Scarisbrick (Lancashire), of which there was no mention in 1608, occurs first in an inventory of 1673. Six years later, the Walmesleys of Dunkenhalgh had a "Little Dineing Room" of their own, as well as the "Greate Dineing Room" and earlier hall.[26]

"A great hall, and a great kitchen, and afterwards a parlour, was the establisht grandure of the English gentry", reported Roger North. But he wrote of a new world in 1698, for which the old was a habitat of dinosaurs. Thus:

In the ancient or Gothick times it was the mode for numerous familys to eat in the same room at severall tables and have few waiters; the butler for serving the master's table, and the porter the others (for the gates were all closed at that time) was sufficient. . . . But that way of a comon eating room made great halls open to the roof, with a lanthorne, to lett out smoak and stench, a laudable fashion, and consequently an indication of great dignity and plenty, and excuseth the unclenlyness of it; but at present the way of the world is chang'd, and the eating is devided, many servants wait, and take their repast after the master, who is served at a table in a room layd out for that porpose. Therefore those wide halls are layd aside, and in the room of them comes the *grand salle*, which is a place to entertein persons coming to the house, and therefore ought to be well adorned, and neat. For the affectation of cleanness hath introduc't much variety of rooms, which the ancients had no occasion for, who cared not for exquisite neatness.[27]

That much variety of rooms – 750 by repute – was what Celia Fiennes remarked at Audley End, one of the grandest private palaces ever built.[28] But Audley End, begun by Thomas Howard in 1603, was already in decay by the time Celia came there in 1697. And more obviously to her taste was the innovatory country house she had previously seen at Coleshill, built in in the mid-century for Sir George Pratt by his architect cousin, Sir Roger. Coleshill was a modern "double-pile" house of that rectangular plan, with central corridor, which Roger Pratt esteemed "of all others to be the most useful". Audley End, in contrast, had been constructed around two courts. And while building "with a court in the middle", Pratt concedes, "is stately indeed", it was also "exceedingly costly, and only fit for the purses of those who are very rich . . . The best forms therefore for a private man I conceive to be that which is an oblong square exactly", One benefit of Pratt's favoured plan was undoubtedly economy: "that we have there much room in a little compass . . . that herein a little ground is sufficient to build upon, and there may be a great spare of walling, and of other materials for the roof". Another clear attraction was the calming at last of that old fear of the English, of being either too hot or too cold – for, says Pratt, "I conceive a double building to be the most commodious of any other for so the rooms will neither be so hot in summer, nor cold in winter, besides when any side of the house is inconvenienced by any ill weather you may retire to the other, and have in your power always to make use of that, which you will find to be most pleasant".[29]

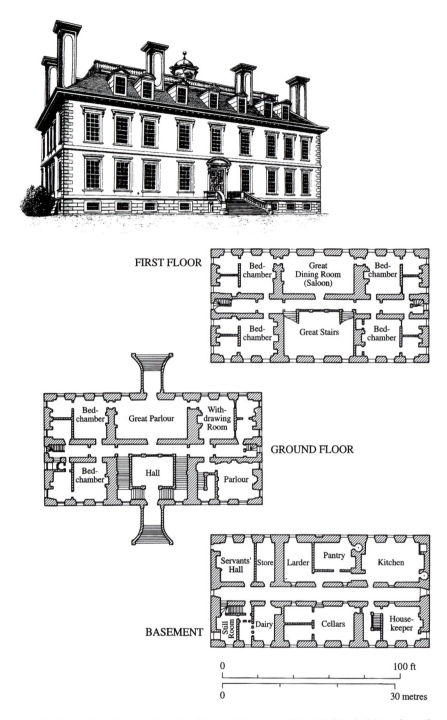

FIRST FLOOR

Bed-chamber | Great Dining Room (Saloon) | Bed-chamber

Bed-chamber | Great Stairs | Bed-chamber

Bed-chamber | Great Parlour | With-drawing Room

GROUND FLOOR

Bed-chamber | Hall | Parlour

Servants' Hall | Store | Larder | Pantry | Kitchen

BASEMENT

Still Room | Dairy | Cellars | House-keeper

0            100 ft

0            30 metres

12   *Roger Pratt's pioneering "double-pile" house at Coleshill (Oxfordshire, formerly Berkshire) was built in the 1650s after his return from Italy and in consultation with Inigo Jones. Pratt's service basement, his central corridor plan, and his balustered roof with viewpoint cupola, were all subsequently repeated at other influential houses by Sir Roger and his imitators, including Belton and Clarendon House. In the 1690s, when Celia Fiennes visited Coleshill, some of its bedchambers (as shown here in plan) were in use as sitting rooms. Coleshill was demolished after a fire in 1952.*

It was Pratt's declared belief that "no [gentleman's] house to which you ascend not by some competent number of steps, can well be graceful nor indeed convenient, nor yet healthful".[30] And Celia Fiennes would find the offices at Coleshill "partly under ground – kitchin pantry buttlery and good cellers", whereas "the entrance of the house is an ascent of severall steps into a hall so lofty the rooff is three storyes [above]". That hall – already more formal vestibule at Coleshill than place of entertainment – carried the "great Staires [which] goes out of the hall on each side, spacious and handsom, [these] staires runs up and meetes on the landing place which is a passage, that runs on both sides to each end of the house". Below, at the back of the hall, was "a large dineing roome or great parlour which has a door thourough into the garden that gives a visto through the house [from the front door]"; on its left was the "drawing roome", on its right, the "little parlour". And there was another big dining room (over the great parlour) at the top of the stairs, with a drawing room on the left and three equal-sized bedchambers at the other corners of the building, having "two closets to each, bigg enough for a little bed with chimney's convenient for a servant and for dressing roomes". Then:

Over this runs a gallery all through the house and on each side severall garret roomes for servants furnished very neate and genteele; in the middle are staires that lead up to the Cupilow [cupola] or large Lanthorn in the middle of the leads, the house being leaded all over and the stone chimney's in severall rows comes up in them on each side; the Cupilow it shewes exact and very uniform, as is the whole Building. This gives you a great prospect of gardens, grounds, woods that appertaine to the Seate, as well as a sight of the Country at a distance.[31]

Coleshill, begun in the early 1650s, was almost finished by 1662. And it was just a year or two later that Roger Pratt was again engaged on major building projects, for Sir John Bankes at Kingston Lacy (1663–65) and for the lord chancellor, Edward Hyde, at Clarendon House (1664–65), on Piccadilly. Both were double-pile houses, grander than Coleshill but of the same basic plan. And like all five of Pratt's houses, they were hugely influential in their day. Most particularly, this was the case with Clarendon House, seen by every potential builder who came to London.Yet Clarendon, that "costly & onely sumptuous Palace of the late L. Chancellor Hydes, where I have often ben so cherefull with him, & so sad", was to be demolished, already in 1683 fallen victim (Evelyn tells us) to the developers – "certaine inferior people, rich bankers & Mechanics, who gave for it & the ground about it 35,000 pounds".[32] Sad indeed though this was for the late lord chancellor's friends, and tragic again that Coleshill itself has since been lost, the example of Pratt's houses was not wasted. Between Coleshill, his comparatively modest original, and Belton House (Lincolnshire), Clarendon's nearest surviving clone, Sir Roger had created "a type of house perfectly acceptable to the noblemen and gentlemen of the later Stuart epoch – a type [Summerson concludes] which, in spite of much indebtedness to the Continent, we may, without much exaggeration, call essentially English".[33]

*13 Belton House (Lincolnshire), built for Sir John Brownlow (probably by William Winde) in 1685 the most perfect survivor of the many important post-Civil War houses directly influenced by Roger Coleshill and by his larger Clarendon House.*

Acceptably English though Pratt's houses might have seemed, *traditional* they most certainly were not. Less than a generation earlier, in 1624, Sir Henry Wotton had taken the view that some foreign practices were not importable. He had said this already about the "aspect" of English houses, and he said it again about basements:

> I have marked a willingnesse, in the Italian Artisans, to destribute the Kychin, Pantrie, Bakehouse, washing Roomes: and even the Buttrie likewise, under ground; next above the Foundation, and sometimes Level with the plaine, or Floore of the Cellar: raysing the first Ascent into the house Fifteene Foote or more for that Ende, which besides the benefit of removing such Annoyes out of sight, and the gayning of so much more roome above, doth also by elevation of the Front, adde Majestie to the whole Aspect. . . . But the Definition (above determined) doth call us to some considera-tion of our owne Countrie, where though all the other pettie Offices (before rehearsed) may well enough bee so remote, yet by the natural Hospitalitie of England, the Buttrie must be more vis-ible; and wee neede perchance for our Raunges, a more spacious and luminous Kitchin, then the foresaid Compartition will beare; with a more competent neerenesse likewise to the Dyning Roome. Or else besides other Inconveniences, perhaps some of the Dishes may straggle by the way.[34]

In Pratt's houses, Wotton's reservations were dismissed. There would be no automatic welcome, in Sir John Bankes's dining room at Kingston Lacy, for those "honest neighbours" and "yeomen of the countrey" who had filled Squire Vincent's hall with rustic talk. And those same "tall fel-lows" who had served the squire well in Elizabethan England were more likely to be categorized by Roger North and his associates as contempt-ible "hang-bys", deservedly banished below stairs – "idle fellows who will be spunging" in the kitchen.[35] Pratt himself advised that "the kitchen and all its offices [should] lie together, and the buttery and cellar with theirs, etc. and all these to be disposed of in a half ground [base-ment] storey, with their backcourts, convenient to them; in that no dirty servants may be seen passing to and fro by those who are above, no noises heard, nor ill scents smelt". In the double-pile house, the servants once accommodated in the ranges of the outer court slept above the family quarters in the garrets – women in one chamber, men in another; "but let none of the house be lodged over the strangers' [guest] quarters, that they may not disquiet them either by their going to bed

*14  The first-floor landing of the main stair at Tyttenhanger House (Hertfordshire), where the "great ones" might pause for conversation and salutes, undisturbed by the "passing to and fro" of their servants.*

late at night, or early rising in the morning". Service corridors and back stairs ensured that "the ordinary servants may never publicly appear in passing to and fro for their occasions". And even the personal servant, lodged in the closet next to his master's bedroom, must use a back stair, "so that he need not foul the great ones [passing up and down the main stair] and whatsoever is of use may be brought up or carried down the back way".[36]

Hiding away the servants was no part of the old style, which indeed had made more point of their display. And the houses Celia Fiennes admired for being built "all the new fashion way" were unquestionably very different from their predecessors. Among the works she so described was Roger North's remodelling of Wroxton Abbey (Oxfordshire) for his successful lawyer brother, Lord Guilford (d.1685). "I took upon me the honour of being prime architect [at Wroxton]", boasted Roger North. And high in his list of proposed amendments for Lord Guilford was the newfangled luxury of back stairs.[37] Other improvements at Wroxton were refurbished rooms of state, a new drawing room, and the symmetrical stable block (with classical pediment at the centre) which still survives. Celia Fiennes, at Wroxton with her mother not long after Lord Guilford's death, found those stables "handsome" and the house "good". The two ladies were shown the still-surviving hall of Sir William Pope's original Jacobean mansion of the 1620s. But Pope's private parlour, at the upper end of that hall, had now become a "dineing room" for the Norths. There was a "large staire-case with good pictures, [and] there you enter another large dineing roome with great compass windows, fine Pictures of the family; within is a drawing roome and chambers and closets well proportioned, [though] little or no furniture was up".[38]

Celia Fiennes's next journey was into eastern Hampshire, where she stayed at Nursted House with the Holts. Margaret Holt was her mother's

*15 At Tyttenhanger, begun in the mid-1650s, this second (or back) stair was not yet designed exclusively for service use, but rose the full height of the house to the servants' fourth-floor garrets and was already the normal passage for their "occasions".*

younger sister. And Richard and Margaret, at the time their niece came visiting, had recently rebuilt their family home. As Celia described it in *c*. 1690, Nursted was:

A neat new built house with brick and stone; a hall, little parlour on the left side and back door into a court built round with all the offices out to the stables barnes; on the right side a great parlour and drawing roome that opened into the garden, which were fine gravel walkes grass plotts and beyond it a garden of flower trees and all sorts of herbage, store of fruit, a freestone broad walke in the middle to the house; the [bed]chambers are very good and convenient, and in the front is a place walled in, beyond is a long ground sett with rows of trees; on the right side of the house is a large grove of firrs halfe scotts halfe norroway which lookes very nobly.[39]

Country houses such as Nursted, comfortable and well-mannered, have never ceased to content their gentry owners. But they were already too familiar, even in Celia Fiennes's day, to attract much contemporary attention. Far different was the case with William Cavendish's palatial Chatsworth, triumphing over a site "where the mountains insult the clouds, intercept the sun . . . a country [Derbyshire] so out of the way, so concealed from the world, that whoever sees it must take a journey for the purpose". Early in the 1720s, it was Daniel Defoe who described Chatsworth thus. But Defoe himself made the pilgrimage at least twice to Chatsworth, finding it "indeed a palace for a prince, a most magnificent building . . . [of which] the front to the garden is the most regular piece of architect[ure] I have seen in all the north part of England".[40]

Celia Fiennes had come to Chatsworth before Defoe, noting (as he did) the duke's new-style sash windows and counting 12 of the great sashes ("4 panes broad 8 long") across its symmetrical garden front. "The sashes of the second story", Defoe later remarked, "are seventeen foot high, the plates polish'd looking-glass, and the woodwork double gilded; which, I think, is no where else to be seen in England".[41] But whereas he then said little about Chatsworth's fine interiors, pleading "want of time, and having so long a journey to go", Celia found much more to report. "The hall", she wrote, "is very lofty painted top and sides with armory . . . the floores of the roomes are all finely inlaid,

6  William Cavendish's suite of inter-connecting state rooms at Chatsworth (Derbyshire) included this State
Dining Room, or Great Chamber. Here the fine woodcarvings are by Samuel Watson, a local sculptor; but the
painted ceiling is by Antonio Verrio, a fashionable Italian history-painter who also worked at Windsor and
Hampton Court (p. 124); and the tall sash window, "4 panes broad 8 long", is one of the earliest of its kind.

there is very curious carving over and round the Chimney pieces and round the Looking-glasses that are in the peers between the windows . . . every roome is differring work and all fine carving and over the doores some of it is of the naturall coullour of the wood and varnish'd only, others painted; . . . the roomes are all painted very finely on the top, all the windows the squares of glass are so large and good they cost 10s a pannell; there was sweete tapistry hangings with small figures and very much silk".[42]

When Celia was at Chatsworth in 1697, "they were just painting the cielings and laying the floores" on the "other side" of William Cavendish's palace. But at least one of the duke's fantasies had been realized:

There is a fine grottoe all stone pavement roofe and sides, this is design'd to supply all the house with water besides severall fancyes to make diversion; within this is a batheing roome, the walls all with blew and white marble the pavement mix'd one stone white another black another of the red rance [variegated] marble; the bath is one entire marble all white finely veined with blew and is made smooth, but had it been as finely pollish'd as some, it would have been the finest marble that could be seen; it was as deep as ones middle on the outside and you went down steps into the bath big enough for two people; at the upper end are two Cocks to let in one hott the other cold water to attemper it as persons please; the windows are all private [ground] glass.[43]

Running hot-and-cold is with us still. However, there was another new fashion (also seen at Chatsworth) for the *visto* or enfilade, which has since gone the way of the Stuart palaces. One expert witness who knew those palaces well was the Yorkshire baronet, Sir Henry Slingsby (d.1658). "I was much taken with the curiosity of the house", Slingsby wrote of the now lost Holland House in 1639, after supping there with Henry Lord Kensington, "& from that house I took a conceite of making a thorough house in part of Red-house [Scriven] which now I build; & that by placing the Dores so one against another & making at each end a Balcony that one may see cleare thro' the house".[44] But honest squire though he was, Slingsby could see the trap for himself in such competitive building, and he used it in his *Diary* to develop a short homily on "the vanity of all worldly things which men do so much rest upon". No man, Slingsby lectured, could hope to win that race, for though "he build his house like Nebuchodonoser . . . yet shall another come that may exceed him & go beyond him . . .We see [such] an emulation in the structure of our houses, if we behold that at [Lord Burghley's] Tibbalds, & that of my Lord of Suffolk's at Audley end. So, in this country [Yorkshire] my Lord Everie's at Maulton; my Lord Savil's at Howley; Sir Arthur Ingram's at Temple Newson".[45]

A few years earlier, Sir Henry Wotton had taken against the *visto* on sounder principles. "I must here take leave to reproove a fashion", Wotton wrote crossly in 1624, "which I know not how hath prevailed through Italie, though without ancient examples, as farre as I can perceive by Vitruvius. The thing I meane, is, that they so cast their partitions as when all Doors are open, a man may see through the whole House; which doth necessariely put an intollerable servitude upon all the Chambers save the Inmost, where none can arrive, but through the rest".[46] Draughts, Wotton pointed out, were another obvious disadvantage of the plan in "cold & windie Regions".Yet, in the very next generation, it would be one of Sir Roger Pratt's first rules "*especially* that there be a clear vista through the very middle of the building".[47] And Roger North again would find particular merit in the "exquisite" placing of the Lauderdales' "rooms of parade" at Ham House (Richmond), "so the visto is compleate from end to end".[48]

Not to be outdone, William Cavendish must have his enfilade. But Chatsworth (like Ham House) was a rebuilding of an existing house. And there was no room behind the facade of Bess of Hardwick's earlier mansion for the full formal suite of state apartments. Cavendish's solution was to use mirrors. Thus when Celia Fiennes moved on from Chatsworth's hall, what she then entered was "a dineing roome two drawing roomes a bed chamber and closet, which opens quite thro' the house a visto, and at the end of the dineing roome is a large door all of Looking-glass, in great pannells all diamond cutt, this is just opposite to the doores that runs into the drawing roome and bed chamber and closet, so it shews the roomes to look all double".[49] As Wotton had foreseen, such *vistos* were "meerely grounded upon the fond ambition of displaying to a Stranger all our Furniture at one Sight, which therefore is most maintained by them that meane to harbour but a few; whereby they make onely advantage of the vanitie, and seldome prove the Inconvenience".[50]

17 *This Dutch perspective painting –* A view down a corridor *by Samuel van Hoogstraeten, dated 16( – continues the real-life enfilade at Dyrham Park (Gloucestershire), built for William Blathwayt in the 169(*

That inconvenience, in Derbyshire today, is hardly worse than in other, mellower regions. But the taming of Chatsworth's landscape – "Black Heaths, wild Rocks, bleak Craggs, and naked Hills" – has been comparatively recent, and owes all to a succession of mighty gardeners. Like every other great palace since Renaissance gardening began, Chatsworth was partnered by its grounds. "Who is it", rhymed Charles Cotton in 1681, even before Cavendish began rebuilding, "but must presently conclude/That this is Paradice, which seated stands/In midst of Desarts, and of barren Sands?"[51] Particularly remarkable, then as now, were Chatsworth's water gardens. "Before the gate", Celia Fiennes tells us, "there is a large Parke and severall fine Gardens one without another with gravell walkes and squairs of grass with stone statues in them and in the middle of each Garden is a large fountaine full of images Sea Gods and Dolphins and Sea Horses which are full of pipes which spout out water in the bason and spouts all about the gardens . . . there is one bason in the middle of one Garden thats very large and by sluces besides the Images severall pipes plays out the water, about 30 large and small pipes altogether, some flush it up that it frothes like snow".[52] Cotton, hymning the *Wonders of the Peake*, had praised these too:

> The Ponds, which here in double order shine,
> Are some of them so large, and all so fine,
> That Neptune in his progress once did please
> To frolick in these artificial Seas;
> Of which a noble Monument we find,
> His Royal Chariot left, it seems, behind;
> Whose wheels and body moor'd up with a Chain,
> Like Drake's old Hulk at Deptford, still remain.
> No place on Earth was ere discover'd yet,
> For contemplation, or delight so fit.[53]

Cotton's remorseless couplets celebrate the earlier Chatsworth of Bess of Hardwick and her heirs – already a monument to what "Art could, [in] spite of Nature, do". Cavendish, when his turn came, wanted better. Once, Defoe remembered, "a great mountain" had interrupted the duke's prospect towards Hardwick. But at Defoe's next visit, "this was so entirely gone, that, having taken a strict view of the gardens at my first being there, and retaining an idea of them in my mind, I was perfectly confounded at coming there a second time, and not knowing what had been done; for I had lost the hill, and found a new country in view, which Chatsworth itself had never seen before". Out of the "houling wilderness" of this "difficult desart country", the traveller descended "into the most delightful valley, with the most pleasant garden, and most beautiful palace in the world".[54]

"If a man would be happy for a week", runs the Chinese proverb, "he could take a wife; if he planned happiness for a month, he must kill a pig; but if he desired happiness for ever, he should plant a garden."[55] Sensible advice, one might think; but the garden in post-medieval England was not "for ever". In gardening, as in architecture, fashions changed swiftly. What William Cavendish inherited at Chatsworth was a Jacobean Mannerist garden, terraced and watered in the Italian taste of

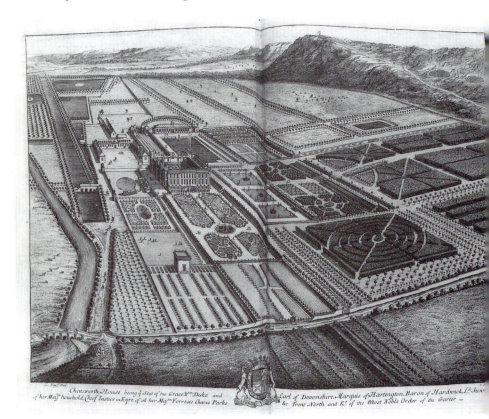

*18  Chatsworth surrounded by its French-style formal gardens as made for William Cavendish, first D*
*Devonshire (d. 1707): a bird's-eye view by Leonard Knyff, engraved and published by Joannes Kip i*
Britannia Illustrata *(1720).*

Thomas Lord Coningsby's expensive new formal gardens of c.1700 at Hampton Court (Herefordshire), great waterworks in the style of Versailles.

the Medici gardens at Pratolino.[56] What he then created was a formal French-style garden of horizon-piercing avenues and lushly planted drives, modelled on Louis XIV's Versailles. To the first duke's Chatsworth, as to the French king's new palace, the "theatre of water" remained central.[57] And Cavendish's huge cascade, constructed in 1694, is still a prominent feature of the Chatsworth gardens. Yet almost everything else was soon removed. By the early 1760s, in the fourth duke's time, formality was out of fashion and a *natural* garden, as English as roast beef, was commissioned from Lancelot (Capability) Brown. When Horace Walpole came visiting in 1768, "many foolish waterworks" had already been demolished, and the gardens (Walpole thought) were "much improved".[58]

None of these new departures was of greater importance than the one that had started them all. Andrew Boorde's *Dyetary* of 1542 had included much sound advice on how "a man shuld buylde his howse or mansyon, in exchewynge thynges that shortneth mans lyfe". But on the subject of gardens, Boorde wrote only: "Furthermore, it is a commodyous and a pleasaunt thynge to a mansyon to have an orcherd of soundry fruytes; but it is more commodiouse to have a fayre gardain repleted wyth herbes of aromatyck & redolent savours. In the gardayne maye be a poole or two for fysshe, yf the pooles be clene kept." There should be a park for deer and rabbits ("a necessarye and a pleasaunt thyng to be anexed to a mansyon"), a dovecot ("a necessary thyng aboute a mansyon-place"), a pair of archery butts ("a decent thynge"), and a bowling alley ("for a great man, necessary it is for to passe his tyme with bowles in an aly").[59] Boorde's ideal garden, even for the great nobleman, was more *commodious* (profitable) than it was fair; it was *necessary* before it was pleasant. Those priorities, almost immediately, were reversed.

"Within these forty years", wrote William Harrison of the 1570s, "if you look into our gardens annexed to our houses, how wonderfully is their beauty increased, not only with flowers . . . and variety of curious and costly workmanship, but also with rare and medicinable herbs . . . so that in comparison of this present, the ancient gardens were but dunghills and laystows [rubbish tips] to such as did possess them". Moreover, "art also helpeth nature in the daily colouring, doubling, and enlarging the proportion of our flowers . . . [and] it is a world also to see how many strange herbs, plants, and annual fruits are daily brought unto us from the Indies, Americans, Taprobane [Ceylon], Canary Isles, and all parts of the world . . . [so that] there is not almost one nobleman, gentleman, or merchant that hath not great store of these flowers".[60]

Harrison, like Boorde, was a herbalist. He would probably have agreed with the Montpelier-trained physician that parsley "is good to breke the stone, and causeth a man to pysse"; that sorrel "is good for a hote lyver, and good for the stomacke"; that rosemary "is good for palses [palsey], and for the fallynge syckenes, and for the cowghe, and good agaynst colde"; that sage "is good to helpe a woman to conceyve, and doth provoke uryne"; and that "there is no Herbe, nor weede, but God have gyven vertue to them, to helpe man".[61] In any event, he was an assiduous collector. "For my own part, good reader", Harrison tells us comfortably, "let me boast a little of my garden, which is but small and the whole area thereof little above three hundred foot of ground, and yet, such hath been my good luck in purchase of the variety of simples [herbs and the like] that, notwithstanding my small ability, there are very near three hundred of one sort and other contained therein, no one of them being common or usually to be had. If therefore my little plot, void of all cost in keeping, be so well furnished, what shall we think of those of Hampton Court, Nonsuch, Theobalds, Cobham Garden, and sundry other appertaining to divers citizens of London?"[62]

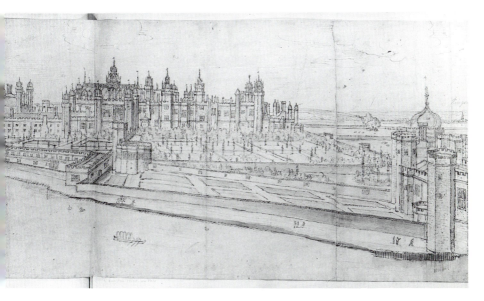

*prospect of the royal palace and heraldic privy garden at Hampton Court (Middlesex), drawn by Anton*
*er Wyngaerde in c.1560.*

53

The answer is that Harrison himself thought very highly of such gardens. "I am persuaded", he had just before concluded, "that albeit the gardens of the Hesperides were in times past so greatly accounted of because of their delicacy, yet if it were possible to have such an equal judge as by certain knowledge of both were able to pronounce upon them, I doubt not but he would give the prize unto the gardens of our days [in England] and generally over all Europe, in comparison of those times wherein the old exceeded".[63] Certainly, the four gardens he named were all of them very remarkable. Cobham Hall, in North Kent, was the seat of Harrison's patron, William Lord Cobham. There was a "rare" garden at Cobham in 1587, "in which no varietie of strange flowers and trees do want, which praise or price maie obtaine from the furthest part of Europe or from other strange Countries".[64] Henry VIII's great formal gardens at Hampton Court, although old-fashioned by this date, were yet so abundantly furnished with ingenious topiary and with fountains "that time shall not drag in such a place".[65]

At Theobalds and at Nonsuch, even while Harrison wrote, huge new gardens were in course of creation. Their models were French and Italian. Thus the French-style canals at Lord Burghley's Theobalds were "large enough for one to have the pleasure of going in a boat and rowing between the shrubs".[66] And Lord Lumley's allegorical groves at Nonsuch drew on personal recollections of Italian Mannerist gardens to pay elaborate tribute to his queen. Elizabeth depicted as Diana the Huntress was a favourite contemporary image. "At the entrance to the garden [at Nonsuch] is a grove called after Diana, the goddess", records Thomas Platter, who was shown Lumley's works in 1599 when the Virgin Queen herself was in residence; "from here we came to a rock out of which natural water springs into a basin, and on this was portrayed with great art and life-like execution the story of how the three goddesses took their bath naked and sprayed Acteon with water, causing antlers to grow upon his head, and how his own hounds afterwards tore him to pieces." Platter also saw "a small vaulted temple, where was a fine marble table" and "a pointed tower spurting out water". He was taken into a wood, cleared in the middle to form "fine straight long alleys . . . so that there is a vista from one end to the other". Of an earlier taste were the maze and naturalistic topiary of the Henrician pleasure gardens – "dogs, hares, all overgrown with plants, most artfully set out, so that from a distance, one would take them for real ones".[67]

The purpose of these great gardens was to distract and to entertain. And whereas all were laid out formally, as convention still required, there was room now also for that deliberate irregularity of which Sir Henry Wotton was among the earliest theoreticians. "First", Wotton wrote in 1624, "I must note a certain contrarietie between building and gardening: For as Fabriques should bee regular, so Gardens should bee irregular, or at least cast into a very wilde Regularitie."[68] What he then described was the "delightfull confusion" of a garden he had once visited in Italy. But that Mediterranean labyrinth of terraces, stairs and secret spaces – furnishing "various entertainemens of his [the beholder's] scent and sight" – was itself artificially contrived. And Wotton's next example was a friend's Hertfordshire garden, where what impressed him chiefly was the ingenuity of the planting, "like a piece not of Nature, but of Arte".[69]

The garden at Ware Park, created for Sir Henry Fanshawe, was also widely celebrated for its water effects.[70] Fanshawe was a scholar and an Italianist, as was Wotton himself. And they both belonged to that close circle of office-holding intellectuals of which Francis Bacon was still the reigning luminary. Wotton describes a fountain – its sprays arching over the promenader like swords at a wedding – which he thought "an invention for refreshment, surely farre excelling all the Alexandrian delicacies, and Pneumatiques of Hero".[71] And if Bacon himself was more dubious of the worth of "fine devices, of arching water without spilling and making it rise in several forms (of feathers, drinking glasses, canopies, and the like)", he nevertheless found fountains of "great beauty and refreshment", while warning repeatedly of the dangers of stagnant pools. Bacon's essay *Of gardens*, published in 1625, was one of the last things he wrote. He had grown impatient by that time of topiary menageries: "they be for children". And he dismisses as mere toys such familiar Tudor conceits as "the making of knots or figures with divers coloured earths", for "you may see as good sights many times in tarts". Yet his ideal "prince-like" garden was still a formal place of "pretty pyramides", of "fair columns upon frames of carpenter's work", and of "alleys spacious and fair". What was new was his provision for a wilderness:

For the heath, which was the third part of our plot, I wish it to be framed, as much as may be, to a natural wildness. Trees I would

55

have none in it, but some thickets, made only of sweet-briar and honeysuckle, and some wild vine amongst; and the ground set with violets, strawberries, and primroses. For these are sweet, and prosper in the shade. And these to be in the heath, here and there, not in any order.[72]

From such small beginnings, in a deliberate lack of order, the garden gate would one day open to the "wide Fields of Nature". Not yet. It was Joseph Addison, the essayist, who contrasted those fields, where "the Sight wanders up and down without Confinement", with the "narrow Compass" of "the most stately Garden or Palace". For "there is something more bold and masterly in the rough careless Strokes of Nature than in the nice Touches and Embellishments of Art".[73] But that was as late as 1712, and Addison even so was a pioneer. In Addison's garden, there was a "Confusion of Kitchin and Parterre, Orchard and Flower Garden, which lie so mixt and interwoven with one another, that if a Foreigner who had seen nothing of our Country should be conveyed into my Garden at his first landing, he would look upon it as a natural Wilderness, and one of the uncultivated Parts of our Country".[74]

Not all foreigners would have been so bemused. Two decades earlier, the diplomat and essayist, Sir William Temple, had reflected *Upon the gardens of Epicurus* (1692). Temple's declared "Pattern to the best Gardens of our Manner" was Lucy Russell's Moor Park (Hertfordshire), "the perfectest Figure of a Garden I ever saw, either at Home or Abroad, when I knew it about thirty Years ago". But Moor Park was a Jacobean sculpture garden, Italian in style. And Temple himself, of the next generation, inclined to French formal alleys and parterres. Already, though, he recognized another level of sophistication:

What I have said, of the best Forms of Gardens, is meant only of such as are in some Sort regular; for there may be other Forms wholly irregular, that may, for aught I know, have more Beauty than any of the others . . . Something of this I have seen in some Places, but heard more of it from others, who have lived much among the Chineses; a People, whose Way of Thinking seems to lie as wide of ours in Europe, as their Country does. Among us, the Beauty of Building and Planting is placed chiefly in some certain Proportions, Symmetries, or Uniformities; our Walks and our

Mutton Davies who, as a Royalist, had spent some years in Italy during the 1650s, created this expensive
ed water-garden at Llanerch, near St Asaph's Cathedral (top right) in North Wales. This painting, by an
own artist, is of c.1662.

Trees ranged so, as to answer one another, and at exact Distances.
The Chineses scorn this Way of Planting, and say a Boy, that can
tell an Hundred, may plant Walks of Trees in straight Lines, and
over-against one another, and to what Length and Extent he
pleases. But their greatest Reach of Imagination is employed in
contriving Figures, where the Beauty shall be great, and strike the
Eye, but without any Order or Disposition of Parts, that shall be
commonly or easily observ'd . . . But [Temple cautions] I should
hardly advise any of these Attempts in the Figure of Gardens
among us; they are Adventures of too hard Achievement for any
common Hands; and though there may be more Honour if they
succeed well, yet there is more Dishonour if they fail, and 'tis
Twenty to One they will; whereas in regular Figures, 'tis hard to
make any great and remarkable Faults.[75]

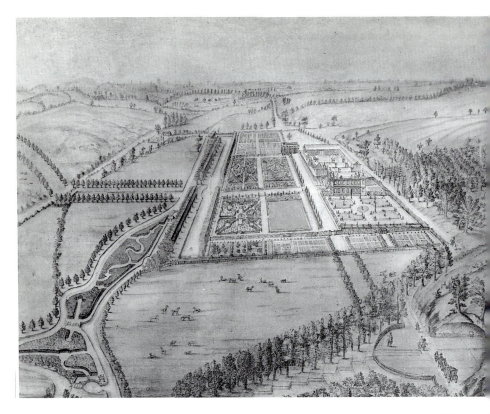

22 When he bought Compton Hall (near Farnham) for his retirement from public life, Sir William Te (d.1699) changed its name to Moor Park, after Lucy Russell's celebrated Hertfordshire garden. Here in S* Temple made a second great garden – his first was at Sheen – combining French-style alleys and parterres the irregular "figures" (bottom left) he so admired in the gardens of China.

If prudence in gardening has its advocates even now, it has never stopped the committed gardener or plant collector. William Temple himself developed a specialism in espaliers. At Temple's garden in Sheen, "the most remarkable thing", wrote the diarist John Evelyn in 1688, "is his Orangerie & Gardens; where the wall Fruite-trees are most exquisitely nailed & applied, far better than in my life I had ever noted".[76] And Evelyn spoke from considerable experience of gardens both at home and on the Continent. At Sayes Court (Deptford), which he bought in 1653, Evelyn had his own huge garden where, even before completion, "I began to set out the Ovall Garden, which was before a rude Ortchard, & all the rest one intire fild of 100 Ackers, without any hedge . . . & this was the beginning of all the succeeding Gardens, Walkes, Groves, Enclosures & Plantations there".[77]

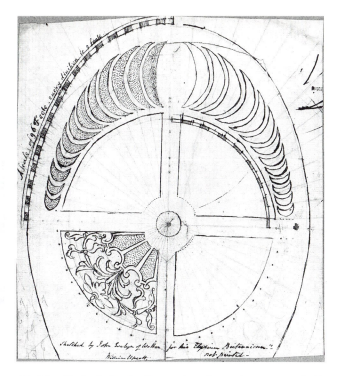

23 *John Evelyn's sketch of an oval garden and parterre, probably based on his own garden at Sayes Court (Deptford) and drawn for his unpublished* Elysium Brittanicum.

It was John Aubrey's opinion that it was "in the time of King Charles the Second [that] gardening was much improved and became common". Fully a century before, in the late 1570s and 1580s, William Harrison had made a near-identical claim. Nevertheless, "I doe believe", wrote Aubrey in his *Natural history of Wiltshire*, "I may modestly affirme that there is now, 1691, ten times as much gardening about London as there was Anno 1660; and wee have been, since that time, much improved in forreign plants, especially since about 1683, there have been exotick plants brought into England no lesse than seven thousand".[78]

And so it would go on. After the Italian secret gardens of pre-Civil War England had come the Gallic vistas and plantations of the returned exiles. Then, shortly before Aubrey wrote, William and Mary brought a whiff of Holland's fragrance to English gardens; following which, through the great Marlborough's wars, a growing abhorrence of all things French made *natural* gardening another form of patriotism. For Alexander Pope, bard of the "brave Britons [who] Foreign Laws despis'd", there was (echoing Addison) "certainly something in the amiable Simplicity of unadorned Nature, that spreads over the Mind a more noble sort of Tranquility, and a loftier Sensation of Pleasure, than can be raised from the nicer Scenes of Art".[79] Away with caution, with engineered terraces and "vast Parterres":

> Begin with Sense, of ev'ry Art the Soul,
> Parts answ'ring Parts, shall slide into a Whole,
> Spontaneous Beauties all around advance,
> Start, ev'n from Difficulty, strike, from Chance;
> Nature shall join you; Time shall make it grow
> A Work to wonder at – perhaps a STOW.
> Without it, proud Versailles! thy Glory falls,
> And Nero's Terrasses desert their Walls.[80]

Viscount Cobham's grounds at Stowe (which Pope knew well) were indeed among the most extensive and successful of all English templed gardens. But they too would fall from fashion, as would the "dull and vapid" landscapes of the mid-century Capability Brown, and, only slightly later, the "unmeaning falballas of Chinese chequer work" of Sir William Chambers, architect of the Pagoda at Kew.[81] Of that forever unattainable Chinese garden, creature of myth though it always was, let Chambers have the last word:

> European artists must not hope to rival Oriental splendor; yet let them look up to the sun, and copy as much of its lustre as they can, circumstances will frequently obstruct them in their course, and they may often be prevented from soaring high: but their attention should constantly be fixed on great objects; and their productions always demonstrate, that they knew the road to perfection, had they been enabled to proceed on the journey.[82]

## CHAPTER 3

# Social space

"Necessary it is", we have heard Boorde say, "for a great man to passe his tyme with bowles in an aly".[1] But playing at bowls could be the least of his accomplishments. Another relaxation might be music, preferably "singing to the lute". A third would be dance: not that wanton "dauncing in the sunne" which young men do, but rather keeping "a certaine dignitie, tempered notwithstanding with a handsome and sightly sweetenesse of gestures".[2] It was Federico Fregoso (later archbishop of Salerno) who counselled thus, in Castiglione's best-selling *Il cortegiano* (1528). And while English readers had to wait until 1561 for Sir Thomas Hoby's translation of *The book of the courtier,* many had learnt its principles long before. Among the earliest borrowers from *Il cortegiano* was Sir Thomas Elyot, author of *The boke named the governour* (1531). Elyot agreed with Castiglione in preferring monarchy above democracy, in prudent deference to Henry VIII. And there were other matters on which their views coincided. One of these was "the Good Order of Dancing", to which Elyot gave wearisome attention. "I am nat of that opinion", he began four prolix chapters, "that all daunsinge generallye is repugnant unto vertue: al though some persones excellently lerned, specially divines, so do affirme it". Rather, he eventually concludes, "these qualities [of severity and magnanimity, constancy and honour, sapience and continence], in this wise beinge knitte to gether, and signified in the personages of man and woman daunsinge, do expresse or sette out the figure of very nobilitie; whiche in the higher astate it is contained, the more excellent is the vertue in estimation".[3]

In Dr Johnson's reckoning, Castiglione's *Il cortegiano* was "the best book that ever was written upon good breeding . . . and you [Boswell] should read it".[4] Next was the *Galateo* of Giovanni della Casa, "done into English" in 1576 by the lawyer Robert Peterson, of Lincoln's Inn. The *Galateo* was a straightforward courtesy-book: "A Treatise of the Manners and Behaviours, it behoveth a Man to use and eschewe, in his Familiar Conversation. A Worke very necessary & profitable for all Gentlemen, or Other." And it covered every sort of situation. "When thou hast blowne thy nose", is one of della Casa's earlier and more unpleasant advices, "use not to open thy handkercheif, to glare uppon thy snot, as if thou hadst pearles and Rubies fallen from thy braynes".[5] However, it was always less for polite behaviour than for the gentle art of conversation that most would have consulted the *Galateo*. Here della Casa, a sophisticated career churchman with no family of his own, is equally blunt. Avoid "sorrowfull matters", he urges, for "it will ill become us to drive men into their dumpes". But

> They doe asmuche amisse too, that never have other thing in their mouthe, then their children, their wife, and their nourse. "My litle boy, made mee so laughe yesterday: heare you: you never sawe a sweeter babe in your life: my wife is such a one, Cecchina told me: of troth you would not beleeve what a wit shee hath:" There is none so idle a body, that will either intend to answer, or abide to heare suche foolishe prittle prattle. For it ircks a mans ears to harken unto it.[6]

Truly, "in speach a man may fault many wayes". He must guard against "vaine or filthye" talk; he "must neither embase, nor exalte himselfe too muche out of measure"; he must eschew the orator's "pomp, bravery, & affectation" in his talk, or men will "laughe him to scorne for it"; he should avoid troubling others "with so base and absurde matter as dreames be"; "neither in sporte nor in earnest, must a man speake any thing against God or his Saintes, how witty or pleasaunt so ever the matter be."[7]

Della Casa's advice might have resulted in the silence that he urges on the unfortunate stammerer: "let him not alwayes babble and gabbe, and keepe a courte alone: let him rather amend the defect of his tounge with silence, and hearinge".[8] But that was far from his intention, for "as over muche babble makes a man weary: so doth over muche Silence procure as great disliking. For, to use silence in place where other men talke to and fro: is in maner, as muche a fault, as not to pay your share and scot as other men doe . . . speache is a meane to shewe men your minde . . . [and] mute & still fellowes [are but] coldly welcome to pleasaunt and mery companie, that meete to passe the time away in pleasure and talke".[9]

Never had that talk been more pleasurable, nor the company merrier, than in the ducal palace at Urbino. Duke Guidubaldo, so Castiglione tells us, "set his delight above all thinges to have his house furnished with most noble and valiant Gentlemen, with whome hee lived verie familiarly, enjoying their conversation". But it was in the evenings, in particular, after the duke had retired to bed, that "everie man ordinarily . . . drew where the Dutchesse was", and that debate quickened under the genial eye of Lady Elisabetta. Guidubaldo died in April 1508, and the good times came to an end. But as long as he had lived, "there was then to bee heard", Castiglione sighed, "pleasant communications and merie conceites, and in everie mans countenance a man might perceive painted a loving jocundnesse. So that this house truely might wel be called the very Mansion place of mirth and joy. And I beleeve it was never so tasted in other place, what manner a thing the sweete conversation is that is occasioned of an amiable and loving company, as it was once there".[10]

Those recollected conversations later became the substance of *The courtier*. There had been much cut-and-thrust in the debates, but also a good deal of laughter. On one occasion, the discourse touched upon beauty. "Beautie is not alwaies good", had begun Morello da Ortona. Yet, laughed Pietro Bembo, taking the opposite view, "I say that beautie commeth of God and is like a circle, the goodnesse whereof is the Centre. And therefore, as there can be no circle without a centre, no more can beautie be without goodnesse". Think of the world, Bembo urged:

The heaven rounde besette with so many heavenly lights: and in the middle, the earth environed with the Elements, and upheld with the waight of it selfe . . . Thinke now of the shape of man, which may be called a litle world: in whom every parcell of his bodie is seene to be necessarily framed by arte and not by happe . . . Beholde the feathers of foules, the leaves and boughes of trees

> ... Leave nature, and come to arte ... Pillers, and great beames
> upholde high buildings and pallaces, and yet are they no lesse
> pleasurefull unto the eyes of the beholders, than profitable to the
> buildings ... It [the world] is praysed, in saying, the beautifull
> heaven, beautifull earth, beautifull sea, beautifull rivers, beautifull
> woodes, trees, gardens, beautifull cities, beautifull churches,
> houses, armies. In conclusion this comely and holy beautie is a
> wondrous setting out of everie thing.[11]

In Art as in Nature, there is beauty in utility and in appropriateness, in
harmony and in graceful proportions. If "it be a hard matter", says della
Casa, "to shewe precisely, Bewtie, what maner of thing it is: yet that you
may have some marke, to know her by: you must understand, that
where jointly & severally, every parte & the whole hath his due proportion and measure, there is Bewtie."[12]

Della Casa found the "saide proportion and measure" in the faces of
"faier and goodly women". And it was the *natural balance and symmetry*
of the human face and body, desirable in love but attainable also in so
much else, which set a new agenda for the arts. "In Architecture", wrote
Sir Henry Wotton in 1624, "there may seem to be two opposite affecta-
tions, Uniformitie and Varietie, which yet will very well suffer a good
reconcilement, as we may see in the great Paterne of Nature, to which I
must often resort: For surely there can be no Structure, more uniforme,
then our Bodies in the whole Figuration: Each side, agreeing with the
other, both in the number, in the qualitie, and in the measure of the
Parts: And yet some are round, as the Armes, some flat, as the Hands,
some prominent, and some more retired: So as upon the Mater [of
Architecture], wee see that Diversitie doth not destroy Uniformitie, and
that the Limmes of a noble Fabrique, may be correspondent enough,
though they be various; Provided alwayes, that we doe not runne into
certaine extravagant Inventions."[13]

A very similar parallel had occurred to Inigo Jones, annotating his
Roman sketchbook of 1614. Much of that book was given over to ana-
tomical drawings, among them studies from Michelangelo's *Last Judgement*. Inigo Jones tells us why:

> As in Design first one studies the parts of the body of Man as eyes,
> noses, mouths, ears and so of the rest to be practised in the parts

separate before one comes to put them together to make a whole figure and clothe it, and consequently a whole story with all the ornaments. So in Architecture one must study the parts as loggias, entrances, halls, chambers, stairs, doors, windows, and then adorn them with columns, cornices, *sfondati* [painted door-cases?], statues, paintings . . . [etc.]

But like Wotton, Jones was wary of "extravagant invention". The rich Mannerist designs of Michelangelo and his followers – so often misapplied by even the best of their English imitators, at Smythson's Wollaton, for example, or at Audley End – "in my opinion do not well in solid Architecture and the facades of houses":

For as outwardly every wise man carrieth a gravity in Public Places, where there is nothing else looked for, yet inwardly hath his imagination set on fire, and sometimes licentiously flying out, as Nature herself does oftentimes extravagantly, to delight, amaze us, sometimes move us to laughter, sometimes to contemplation and horror, so in Architecture the outward ornaments ought to be solid, proportionable according to the rules, masculine and unaffected.[14]

Within a year, Inigo Jones was the new Surveyor of the King's Works. And uncompromisingly classical buildings such as the Queen's House (Greenwich) and the Banqueting House (Whitehall) swiftly followed. Still a generation ahead of their time, they had no precedents in England and few immediate imitators. But their context also was changing radically. Inigo Jones was in Florence in the early 1600s, when travel remained only for the dedicated. He probably met Wotton while he was there. On his second (and crucially important) Italian journey of 1613–14, Jones travelled in the suite of Thomas Howard, Earl of Arundel, statesman and art connoisseur. Between those visits, the Wars of Religion had sputtered out. There was peace with Spain from 1604. And the pacification of France and The Netherlands increasingly opened continental Europe to English travellers. "Of all other famous and glorious Nations separated from the maine Continent of the world", Sir Thomas Palmer told Prince Henry in 1606, "the people of Great Britain are by so much the more interested to become Travailers".[15] They had a great deal of lost ground to make up.

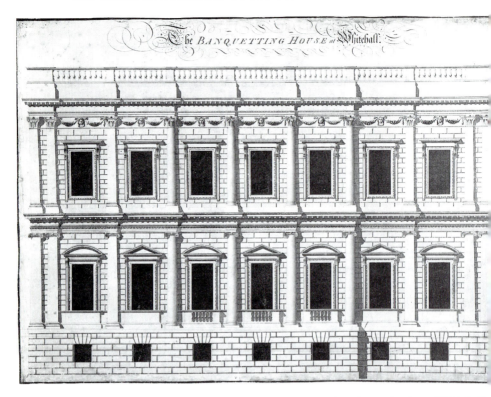

24  Inigo Jones's strictly classical Banqueting House (begun in 1619) at the royal palace of Whitehall.
elevation by John Soane was awarded the Royal Academy's silver medal in 1772.

It was not that overseas travel had ever been entirely denied to Elizabeth's subjects. However, its dangers, not least of moral and religious
corruption, were well known. And travel was left to those – Wotton (the
linguist), Jones (the architect) – who had something specific to learn
from it. Back in 1563, after a conversation at Windsor as lively as any at
Urbino, Sir Richard Sackville had taken the educator, Roger Ascham,
to one side. The company had spoken eloquently about schooling. And
Sackville wanted Ascham to record the debate; in particular, to show
what he thought even then "of the common goinge of Englishe men
into Italie". What resulted was Ascham's posthumously published *The
scholemaster* (1570). But Ascham was no friend of abroad. "I was once in
Italie my selfe", he confides, "but I thanke God, my abode there was but
ix days: And yet I sawe in that litle tyme, in one Citie, more libertie to
sinne than ever I hard tell of in our noble Citie of London in ix yeare".
Renounce travel (Ascham advises) and read *The courtier* instead, where:

To joyne learnyng with cumlie exercises, Conto Baldesaer
Castiglione in his booke, *Cortegiano*, doth trimlie teache: which
booke, advisedlie read and diligentlie folowed but one yeare at
home in England, would do a yong jentleman more good, I wisse,
then three yeares travell abrode spent in Italie. And I mervell this
booke is no more read in the Court than it is, seyng it is so well
translated into English by a worthie Jentleman Syr Th. Hobbie,
who was many wayes well furnished with learnyng, and very
expert in knowledge of divers tonges.[16]

Hoby had become expert in "divers tonges" when training for a
career in diplomacy. And there would always be those who, rejecting
Ascham's counsel, followed similar career paths of their own. "Travel in
the younger sort is a part of education", declared Francis Bacon, himself
an observant tourist in his youth.[17] And Philip Sidney, likewise, had travelled purposefully as a young man, beginning a meticulously planned
*giro* in 1572, which would take him almost everywhere but Rome.[18]
When Henry Wotton had completed his education at Oxford, his biog-
rapher tells us, "he then laid aside his Books, and betook himself to the
useful Library of Travel, and a more general Conversation with Man-
kind; employing the remaining part of his Youth, his industry and fortune, to adorn his mind, and to purchase the rich Treasure of Foreign
knowledge".[19]

It could scarcely be imagined that such a treasury of knowledge – of
courts, churches and monasteries, of walls and fortifications, of antiquities and ruins, of houses and gardens "of state and pleasure", of cabinets
and rarities, and much else – could be gained (*pace* Ascham) just from
books. "True it is", admitted Roger Pratt as late as 1660, "that a man
may receive some helps upon a most diligent study from those excellent,
and most exact designs of Palladio, Freart, Scamozzi, and some few
others, yet never having seen anything in its full proportions, it is not to
be thought that he can conceive of them as he ought".[20] He himself was
fully expert in both areas.

Providentially, Roger Pratt and a few others had escaped the Civil
War: "to avoid which storm, & give myself some convenient education,
I then went out of England about April anno 1643 and continued travelling in France, Italy, Flanders, Holland, etc. till Aug. 1649 viz. about
six years and a half, at which time I againe returned after the end of the

war and the death of the King". Among those who had been less lucky was Inigo Jones, trapped in the long siege of Basing House. Nevertheless, the two were off together, soon after Pratt's return, to consult on the rebuilding of Coleshill. It was probably that experience which afterwards inspired Pratt's advice to intending house-builders: "If you be not able to handsomely contrive it [the design] yourself", he warned in 1660, "get some ingenious gentleman who has seen much of that kind abroad and been somewhat versed in the best authors of Architecture: viz. Palladio, Scamozzi, Serlio etc. to do it for you, and to give you a design of it in paper, though but roughly drawn, (which will generally fall out better than one which shall be given you by a home-bred Architect for want of his better experience, as is daily seen)". Houses may be square or oblong, of H-plan or E-plan, on either three or four sides of a central court, "with pavilions at the corners, after the manner of France, or without, as that of England, Italy, etc." But:

> As to the several forms of building, it is most certain, that no man deserves the name of an Architect, who has not been very well versed both in those old ones of Rome, as likewise the more modern of Italy and France etc. because that with us, having nothing remarkable but the banquetting house at Whitehall and the portico at St Paul's [both by Inigo Jones], it is no ways probable that any one should be sufficiently furnished with the variety of invention, and of excellent ideas, which upon several occasions it will be necessary for him to have, who has had but so great a scarcity wherein to employ his judgment, neither can it be supposed that anything should be in the Intellect, which was never in the senses.[21]

Travel abroad is no guarantee of sensibility. And there may still be some truth in the "ancient complaint", commonly made (said Jerome Turler in 1574) that "our countrymen [more] usually bring three things with them out of Italy, a naughty conscience, an empty purse, and a weak stomach".[22] However, that "new way of Architecture" to which Sir Roger Pratt himself adhered owed almost everything to the inspiration of English travellers. One of those, John Evelyn, was an old friend of Roger Pratt's. They had been together in Rome during the winter of 1644–45. And Evelyn's exact account of that visit – while Archbishop Laud went to the scaffold back at home in England, and Oliver

Cromwell prepared for victory at Naseby – is both an exceptionally complete record of everything he saw and important evidence of the shaping of his taste.[23]

When in Rome, Evelyn was as ready to inspect the "modern" churches and palaces of the papal city as to visit its imperial antiquities. Consequently, his first impressions of Roger Pratt's new mansion for Edward Hyde, Earl of Clarendon, are worth recalling. "Let me speak ingenuously", wrote Evelyn in January 1666 to Lord Cornbury (Clarendon's heir) who, before too long, would sell on his father's house to pay his debts:

> I went with prejudice, and a critical spirit; incident to those who
> fancy they know any thing in art: I acknowledge to your Lordship

*Clarendon House (Piccadilly), built for Edward Hyde to a design by Roger Pratt: "without hyperbolies, best contriv'd, the most usefull, gracefull, and magnificent house in England" (John Evelyn, in 1666). ; engraving is of Clarendon House shortly before its demolition in 1683, between Christopher Monck's lase and re-sale to developers.*

that I have never seene a nobler pile: my old friend and fellow traveller (cohabitant & contemporarie at Rome) has perfectly acquitted himselfe. It is, without hyperbolies, the best contriv'd, the most usefull, gracefull, and magnificent house in England, – I except not Audly-end; which, though larger, and full of gaudy &

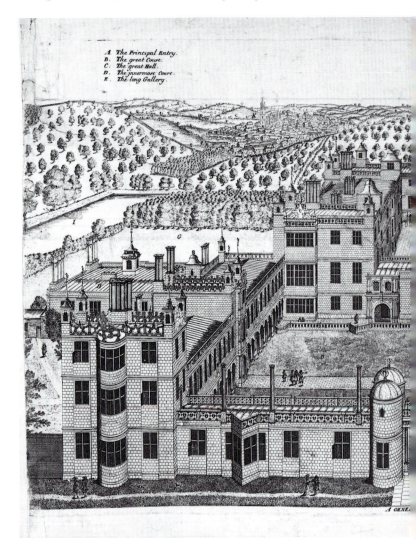

*26  Henry Winstanley's fine perspective view of Audley End, near Saffron Walden (Esse drawn for Charles II in 1676, shortly after Charles had bought the palace for himself. I this extravagant double-courtyard house, built at huge cost by Thomas and Catherine Ho 1604–14, that James I once commented that it was "too big for a King but might do for*

barbarous ornaments, dos not gratifie judicious spectators. As I sayd, my Lord: here is state and use, solidity & beauty most symetricaly combin'd together: Seriously there is nothing abroad pleases me better; nothing at home approches it . . . I pronounce it the first Palace of England.[24]

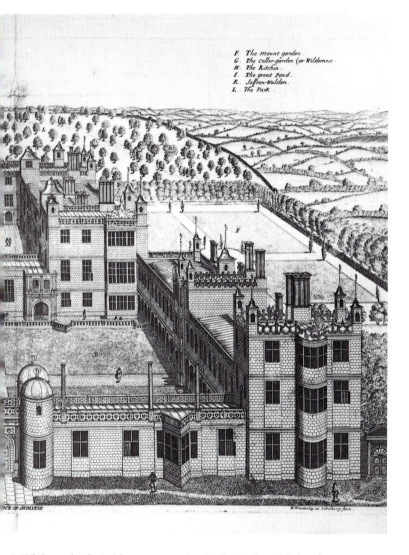

*r". While much admired by contemporaries, Audley End quickly lost favour to more com-*
*…ses like Coleshill, Belton and Clarendon. Today, only the central hall and its attached*
*…rvive intact at Audley End. The rest – including the entire outer court and most of the*
*…vas demolished soon after 1701, when the palace reverted to the Howards.*

Della Casa had recognized beauty "where jointly & severally, every part & the whole hath his due proportion and measure". Inigo Jones welcomed architecture that was "solid, proportionable according to the rules, masculine and unaffected". Solidity and symmetry were again the "modern" qualities that Evelyn most admired at Clarendon House. Their opposites were "Gotique" or "barbarous".

Audley End, built for Thomas Howard, Earl of Suffolk, in 1604–14, was already the target for such epithets. Evelyn, fresh from Rome, was among Audley End's earliest critics. He had visited the house in 1654, when he declared it "without comparison one of the statliest Palaces of the Kingdome". On that occasion, he had especially liked Howard's vaulted cellars: "I never saw any so neate & well dispos'd". However, the great gallery also was "the most cherefull, & I thinke one of the best in England"; there was "a faire dining-roome, & the rest of the Lodgings answerable with a pretty Chapell"; the gardens were "well inclosed"; the park was "nobly well walled, wooded & watred"; the entire structure was "perfectly uniforme". Nevertheless, he found Audley End a "mixt fabric, 'twixt antique & modern": the sort of pile that, only 16 years later (with Clarendon House in between), he would more readily dismiss as a "cherefull piece of Gotic-building, or rather *antico-moderno*".[25]

Samuel Pepys underwent the same conversion. Pepys's first visit to Audley End was on 27 February 1660, when "the housekeeper shewed us all the house, in which the stateliness of the ceilings, chimney-pieces, and form of the whole was exceedingly worth seeing. He took us into the cellar, where we drank most admirable drink, a health to the King [about to return]. Here I played my flageolette, there being an excellent echo."[26] The next time Pepys came visiting was on 8 October 1667, and again the party went "all over the house and garden: and mighty merry we were". But experience of Clarendon House – as with Evelyn, his fellow diarist – had intervened. Just five months before, Pepys had been called to the lord chancellor's new mansion, to attend the Committee for Tangier. And it was then that he pronounced himself "mightily pleased with the nobleness of this house, and the brave furniture and pictures, which indeed is very noble".[27] Audley End, in contrast, was ill-furnished, overblown, *retardataire*:

> The house indeed do appear very fine, but not so fine as it hath heretofore to me; particularly the ceilings are not so good as I

always took them to be, being nothing so well wrought as my Lord
Chancellor's are [at Clarendon House]; and though the figure of
the house without be very extraordinary good, yet the stayre-case
is exceeding poor; and a great many pictures, and not one good
one in the house but one of Harry the Eighth, done by Holben;
and not one good suit of hangings in all the house, but all most
ancient things, such as I would not give the hanging-up of in my
house; and the other furniture, beds and other things, accordingly.
Only the gallery is good, and, above all things, the cellars, where
we went down and drank of much good liquor; and indeed the
cellars are fine: and here my wife and I did sing to my great content.[28]

Towards the end of the century, when Celia Fiennes made her visit,
Audley End seemed to her "altogether a stately palace", making "a noble
appearance like a town". Inside, "the roomes are large· and lofty with
good rich old furniture tapistry etc.". But there were "noe beds", Celia
noted, "in that part we saw"; William III (who then owned it) had
ceased to come to Audley End; and the palace was widely rated a curiosity.[29] Roger North, while perfectly aware of the original purpose of
Suffolk's pile, pointed the contrast between Audley End and the houses
becoming fashionable in his day. "I have often wish't", North confessed
in 1698, "to see an house built *alla moderna*, composed of greater and
smaller orders of rooms compact well together, with regard to use, state,
and decorum". But the new-style suburban villa failed this test:

A villa is quasy a lodge, for the sake of a garden, to retire to injoy
and sleep, without pretence of enterteinement of many persons;
and yet in this age, the humour takes after that, and not the other.
And the inconveniences [i.e. lack of space] are not dreamt of till
experience shews them. The ancients, I mean our elder country
men, took another course; they built in different orders, so as to
accomodate all orders of persons and occasions; of this among
many other instances I shall mention Audley Inn house; which
hath a court at first entrance, of low building and portico walks,
which serves for *passer tiempo* and lodging of officers and servants.
The next court is for parade, and a loftyer order. This may be
esteemed out of fashion, but it is not to be for that disesteemed,

when reason justifies it. For what is more necessary to a numerous court [household], than walks, and numerous apartements; and to dispose in them in order so that you have a pompous walk, from the port to the grand-sall, the building rising as you advance.[30]

However, in these "latter ages" to which North himself belonged, great men "have bin more addicted to a citty life, after the French way. And that recourse to London hath encouraged the trade of building, and that led into ways of compendium [saving] and thrift for gain sake; and not onely in the cittys and townes, a compact model is used, but in all country seats of late built, the same method is practis't, to the abolishing grandure and statlyness of that sort the former ages affected".[31]

It was James I's *bon mot*, when he learnt how much it cost, that Audley End was "too big for a King but might do for a Lord Treasurer". But the Prince who failed to "set a stint to the over sumptuous buildings of private men" had only himself to blame for the excess.[32] Audley End would stretch the means of any owner. No sooner had Charles II bought it in 1667 than he lost interest in the palace. And in 1701 – "very much out of Repaire" and become a "Place his Majesty [William III] in all likelihood will never make Use off" – Audley End reverted to the Howards. They began almost at once to reduce it. Thus by 1713 the Lord Treasurer's flamboyant outer court was "most of it pulled down, there remaining only one large court, which however makes a Noble Palace to the present Earl [Henry Howard] that resides there". The much-admired Long Gallery, already a relic of the past, was demolished in 1752.[33]

Audley End's slide in public favour, having further than most to fall, was precipitous. "Superb" was once the verdict of the German traveller, Hans Jacob Wurmsser von Vendenheym, on seeing the palace in 1610 when half complete; while "said to be the finest in England . . . it is not yet finished, and has cost 100,000 pounds sterling, and it is supposed that the remainder will not come to less".[34] Justus Zinzerling, visiting England that same year, added his voice to the chorus. Zinzerling's special interest was in royal palaces. "Nonesuch we could not see", he later regretted in his *Description of England* (1616), "but it is a very pleasant place; the grounds are highly praised." On the outside, Whitehall "is not very magnificent", but "in the new building is the spacious hall where the Knights of the Garter are accustomed to banquet". St James's Palace is "a pleasant and splendid residence, formerly an abbey". At Richmond Palace "the most curious thing to be seen is Henry VII's Library . . . [and] his bed-chamber sprinkled with his blood". Finest of the many fine apartments at Hampton Court is the Paradise Room, for "it captivates the eyes of all who enter, by the dazzling of pearls of all kinds". Theobalds, too, is "very pleasant"; there you may "pass through two halls, in one are forty trees representing the counties of England; in another are painted the large cities of Europe". But it is to Audley End, still only "a good part built", that Zinzerling, the connoisseur, awards the palm. When finished, "no other palace in the kingdom will compare with it".[35]

If Inigo Jones, as Charles I intended, had rebuilt Whitehall, Audley End would very soon have been out-classed. But the king ran out of money, the Civil War began, and Suffolk's palace was left alone without competitors. When Charles II viewed it, in March 1666, Audley End was old-fashioned but unique. "Many ancient houses of the Crown having been demolished", said Charles, "we have taken a liking to Audley End."[36] And if what he most appreciated was its convenient situation (handy for Newmarket) and bargain price (less than a quarter of the earl's original outlay), the famous Long Gallery, the exactly matching private apartments of the King's Side (south) and the Queen's Side (north), and the French-style dispositions of the great outer court, must all have played their parts in his decision.

Audley End, like a meteor, flared and was gone. Suffolk's Long Gallery, among the grandest ever built, was also one of the first to be demolished. His modish outer court – the nearest English equivalent to Jacques Androuet du Cerceau's Mannerist palaces at Verneuil and Charleval – lives only in the contemporary plans of John Thorpe, its probable builder, and in the 1676 engravings of Charles II's clerk of works, Henry Winstanley.[37] Yet Audley End's importance is undiminished. John Thorpe, of a family of Midlands builders, was a thoroughgoing professional, trained over many years in the royal works and an "excellent Geometrician and Surveiour . . . not onely learned and ingenuous himselfe, but a furtherer and favorer of all excellency whatsoever".[38] But there is no reason to believe he ever travelled. And certainly that purposeful "visiting of forraine countries, and observing of strange fashions" urged by Montaigne on the noble youth "even from his infancie" played no obvious part in Thorpe's career.[39] Like his father before him, Thorpe found inspiration at home or from pattern-books. But what had suited the older Thorpe at Kirby Hall (Northamptonshire) was less than ideal for his son. Thomas Thorpe, building Kirby in the 1570s for Sir Humphrey Stafford and Sir Christopher Hatton, had

27 *Much of the classical ornament and the full height (giant order) pilasters of Sir Humphrey Stafford's inner court at Kirby Hall (Northamptonshire) were copied by Thomas Thorpe, a local mason, from imported architectural treatises by Sebastiano Serlio and Philibert de l'Orme. In the centre, Stafford's displayful Anglo-French porch is dated 1572, but the more correct Italianate balcony-window over the main door is a 1638 insertion by the King's Master Mason, Nicholas Stone, for the antiquary Sir Christopher Hatton III (p. 88).*

worked from Sebastiano Serlio's *L'Architettura* and the *Premier tome de l'architecture* of Philibert de l'Orme. What resulted was an innovatory francophile mansion of fine restraint.[40] In contrast, when John Thorpe, in 1608–1609, began the extension of Audley End, he took as his starting-point the extreme ornamental licence – misuse of the classical orders "in the most wanton manner" and elevations of "the highest degree fantastic" – of du Cerceau's *Les plus excellents bastiments de France*.[41] It was in 1614, when Audley End's outer court was almost done, that Inigo Jones left for his second journey into Italy, inaugurating a new era of refined classicism.

Thus it came about that the first and fiercest critics of Audley End, finding it least able to "gratifie judicious spectators", were committed travellers such as John Evelyn and Roger Pratt. Others, at a greater distance, could find more merit in it. But what they saw was less a building than a life-style. Certainly, the young Ralph Thoresby's first sight of Audley End, in the autumn of 1680, was coloured by the fact that, just the day before, he had "had the honour to see his Majesty and the Duke of York" at Newmarket. To Thoresby, 23 at the time, majestic Audley End remained "the greatest house in England . . . a vast building, or rather town walled in; it is adorned with so many cupolas and turrets above, walks and trees below, as render it a most admirably pleasant seat".[42] Roger North, by the 1690s, was more expert. Yet he too found much to praise in the "different orders" of Audley End, lost in the modern compact houses of Roger Pratt. Howard's huge and rambling palace had at least provided accommodation for all persons and occasions, along with rooms of state and of parade. But "it is the use now, to carry all storys thro in the same levell between floor and ceiling. So was Clarendon house . . . and many, I might say most, of the new and more elegant fabricks of this latter age. The consequence is thatt all rooms in the same story, are equally high pitch't; the inconvenience is, that if you have any great rooms with fitt height your lesser rooms are all like steeples".[43] The obligatory external symmetry of the Coleshill-type facade might exact a heavy toll on life within.

One inevitable casualty of the new compact plan – where "the great rooms are too low, and the small ones too high" – was the traditional open hall of the Middle Ages. But that style of communal living was already almost lost. And more serious was the threat to the Henrician Long Gallery: "that noble accomplishment to an house", first provided

*28  In Elizabethan England, even a relatively small and remote country house like Little Moreton Hall (Cheshire) would be furnished with a top-floor exercise gallery. John Moreton's fashionable walking-space – "for no other use but pastime and health" – was nearly 70 feet long. It ran the full length of the third storey of a new guest-wing at Little Moreton, added in the 1570s, not long after John inherited from his father.*

for promenading Tudor courtiers. "This is a room", North explains, "for no other use but pastime and health." It must be "easy of access, and for that reason should be upon the first floor". But "higher than the next floor it must not be, for such as are in garretts, as I have often seen [at houses such as Montacute, Little Moreton, or Parham], are useless, because none will purchase the use of them with the paines of mounting. And for the same reason, promenades on the topps of houses are useless, and cuppolo closetts and the like [at Coleshill, Kingston Lacy, or Wisbech Castle], because it is irksome even to thinck of climing so high".[44] Matching the state of a prince, Audley End's Long Gallery "is in all respects as one would have it". However,

As the state of a gentleman, or at least his company, may be of a midle condition, or he desires by his enterteinement to raise them above their order, which is allwais pleasing, I should propose a gallery of a midle sort, not wholly dedicated to parade, nor to private use, but such as may serve reasonably to both porposes, and not pretend to the height of grandure, as usually is expected. And I doe not know any superfluity in an house more desirable than this, for it pleaseth all, and is usefull to all, and being tollerable scituated serves as well as the best, few minding nice matters.[45]

Accordingly, to entertainment and health, North's two original purposes of the gallery, was added a civilizing (or even a pedagogic) role: elevating the quality of discourse in a household by furnishing space "for select companys to converse in".

29  *Palladio's Villa Barbaro (1557–58), built for the brothers Marcantonio and Daniele Barbaro at Maser (near Treviso), uses a full-height loggia as always intended in Mediterranean countries: for exercise, conversation, and alfresco eating.*

Such was also the intention of another Renaissance borrowing from the South, of "those portico rooms, which the Italians call the *loggia*, and are with them seldome omitted". Open colonnades, Roger North admits, are not as "generally recomendable to us, because the same reasons doe not hold here, as in Italy, the climats being so vastly different with respect to weather . . . the raines and snows are not so furious, frequent, and driving as here [in England]; nor is the heat so furious". Even so,

> I am a great freind to portico walks abroad . . . [and] I must confess
> it is of use to every individuall person of the family, who hath a
> title to pass time in a degree of idleness. And therefore great
> familys, who for parade maintein many such, ought [even in Eng-
> land] to provide such *promenoirs* for them, that they may be so well
> diverted at home, as not to seek their pastime abroad, and so add
> debauchery to idleness. And I know no place so calculated for this
> end as Audely-End, which hath (as I remember) 2 courts portico'd
> round.[46]

He remembered rightly. And what the builders of Audley End had
most specifically provided was a context for the life of *The courtier*. Far
from Duke Guidubaldo's gentle palace at Urbino, the "sweete conversation" of Castiglione's "amiable and loving company" was, in practice,
impossible to reproduce. Nor has there ever been a time when the patri-
otic Englishman has adopted southern manners without reserve. "A
yong gentleman", warned Roger Ascham in the 1560s, "thus bred up in
this goodly schole [of Italy], to learne the next and readie way to sinne,
to have a busie head, a factious hart, a talkative tonge, fed with discours-
ing of factions: led to contemne God and his Religion, shall cum home
into England, but verie ill taught".[47] Nevertheless, a good education,
whether obtained at home or abroad, was increasingly a requirement of
polite society. Never before had the gentry demanded entry in such
numbers to their own universities.[48] "I have told you often", said Valentine (the Elizabethan courtier) to Vincent (the country squire), "that the
chief and principal studies, and delight of a Gentleman, must be learning and Arms: and therefore such as have [been] civilly brought up, do
seldom muse on other matters". Truly, "so noble knowledges are not
gotten without long labour and perseverance", agreed Vincent; however, "you must understand that the most of us [squires] have gone to
school, and many have seen some part of the wars", so "I pray you tell
me what imperfection you [still] find in the conversation of our Country Gentlemen". Valentine pulled no punches in his reply:

> Touching their conversation, you shall besides the rusticity of their
> houses and garments, find them full of lofty looks, barbarous

behaviour, and undecent doings. As for example, some one will laugh when he speaketh: another will cough, before he tells his tale: and some will gape or yawn when he giveth the hearing. . . . Also if they hap to dine at any table, either they are sullenly silent, or else they fall into speech of their own Ancestors, their own lands, their own wives or children: other subjects of talk ye shall seldom find among these sorts of country men.[49]

There is more than just an echo, in the gapes and yawns of the *Cyvile and uncyvile life* (1579), of the "coffing or neesing", the yawning, spitting and other "yllfavoured fashions" of those who "braye and crye out like Asses" in Peterson's 1576 translation of the *Galateo*.[50] And in Elizabethan England, from this time forward, no sophisticated townee nor would-be courtier could unselfconsciously enjoy the honest country talk of Squire Vincent's good fellows: "of hawks or hounds, fishing or fowling, sowing or grassing, ditching or hedging, the dearth or cheapness of grain, or any such matters, whereof Gentlemen commonly speak in the Country".[51] Rather, he must go the Italian way, "seasoning [his] talke at the table among grave and serious discourses, with conceits of wit and pleasant invention, as ingenious Epigrams, Emblemes, Anagrams, merry tales, wittie questions and answers, mistakings".[52]

It was in another popular manual, Henry Peacham's *The compleat gentleman* of 1622 (revised 1634), that these guidelines were laid down. And it was Peacham again who, in an earlier work, had once praised John Thorpe as "the furtherer and favorer of all excellency whatsoever". But it was Peacham (the educator), not Thorpe (the surveyor), who then took himself abroad, believing "the most eminent and wise men of the world to have been the greatest Travailers". French palaces, Peacham noted, were "very Magnificent". Of Charleval (Thorpe's model for Audley End), "had it beene quite finished, it had beene the chiefe building of France"; indeed, "I know not whether in all Europe, any buildings may for Maiestie and State be compared with those of France . . . they being the best Architects of the world".[53] Frenchmen, Peacham believed, though "quicke witted" and "full of discourse", were too "light and inconstant" to converse well. However, he had found better talk in The Netherlands:

When I was in Utrecht, and lived at the table of that Honourable Gentleman, Sir John Ogle, Lord Governour [1610–18], whither resorted many great Schollers and Captaines, English, Scottish, French, and Dutch, it had beene enough to have made a Scholler or Souldier, to have observed the severall disputations and discourses among many strangers, one while of sundry formes of battailes, sometime of Fortification; of Fire-workes, History, Antiquities, Heraldry, pronunciation of Languages, &c. that his table seemed many times a little Academie.[54]

Ogle, the lord governor, was a successful mercenary, and it was natural enough that fortification, fireworks and "sundry formes of battailes" should feature prominently in the discourse of his company. But the disputations of that "little Academie" at Utrecht ranged more widely. Peacham himself, expert in heraldry, shared with other scholars the pleasure in "venerable" antiquities (statues, inscriptions and coins) "best knowne to such as have seene them abroad in France, Spaine, and Italy, where the Gardens and Galleries of great men are beautified and set forth to admiration with these kinds of ornaments".[55] Just such a patron was Thomas Howard (1585–1646), the pre-eminent English collector:

And here [interjects Peacham] I cannot but with much reverence, mention the every way Right honourable Thomas Howard Lord high Marshall of England, as great for his noble Patronage of Arts and ancient learning, as for his birth and place. To whose liberall charges and magnificence, this angle of the world oweth the first sight of Greeke and Romane Statues, with whose admired presence he began to honour the Gardens and Galleries of Arundel-House about twentie yeeres agoe, and hath ever since continued to transplant old Greece into England.[56]

Before Peacham's second edition of 1634, Earl Thomas had been joined by another: "King Charles also ever since his comming to the Crowne [in 1625], hath amply testified a Royall liking of ancient statues, by causing a whole army of old forraine Emperours, Captaines, and Senators all at once to land on his coasts to come and doe him homage, and attend him in his palaces of Saint James, and Sommerset-house".[57]

Arundel's travelling companion, on a long antiquarian foray into

*Mary Herbert's "curious" lodge at Houghton, in Ampthill (Bedfordshire), in the late eighteenth century, tly before the house was dismantled. On the west facade (right), an Italianate three-tier loggia shows the ence of Inigo Jones and his followers.*

Italy, had been Inigo Jones, appointed Royal Surveyor in 1615. The next year, Jones began building the Queen's House (Greenwich); he was designing a classical gateway for Earl Thomas in 1619, and making a start for the king on Whitehall. Other Englishmen, too, would drink deep of the "warm South".[58] And few, even among those patrons already active in Elizabeth's reign, could remain unaffected by the new optimism. Through the 1580s and 1590s, Mary Herbert, Countess of Pembroke and sister of the soldier-poet Sir Philip Sidney, had been "the greatest patronesse of witt and learning of any lady in her time", keeping a house at Wilton which "was like a College, there were so many learned and ingeniose persons".[59] Widowed in 1601, she was over 40 on James I's accession in 1603; yet would begin again in 1615 on a "curious" house at Houghton, in Ampthill (Bedfordshire), "according to the description of Basilius's house in the firste booke of the *Arcadia* (which is dedicated to her)", for which "the architects were sent for from Italie".[60]

Houghton Lodge, these days, is just a shell. And the parallels are no longer obvious between Lady Mary's great house and the imaginary star-shaped lodge of her brother's *Arcadia* – "having, round about, a garden framed into like points; and beyond the garden, ridings cut out, each answering the angles of the lodge".[61] Nevertheless, King Basilius's four woodland *vistos* were repeated again at Mary's lodge: "each prospect 25 or 30 miles". And we know that at the centre of the west facade at Houghton, looking down the length of one of these drives, was a three-tiered Italian *loggia* of such classical perfection and "solid" Palladian worth as to make it seem that only Inigo Jones could have built it.[62] There is no evidence, in point of fact, that he did so. But on another "Arcadian place and paradise", at Lady Mary's Wilton House, he both counselled and worked in detail for her sons. John Aubrey, who knew Wilton well, takes up the tale:

> King Charles the first did love Wilton above all places, and came thither every summer. It was he that did put Philip first Earle of Pembroke upon making this magnificent garden and grotto, and to

31 *The south garden front at Wilton House (Wiltshire) in its final contracted form, by Inigo Jones and* Webb, *"all* al Italiano*".*

84

new build that side of the house that fronts the garden, with two
stately pavilions at each end, all *al Italiano*. His Majesty intended to
have had it all designed by his own architect, Mr. Inigo Jones, who
being at that time, about 1633, engaged in his Majesties buildings
at Greenwich, could not attend to it; but he recommended it to an
ingeniouse architect, Monsieur Solomon de Caus, a Gascoigne,
who performed it very well; but not without the advice and ap-
probation of Mr Jones . . . [then] The south side of this stately
house, that was built by Monsieur de Caus, was burnt ann. 1647
or 1648, by airing of the roomes. In anno 1648 Philip (the first)
re-edifyed it, by the advice of Inigo Jones; but he, being then very
old, could not be there in person, but left it to Mr. Webb, who
married his niece.[63]

Earl Philip (d.1650) was not the "first" Herbert earl. Aubrey calls him
that to distinguish him from the second Earl Philip (d.1669) and the
spendthrift third (d.1683), succeeded by the "good" Earl Thomas
(d.1733). And Aubrey's narrative sows confusion in other ways, mixing
Solomon with Isaac de Caus.[64] However, Aubrey was a native Wiltshire-
man, born and bred, and although still only a youth when Wilton was
remodelled, would later claim the Herberts as his friends. It was in Earl
Thomas's time, beginning in 1683, that Aubrey was made most welcome at Wilton House. And it was then, before the "architect" Earl
Henry (d.1750) refashioned Wilton's gardens in the English landscape
style, that Aubrey saw them still *al Italiano*:

This garden, within the inclosure of the new wall, is a thousand
foot long, and about four hundred in breadth; divided in its length
into three long squares or parallellograms, the first of which divisions, next the building [the new south range], hath four platts
embroydered; in the midst of which are four fountaines, with statues of marble in their middle; and on the sides of those platts are
the platts of flowers; and beyond them is a little terrass raised, for
the more advantage of beholding those platts. In the second division are two groves or woods, cutt with divers walkes . . . and in
the middest of the aforesayd groves are two great statues of white
marble of eight foot high, the one of Bacchus, and the other of
Flora; . . . At the beginning of the third and last division are, on

either side of the great walke, two ponds with fountains, and two columnes in the middle, casting water all their height; which causeth the moving and turning of two crowns at the top of the same; and beyond is a compartment of green, with divers walkes planted with cherrie trees; and in the middle is the great ovall, with the Gladiator of brasse, [a copy of] the most famous statue of all that antiquity hath left.[65]

One of those who saw Isaac de Caus's garden in process of creation was Lieutenant Hammond in 1635. Accompanied by "the fat Dutch Keeper thereof, a rare artist", Hammond admired in particular the "rare

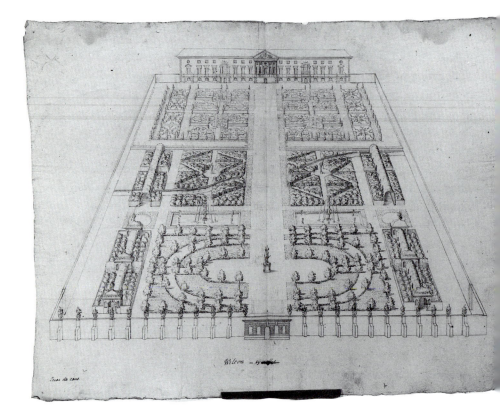

*32 A bird's-eye view of the Herbert gardens at Wilton House, as designed by Isaac de Caus. In the (front) is Hubert le Sueur's cast of the Borghese Gladiator, first made for Charles I and then copied fo* statuary gardens at Wilton. Other Italian features included the fountains (centre) and the elaborate trick w works in the stone pavilions (right and left), which sang like birds and "dowse the unsuspecting onlookers' the top, the elevation is of an earlier projected facade, the full width of the new garden, which was r completed.*

Water-worke now making, and contriving by this outlandish Engineer, for the Singing, and Chirping of Birdes, and other strange rarities, onely by that Element".[66] He also saw Hubert le Sueur's "Romane Gladiator alle in brasse" (later presented by Earl Thomas to Sir Robert Walpole), and noted the many antique-style statues (some still at Wilton) – of Venus "with her sonne Cupid in her armes", Diana "with her bathing sheet", Cleopatra "with the Serpent", Flora and Bacchus "both most artificially cutt" – by the then fashionable monumental sculptor, Nicholas Stone.[67]

Hubert le Sueur, sculptor of the Wilton *Gladiator*, was a self-important Frenchman, best known for his bronze castings from the antique. It was he who brought the "moulds and patterns of certain antiques" from Italy in 1631, which furnished Charles I's palace at St James with its "whole army of old forraine Emperours, Captaines, and Senators".[68] Nicholas Stone, English-born but trained at Amsterdam, was a fresher talent in every way. Both sculptors worked at different times for Inigo Jones – Stone on the Banqueting House (Whitehall) in 1619–22; le Sueur on James I's catafalque in 1626. And all three were to contribute to a Jacobean enlightenment, encouraging radical new departures from Tudor insularism. There is an extraordinary marble memorial, on the floor of Hatfield Church, to Sir William Curle (d.1617), who lies twisted and half-covered by his shroud.[69] Sir William's cadaver image began a new tradition, and was repeated several times on other monuments. But nothing remotely like Nicholas Stone's naturalistic Hatfield effigy had been seen before in England. In its sad and poignant realism, it was as much a culture shock as the Whitehall Banqueting House.

Nor was that, even so, the end of change. Stone's Netherlandish realism was quickly overtaken by an exaggerated regard for the antique. In the 1630s, Stone was providing statuary – a *Diana* in repose, with her Cupid fled – to make a new Olympus for Charles I of Windsor Castle. He carved a *Hercules*, now at Blickling, for the Pastons of Oxnead Hall, with a *Venus*, a *Mercury* and a *Jupiter*.[70] Before the end of that same decade, when rebuilding Kirby Hall, Stone furnished Christopher Hatton III (himself a famous antiquary) with the Roman portrait busts which no self-respecting collector could be without: "6 Emperors heads, with their Pedestals cast in Plaster, moulded from the Antiques"(£7 10s), the "head of Apollo, fairly carved in Portland stone, almost twice as big as life"(£4), and "one head carved in stone of Marcus Aurelius"(£4 again),

*33  Nicholas Stone's shrouded effigy of Sir William Curle (d. 1617) at Hatfield Church (Hertfordshire) is a fine example of Low Countries realism – Stone was trained at Amsterdam – and of the new openness of Jacobean society to foreign influences.*

still preserved in the north facade above the loggia.[71] In 1638, as a start was made on Kirby, Nicholas Stone "the younger" left for Italy. His purpose was educational. He went there to study sculpture under the great Gianlorenzo Bernini, among others. But another important objective of the young Stone's lengthy exile was the purchase of models, casts and drawings for his father's workshop. One consignment from Livorno, in the summer of 1640, included "2 plaister heads, one of Venus the other of Cicero . . . a plaister leg moulded from the antique . . . a plaister head of Satyre . . . [and] a Bacchus in plaister". There were some books: "a book of per[s]pective of Vignola"; another on "the fountaines of Roome" (Maggi's *Le fontane di Roma*); a third on the "Archytecture of Vitruvius". And there were "113 small peeces of severall sorts of marbles" for the London yard, to "send for England according to my fathers commaund".[72]

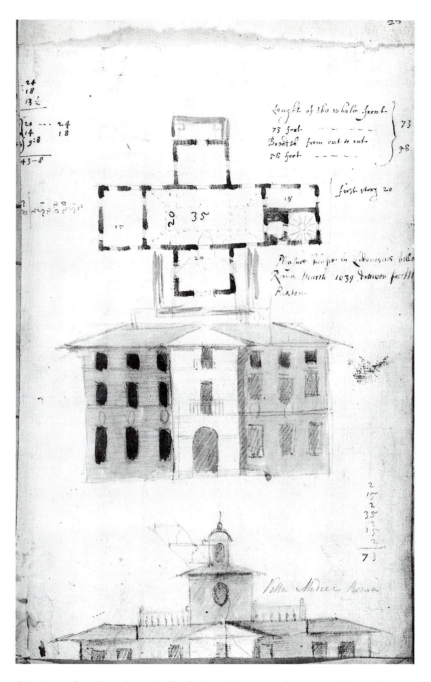

34  A page from the Italian sketchbook of Nicholas Stone the Younger (d.1647), now in
the library of Sir John Soane's Museum. The elevation and plan (with measurements) are
of a "pleasure house" in the famous new gardens of the Villa Ludovisi (Rome), "drawn
for Mr Paston" in March 1639. Nicholas used the bottom of the same page for a sketch
of the cupola on the Villa Medici.

Nicholas Stone the younger only just outlived his father, and much of the point of his long apprenticeship was thus lost. But the Stones's evident conviction of the comparative poverty of English art, fully shared by Inigo Jones and by his more sophisticated royal patrons, was not lost on the Jacobean nobility. Nicholas eventually left Rome in 1642, filling another large chest with casts and drawings. And just two years later, John Evelyn and Roger Pratt were there together. Evelyn's taste, much refined by that exposure, determined his assessment of modern buildings. Christopher Lord Hatton, rebuilder of Kirby Hall, was a personal friend. And Evelyn found Kirby, in the summer of 1654, "a very noble house . . . built *a la moderne*: Garden, & stables agreable". But next to Wilton (visited the month before), even that has to be regarded as faint praise. Kirby's avenue is "ungraceful" and "the seat naked"; Wilton, in contrast, is Arcadian. "After all", concludes Evelyn, "that which to me renders the Seate delightfull, is its being so neere the downes & noble plaines about the Country & contiguous to it." Most "observable" at Wilton is the "Dining-roome in the modern built part towards the Garden, richly gilded, & painted with story by De Creete [Critz], also some other apartments, as that of Hunting Landskips by Pierce: some magnificent chimny-pieces, after the French best manner".[73]

Evelyn, significantly, says nothing whatever about Elizabethan Wilton, choosing even to omit the Holbein porch. Instead, his whole concern is with "the modern built part", and with the gardens de Caus provided to set it off. That "modern built" Wilton was no *English* palace. Earl Philip's new south range was Venetian-inspired: by Inigo Jones, out of Palladio and Scamozzi. Internally, the earl's chimney-pieces and plasterwork were "after the French best manner", from engravings by Barbet and Cotelle.[74] Specially commissioned family portraits lined the great "dineing roome" (the Double Cube Room) of the Herbert house. And in the adjoining "drawing roome" (the Single Cube Room), "the wanscoate is painted with the whole History of the Acardia [sic] romance made by Sir Philip Sidney brother to the then Countess of Pembrooke and composed by him in the fine woods above the house".[75]

In the 1720s, Earl Thomas (Aubrey's patron) still presided at Wilton: "a true patriarchal monarch . . . with an authority agreeable to all his subjects". There, eulogized Defoe, "an exhaulted genius is the instructor, a glorious example the guide, and a gentle well directed hand the governour and law-giver to the whole":

*he Great Dining Room (Double Cube) at Wilton House, with family portraits by Anthony Van Dyck,*
*paintings by Thomas de Critz (the central oval) and Edward Pierce (the coved surround), and a*
*\*y-piece and gilded plasterwork in the newly imported decorative taste, "after the French best manner".*

As the present Earl of Pembroke, the lord of this fine palace, is a nobleman of great personal merit, many other ways; so he is a man of learning, and reading, beyond most men of his lordship's high rank in this nation, if not in the world; and as his reading has made him a master of antiquity, and judge of such peices of antiquity, as he has had opportunity to meet with in his own travels, and otherwise in the world; so it has given him a love of the study, and made him a collector of valuable things, as well in painting as in sculpture, and other excellencies of art, as also of nature; in so much that Wilton House is now a meer musaeum, or a chamber of rarities, and we meet with several things there, which are to be found no where else in the world.[76]

Basilius, king of Arcadia, ruled again.

## CHAPTER 4

# The Grand Tour house

Basilius would have been well content with Wootton Lodge. Wootton, built for Sir Richard Fleetwood at the start of James's reign, was remote from court life in north-east Staffordshire. And it belonged to that period when (as Aubrey once said of Catherine Knyvett's Charlton Park) "architecture was at a low ebbe".[1] But Wootton – "incredibly simple, effortlessly beautiful"[2] – had none of the decorative extravagance of Charlton Park, nor of Catherine's other major residence at Audley End. That simplicity was deliberately Arcadian. And Arcadian again was Wootton's lofty situation – "Truly a place for pleasantness, not unfit to flatter solitariness . . . it gives the eye lordship over a good large circuit . . . with lovely lightsomeness and artificial shadows".[3]

Robert Smythson (d.1614) was probably Fleetwood's architect at Wootton, building there towards the end of his career. And indeed, "there is an atmosphere about Wootton of peace after a battle – the peace [Girouard writes] of achievement".[4] Moreover, Wootton shows maturity in other ways. In one important commission after another, Smythson had emerged as the most creative architectural talent of his generation. From 1568, he had worked for Sir John Thynne at Longleat House. He built Wollaton Hall, in the 1580s, for Sir Francis Willoughby; and designed Hardwick, in the next decade, for Countess Bess. During that time, the modern *compact* plan had first begun to triumph over the medieval *courtyard*; and although still believed less suitable for the grander public projects – Audley End is a case in point – it was

*36  Wootton Lodge (Staffordshire) was one of Robert Smythson's finest country houses, built for Sir Richard Fleetwood in the early years of the seventeenth century as a retreat of Arcadian simplicity. Like other rural pleasure houses of that date, including Lulworth and Bolsover, Wootton was sited where Sir Richard could enjoy distant views, giving his eye "lordship over a good large circuit . . . with lovely lightsomeness and artificial shadows".*

more readily accepted for the lodge. The tall and compact Wootton had its companion lodges in Walter Raleigh's Sherborne, Thomas Howard's Lulworth, Francis Bacon's Verulam, Thomas Tresham's Lyveden, Robert Cecil's Cranborne, and Charles Cavendish's Bolsover. And while none of these private lodges was its builder's principal residence, each was fully – even luxuriously – equipped.

Second homes do not come cheap at any time. But they had never, until then, been more affordable. As Sir Walter Raleigh told Parliament in 1601: "our estates that be £30 or £40 in the Queen's Books, are not the hundred part of our wealth". His reference was to frozen subsidy assessments long favouring the rich, for "persons of very great possessions and wealthe have ben assessed at very meane sommes".[5] However, his own retreat at Sherborne, given to him "as a bôn from queen Elizabeth", was built on other profits also, from higher prices to lower wages and bumped-up rents. Raleigh, as Aubrey says, was "no slug". But a "person so much immerst in action ail along and in fabrication of his owne fortunes . . . could have but little time to study, but what he could spare in the morning". And the privacy of Sherborne, where Raleigh built "a delicate lodge in the park, of brick, not big, but very convenient for the bignes, a place to retire from the Court in summer time, and to contemplate, etc", was very precious to him.[6] It was Montaigne's sensible observation that "solitarinesse, mee seemeth, hath more apparance and reason in those [like Raleigh] which have given their most active and flourishing age into the world". But the rule had a much wider application:

> A man that is able may have wives, children, goods, and chiefly health, but not so tie himselfe unto them that his felicitie depend on them. We should reserve a store-house for our selves . . . altogether ours, and wholy free, wherein we may hoard up and establish our true libertie, and principall retreit and solitarinesse, wherein we must go alone to our selves, take out ordinarie entertainment, and so privately that no acquaintance or communication of any strange thing may therein find place. . . . Let us prepare ourselves unto it, packe wee up our baggage. Let us betimes bid our companie farewell. Shake we off these violent hold-fasts which else-where engage us, and estrange us from our selves. . . . The greatest thing of the world is for a man to know how to be his owne.[7]

"Leading a private life", it was once said of Francis Bacon, "he much delighted to study in the shade of solitariness."[8] And it was "for a place of privacy" that Bacon built Verulam House, to which he could retreat from Gorhambury.[9] Verulam has long since gone, and there is little left of the earlier Gorhambury (his father's mansion) except an "Italianized" porch and other fragments. But what Aubrey saw of the lord chancellor's Verulam, shortly before demolition, confirms its compact plan. "All the tunnells of the chimneys were carried into the middle of the howse", Aubrey reports, and there also "was a delicate staire-case of wood, which was curiously carved, and on the posts of every interstice was some prettie figure, as of a grave divine with his booke and spectacles, a mendicant friar, &c. – (not one thing twice)".[10]

Long before the same device was used again at Chatsworth, Bacon's Verulam had its own internal *visto* done with mirrors; it had a "lovely prospect to the ponds" from a viewpoint on the roof-leads; there were fine panel paintings of Apollo and Jupiter, "bigger then the life and donne by an excellent hand". Yet for all its huge cost – "nine or ten thousand [in] the building" was Aubrey's estimate – Verulam remained the smaller of the lord chancellor's country residences. What it lacked, most significantly, was rooms of state. Those, at Gorhambury, had included a "stately gallerie, whose glasse-windowes", Aubrey remembered, "are all painted; and every pane with severall figures of beast, bird, or flower . . . The windowes looke into the garden, the side opposite to them no window, but that side is hung all with pictures at length, as of King James, his lordship [Francis Bacon], and severall illustrious persons of his time . . . The roofe of this gallerie is semi-cylindrique, and painted in the same hand and same manner [as the gods of classical legend at Verulam House], with heads and busts of Greek and Roman emperours and heroes".[11]

Horace Walpole, a century later, liked Gorhambury less. "There is great taste", he allowed, "in the porticos & Loggias, which tho Italianized, artfully are prevented from swearing with the older parts of the building." It had "many & good rooms, large hall, library-gallery, good Drawing rooms &c. and small Cabinets", where "most of the furniture is the same they [the Bacons] left". But "bad heads" spoiled the ceiling of the "pleasing old Gallery", and the paintings of "remarkable persons" which still lined its walls were no better than "tolerable copies".[12] Walpole knew his paintings well. However, his taste in architecture ran rather to Castle Howard (1699–1726) – "the grandest scene of real magnificence I ever saw"[13] – than to anything (even of high quality) of earlier date. Thus while he listed the Digby portraits at Sherborne Castle, he otherwise said little about Raleigh's lodge which, as greatly enlarged by the first Digby earl (d.1653), was still "an indifferent House, but pretty".[14] And whereas Walpole recognized the worth of a good site at Houghton Park – "beautifully situated on the brow of a high hill commanding the Vale of Bedfordshire" – he found Lady Mary's lodge, although "very picturesque" externally, "a bad & inconvenient house within".[15]

Houghton, by Walpole's inflated standards, was "not a large house". And other Arcadian retreats such as Lulworth and Bolsover – the quintessential "castles" of Spenserian chivalry [16] – were even smaller. They placed little emphasis on public rooms; so that when Thomas Howard required a Long Gallery of his own, he provided it not at his new and "pretty" lodge in Lulworth Park, but at neighbouring Bindon House, his family home.[17] Lulworth, begun by Viscount Bindon in 1608, came to be formal enough. Its great "Dyning Chamber", over the hall, was equipped like a throne-room in 1635, with a canopy or "faire Cloth of State". But Theophilus Howard, Earl of Suffolk (1626–40), who was living at Lulworth when Lieutenant Hammond called, commonly dined alone in a private chamber. And the obvious purpose of Lulworth's plan – compact but multi-floored – was to separate the family quarters from the rest. Hammond was shown the "goodly" basement kitchen, with its "brave archt Cellers for Wine and Beere". He entered by "stately Stayres

*...lworth Castle (Dorset), painted by Theodore de Bruyn (d. 1804). Begun by Viscount Bindon in 1608, ...tress-like lodge at Lulworth was probably still incomplete on Bindon's death in 1611, when it descended ...relatives, the Suffolks. It was Thomas and Catherine Howard, builders of Audley End, who then remod-...ulworth's interior, transforming it from Bindon's Arcadian retreat to the miniature country palace which ...nant Hammond visited in 1635: one of the first compact houses of Stuart England.*

of Freestone", and was encouraged to admire the "stately Hall" and the "faire Lodging Chambers, all richly hang'd and adorn'd", in the four corner towers. But he said nothing of the next (and top) level of family apartments, to which, very probably, he was never admitted. He did, however, go one stage higher, for the view:

> The Top of all this Castle is flat, leaded roundabout and hath also strong Freestone Battlements; on the Leads through a daintie glade, you may see within 2. Mile thereoff, the Ships sayling on the Maine, the most part of the Island of Purbecke; Another statelie Building [Bindon House] of his Lordships neere adjoyning, and all those large and goodly Parkes belonging to this, and that.[18]

Made just for pleasure, Lulworth and Verulam, Sherborne and Wootton were expensive one-off toys. They had little to do with everyday living. But the Jacobean lodge, exceptional though it may have seemed, was already a very modern house. Before long, Lulworth Castle had replaced Bindon House as the principal residence of the Howards' successors, the Welds. And the "elbow-room" that Thomas Howard felt he needed at Lulworth in 1605, enclosing 1000 acres to obtain it, furnished even then one of the earliest examples of the spacious parkland settings obligatory at country houses of later dates.[19] In other ways also, the lodge was a barometer of fashion. Thomas Howard and Francis Bacon, Walter Raleigh and Richard Fleetwood, Thomas Tresham, Robert Cecil and Charles Cavendish were all of the most cultivated class. They had lived abroad, and had read to their advantage in the "great book" of the world, which "none study so much as the Traveler".[20] They knew Castiglione's *Courtier* and della Casa's *Galateo*; they were familiar with the *Essays* of Montaigne. If the remote "store-house for our selves" that Montaigne had preferred was not the only accommodation that they wanted, the retreat to "solitarinesse" had real attractions for them.

That retreat – "there to discourse, to meditate and laugh, as, without wife, without children, and goods, without traine or servants"[21] – was never incompatible with good company. Admittedly, there was now little to bring together the "Country gentleman that never travelled, [and] can scarce go to London without making his Will, at least without wetting his hand-kerchief", and the knowledgeable voyager "wellcome home again to his Neighbours, sought after by his betters, and listened unto with admiration by his inferiours".[22] But "why might not some gentlemen", suggested Evelyn (the botanist) to Boyle (the chemist) in 1659, "whose geniuses are greatly suitable, & who desire nothing more than to give a good example, preserve science, & cultivate themselves, join together in a society, & resolve upon some orders & oeconomy, to be mutually observed . . . [living] profitably and sweetly together".[23] Not long afterwards, the Royal Society was born. But Evelyn's delicious dream of a scholar's rustic hide-away never came any closer to realization. It had envisaged six individual fellows' apartments: "each whereof should contain a small bedchamber, an outward room, a closet, and a private garden, somewhat after the manner of the Carthusians". And two of those retreats, reserved for founders' use, were to have been assigned to Evelyn and his wife, "for we are to be decently asunder". In the Society's main pavilion, separate from this cloister, there was to have been a refectory on the first floor, with a library, withdrawing room and closet; on the second floor, "a fair lodging chamber, a pallet-room, gallery, & a closet; all which should be well & very nobly furnished, for any worthy person that might desire to stay any time, and for the reputation of the college". Then, lest "traine or servants" should disturb the scholars' peace, "we suppose the kitchen, larders, cellars & offices to be contrived in the half story under ground", with another "half story above [the gallery] for servants, wardrobes, & like conveniences".[24]

In protecting the fellows' privacy by hiding away their servants above and below, Evelyn was not describing anything new. Service basements had featured already at the more innovatory Elizabethan houses such as Longleat, Wollaton and Hardwick. And lofts and attic chambers had long been used to accommodate the junior members of great households. However, what remained in flux, even as Evelyn wrote, was the nature and composition of those households. In part, Jacobean "great ones", more secure in their estates, had felt less need of the protection of a retinue. Others had trimmed their households for economy. But all were aware also of a growing chasm between the classes, and increasingly sought the company of their peers. Accordingly, to the earlier "solitariness" of the chamber and privy garden were added new requirements for social space: the exclusive parade space of the long gallery and ground-floor loggia; the straight stair and its broad landings for salutes; the suite of state apartments on the *piano nobile*, and the *visto* prolonged (if necessary) with mirrors.

From the very start of these changes, a distinction arose between the *corridor* gallery of the late-medieval house and the *recreative* gallery of Tudor England. Fully incorporated corridor galleries, as distinct from tacked-on pentices, remained rare in fifteenth-century England. They occurred only at the highest-fashion buildings of the end of the Middle Ages: at Prior Singer's range of lodgings at Much Wenlock Priory and in Archbishop Bourgchier's Brown Gallery at Knole. And some, even so, including the Brown Gallery, were converted to recreational spaces in later times.[25] Nevertheless, the utilitarian gallery ("to convey every man to his loadging") was a very different place from Cardinal Wolsey's new "gallories" at Hampton Court and Whitehall: "fayer, both large and long, to walk in them when that it lyked [him] best". Wolsey used those galleries for work as well as pleasure. They provided him with neutral ground – equivalent to the men's room or office corridor – for informal consultations and private audiences. In Mediterranean countries, under the "splendid silent sun", similar business had been conducted in court or garden. And when a Venetian envoy, in 1531, saw Whitehall's "so-called galleries" for the first time, he could find no words of his own to describe them – "long porticos and halls, without chambers, with windows on each side, looking on gardens and rivers, the ceilings being marvellously wrought in stone with gold".[26] Yet their functions must have been obvious from the start. The closed recreational gallery, probably first seen in northern France, exactly suited the Renaissance lifestyle of the sophisticated Tudor magnate – of the much-travelled churchman like Cardinal Wolsey (at Whitehall) or Archbishop Warham (at Otford); of such wealthy Henrician courtiers as Sir William Fitzwilliam (at Cowdray) or William Lord Sandys (at The Vyne); and, most influentially, of Henry VIII himself, whose great gallery at Nonsuch was "magnificent with every device and the most sumptuous appointment, comparable with the best of the Greek ones".[27]

Henry had been king for 30 years when he began Nonsuch in 1538. And the way he liked to see himself – and so chose to be represented – was equal in rank and dignity to Roman emperors. Prominent at Nonsuch was a great stucco sculpture of Henry VIII, with Prince Edward at his side, enthroned on the curule chair of the Roman magistracy. And every other Nonsuch figure, from Scipio to Socrates and Hercules to Julius Caesar, flattered Henry's learning and promised the same accomplishments in his son.[28] These repeated classical reminders were, of

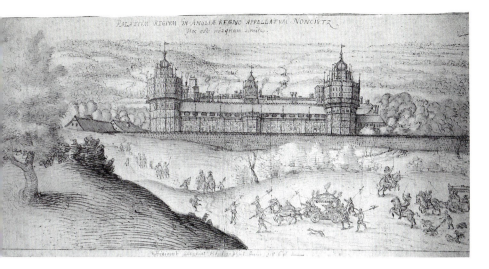

Henry VIII's "privy palace" at Nonsuch (Surrey) was a favourite project of the king's declining years. Its ~~ly ornamented upper storeys and sculptured sheath of stucco panels show clearly in this rare view, over the ~~n wall, by Joris Hoefnagel (1568). The palace, timber-framed on this south facade and impossibly expen-~~o maintain, fell into decay in the seventeenth century, and was demolished in the 1680s.

course, political. By obliterating the Middle Ages, they helped diminish some of the pain of Henry's policies. But their effect was to encourage a precocious classicism at Court, which found clear expression in the arts. One outlet was a new purity in architecture. Nonsuch itself had shown nothing of this restraint; it was as flamboyant and grotesque as its builder. Yet it set the scene for an educational programme that was carefully phased to groom the young prince for his accession. Edward, as he tells us in his *Chronicle*, was tutored by "two well-learned men [Richard Cox and John Cheke], who sought to bring [me] up in learning of tongues, of the scripture, of philosophy, and all liberal sciences".[29] Cox (a former headmaster of Eton) and Cheke (a professor of Greek) were noted classical scholars, leading humanists, and committed Protestants. And these were the separate strands that came together again in the new building ethos of the king's circle. Especially prominent among the builders of Edward's short reign were the two Protectors: Edward Seymour, Duke of Somerset (at Berry Pomeroy, Syon and Somerset House) and John Dudley, Duke of Northumberland (at Dudley Castle). Another was Sir William Sharington (at Lacock Abbey). For them and for those of the same circle who survived Mary's reign to continue the same tradition under Elizabeth – John Thynne (at Longleat), Thomas Smith (at Hill Hall) and William Cecil (at Theobalds and Burghley

House) – classical precision in architecture and Protestant restraint in religion coincided.[30] At Somerset House, for the first time, exact proportions were observed, the classical orders were respected, and the loggia (later so widely imitated) was correctly used. The Protector's London palace, it has been rightly said, "was probably the first deliberate attempt to build in England a house composed altogether within the classical discipline. And the models for several parts of it were French."[31]

Certainly, very few of its guiding principles were English. As a young man, Edward Seymour had spent much time in northern France; and so had Dudley. John Thynne and Thomas Smith, before joining the Protector's service, had been dedicated travellers, equipping themselves thus for public duties. It was Dudley who sent John Shute ("Paynter and Archytecte") to Italy in 1550, "to confer with the doinges of the skilful maisters in architectur, & also to view such auncient Monumentes hereof as are yet extant", and who arranged for him, on his return, to

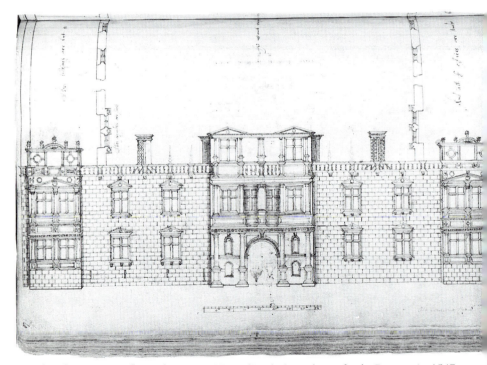

*39  Edward Seymour's influential Somerset House (London) was begun for the Protector in 1547, soon*
*the old king's death. French influence shows in the set-piece "triumphal" entrance and in the classic*
*inspired double-height bays – later used again at Sir John Thynne's Longleat – to right and left. This elev*
*of the Strand front, with plan behind, is by John Thorpe, son of the builder of Kirby Hall (p. 75).*

show his work to Edward VI "whose delectation and pleasure was to see it". In point of fact, Shute learnt less than he later claimed from those travels. His *The first & chief groundes of architecture* (1563) owes more to Sebastiano Serlio's *Regole generali di architettura* than to any personal "experience and practise, gathered by the sight of the Monumentes in Italie".[32] Nevertheless, Sir Thomas Tresham had a copy of Shute's book in his library at Rushton Hall, along with every other architectural treatise – Alberti, Vignola, Palladio, Serlio, and many more – he could lay his hands on. And Sir Thomas Smith would buy another before beginning the classicizing reconstruction of his mansion at Hill Hall which closely followed his 1560s embassies to France.[33]

Smith (like Tresham) also owned copies of the latest French treatises, including the *Livre d'architecture* (1559) of Jacques Androuet du Cerceau, and Philibert de l'Orme's *Nouvelles inventions pour bien bastir* (1561). And it was the Mannerism of these and other northern sources, only partially absorbed, which was ultimately most influential on Elizabethan builders. But Smith belonged to an earlier, more travelled generation. He was

*Sir John Thynne's Longleat (Wiltshire), of 1567–80, is the best and most complete survival of the country es influenced by Edward Seymour's Somerset House and built by former members of his circle.*

*41 The classicizing courtyard facades of Sir Thomas Smith's Hill Hall (Essex) came not firsthand from Italy but from Smith's study of French Renaissance buildings while ambassador to Paris in the 1560s, and from the architectural treatises in his own library.*

bred, Fuller tells us, "in Queens' College in Cambridge, where such [was] his proficiency in learning, that he was chosen out by Henry the Eighth to be sent over and brought up beyond the seas. It was fashionable in that age that pregnant [promising] students were maintained on the cost of the state, to be merchants for experience in foreign parts; whence returning home with their gainful adventures, they were preferred (according to the improvement of their time) to offices in their own country."[34] Lengthy foreign travel was as influential also in the shaping of the tastes of John Thynne. And there is an archaeological correctness in Smith's courtyard elevations (at Hill Hall) and Thynne's garden facades (at Longleat), which reflects the superior quality of that training. Nothing as comprehensive would be possible again during the turmoil of the Wars of Religion.

As a result of those wars, what was chiefly missing in Elizabeth's reign was personal exposure to foreign architecture. There were some – and Elizabeth's principal secretary, William Cecil, was among them – whose learning made up the deficiency. Cecil went first abroad as late as 1554, and seldom had occasion to go again. Yet he would pack off both his sons on educational visits to France; and his own "Roman" staircase at Burghley House is as notable a Renaissance *tour de force* as Sir John Thynne's Longleat.[35] Cecil, even so, sent away his sons with a heavy heart. And there were few caring fathers in Elizabethan England who dared risk their heirs in such a fashion. What ensued at home was a deep-seated provincialism, exhibited even at Cecil's Burghley House in later years. Its characteristics were a mindless copying of Italian *grottesche,* and the misapplied "flummery" of Flemish strap-work.[36]

The continent-wide alliances of 1598, which England (at peace with Spain) entered only in 1604, brought no permanent end to the killing. In 1618, the Bohemian Rebellion launched the Thirty Years' War, and there was hardly a year through the entire seventeenth century when Europe was wholly at peace. Nevertheless, those two decades of general tranquillity, from 1598 to 1618 – "the extravagant, magnificent years" of Rudolf II (Holy Roman Emperor) in Prague, of Philip III (of Spain) and Henry IV (of France), of Maximilian I (of Bavaria) and Archduke Ferdinand (of Styria), and of our own James I at Whitehall – established new parameters in princely patronage. [37] England's long isolation, ended by James I, was succeeded at once by foreign travel and by the start of competitive collecting. Addicted noble collectors included the Herbert Earls of Pembroke (furnishing Wilton House), George Villiers, Duke of Buckingham (d.1628), and the obsessive Thomas Howard, Earl of Arundel (d.1646).[38] When Arundel first came to Italy in 1613–14, bringing Inigo Jones in his company, English tourists of his quality were still rare. But the earl's missionary zeal for fine art and his free-spending ways left his name one to be conjured with. In the travel diary of the young sculptor Nicholas Stone "junior", sent to Italy by his father for his art, there is a charming description of an encounter with Grand Duke Ferdinand II of Tuscany. Nicholas and his brother Henry (the painter) had been living and working in Florence for almost a month when, on 15 July 1638, "thaire came [into the gallery] the great Duke of Tuscany, who with a smiling countenaunce demaunded who wee were; answere made we were straungers (English) come his favour to learne after the rare paintings and statues; he passing by us foure times (walking and loking on the statues) every time as he came nye smiled (att his first coming he askt whether the Kings of England had many rare thinges, and my Lord of Arundell) . . . about an houre afterward came the

Marquesse [the brothers' contact at court] who very frendly gave commission to the gallery keper to deliver to my brother [for copying] any
peice he should chuse; then we went into the tribunas, being the
principall cabbinett, [where] were the rarest peeces of Raphyell and
Titian, Andrea Dell Serto, Michaell Agnolo, Holbin and of other great
masters (so he made choice of a head of Titian)". The next day, "I went
to draw in the gallery after a statua of Bachus of Michell Agnoloes
worke, the great Duke passing by looke on my drawing and said, *Faci est
un bella statua.*"[39]

In Grand Duke Ferdinand's gallery, "being about 520 foot long and
20 brod", Nicholas counted "52 heads, 27 statues, a wild boare antique,
2 wolves antique, whereof 24 are antiques and 3 moderne". And it was
for just such displays of sculpture, both old and new, that Thomas
Howard used the lower of his two galleries at Arundel House. "The lord
of the house, the Earl of Arundel and Surrey", remarked Abram Booth
(a visiting Dutch envoy) in 1629, "is a great lover of paintings and antiquities – against the nature of most Englishmen". There:

> In a very long gallery standing below and opening on to the
> Thames, one sees an extraordinary number of very antique statues,
> epitaphs in Greek and Latin on square and other antique grave-
> stones, which were brought here from every corner of Christen-
> dom at the expense of the aforementioned Earl. Yes, even from
> Egupt and Greece. Besides this lower gallery is another of the same
> size and length, where one finds the most beautiful paintings of all
> manner of famous masters that one can imagine; so much so that
> the curious will need a day to view it all.[40]

If Arundel's collections were in every way exceptional, less so was his
method of display. Back in the 1570s, when William Cecil built
Theobalds, he had furnished his galleries as Italian-style parade spaces,
decorated chiefly with frescoes: with "divers citties rarely painted and sett
forth" in the Great Gallery, and with "the Armes of the Noblemen and
Gentlemen of England in trees", all "excellentlie well painted" in the
Green Gallery.[41] That also was the choice of Sir Thomas Smith at Hill
Hall, commissioning tapestry-style frescoes – a *Cupid and Psyche*
sequence and a *Life of Hezekiah* – for the chambers he contemporaneously refurbished there.[42] But the "properest" place for frescoes, as Sir

Henry Wotton pointed out, was on friezes and borders; "as for other Storied Workes upon Walles, I doubt our [English] Clime bee too yeelding and moist, for such Garnishment".[43] His worries were exaggerated; and frescoes continued to do very nicely, even in the dank and moisty North, for the decoration of awkward spaces such as stair-wells. However, by the time Wotton published his *Elements of architecture* in 1624, England's aristocratic collectors were already busy. The Jacobean Long Gallery – as a repository for art – had been given a new lease of life.

Wotton, three times ambassador to Venice, knew a good deal about paintings. "No Roome", he warned, "[should] bee furnished with too many, which in truth were a Surfet of Ornament, unlesse they bee Galleries, or some peculiar Repository for Rarities of Art". He counselled how to hang them: "not where there is the least, but where there are the fewest lights". And he was the first to publish guidelines about which paintings should go where, having a view to their content: "chearefull Paintings in Feasting and Banquetting Roomes; Graver Stories in Galleries, Land-schips and Boscage and such wilde workes in open Tarraces, or in Summer houses (as we call them) and the like".[44] Later, in the great houses of Restoration England, where paintings crowded every wall, such conventions were even more desirable. Thus "histories, grave stories, and the best works become *Galleries*", writes William Salmon in 1675, "where one may walk and exercise their senses in viewing, examining, delighting, judging and censuring". But "let the *Hall* be adorned with Shepherds, Peasants, Milk-maids, Flocks of sheep and the like"; "let the *Staircase* be set off with some admirable monument or building, either new or ruinous, to be seen and observed at a view passing up"; let there be landscapes in the *Great Chamber* and portraits of close friends in the *Withdrawing Chambers*; in the *Banqueting-room*, "put cheerful and merry paintings of Bacchus, Centaurs, satyrs, syrens and the like, but forbearing all obscene pictures"; and lastly in the *Bedchamber*, "put your own, your wives and childrens pictures; as only becoming the most private room, and your modesty".[45]

Paintings of every subject were what John Evelyn admired in 1696 in William III's collections at Kensington Palace: "the Gallerys furnished with all the best Pictures of all the [royal] Houses, of Titian, Raphel, Corregio, Holben, Julio Romano, Bassan, V[an] Dyke, Tintoret, & others".[46] But the more usual gallery furniture, both before and after Evelyn wrote, was the portrait. "Long time thy shadow hath been thrall to me", says the Countess of Auvergne to gallant Talbot in *Henry VI Part One*, "for in my gallery thy picture hangs."[47] And in this earliest of Shakespeare's histories, dating to about 1590, a contemporary London audience could already be assumed to recognize the gallery as portrait space. One London model was Dudley's "great" (or "high") gallery at Leicester House. Robert Dudley, Earl of Leicester, died on 4 September 1588. And two years later, on 3 April 1590, his paintings were valued for the Queen:

In the High Gallery . . . Two cards or Mapps, xxs. A picture of the Quenes Majestie, xxs. Three pictures in Large Tables, one of the Earle of Leicester, one of the Earle of Warr[enne], and the third of the Lord Admirall, ls. Other pictures in tables, viz. of the Prince of Oringe, Duke Cassimere, Sir Phillipp Sidney, Mr Henry Knowles, the Earle of Leicester twise, a picture of Beachampe, of the Lady Dacres Daughter, the yonge Baron of Denbigh, one other childes picture, three smale pictures, two of men and one of a woman, a greate picture of a woman, six small mapps in frames, a table of a woman with fruytes and other thinges, the picture of a yonge gentleman, of Penelope, of two yonge ladies, of the ffrench Kinge and of Julius Cesar, vj*li*. [48]

Some of Dudley's paintings may have passed to Bess of Hardwick, for she was in London soon afterwards on a shopping spree, buying the plate, the tapestries, and the other fine furnishings for her last and greatest project at Hardwick Hall. Among the bargains Bess struck in the spring and summer of 1592, before returning north again to Derbyshire in late July, was the purchase of the 13 great tapestries of the *Story of Gideon* originally woven in 1578 for Sir Christopher Hatton (of Holdenby House and Kirby Hall). Those tapestries still hang in Hardwick's Long Gallery, as do historical and family portraits, some of which Bess may have bought or commissioned while on that same visit to the capital. All were listed in her inventory of 1601:

In the Gallerie: Thirtene peeces of deep Tapestrie hanginges of the storie of Gedion everie peece being nyntene foote deep . . . The Pictures of Quene Elizabeth, Edward the second, Edward the third, Rychard the third, Henry the fourth, Henry the fyft, Henry

*Bess of Hardwick's* Story of Gideon *tapestries, woven in 1578 and bought secondhand for her new* dwick Hall (Derbyshire) in 1592, still hang in the Long Gallery on the top floor of the house, as does her *ction of portraits.*

the sixt, Edward the fourth, Rychard the third, Henry the seaventh, Henry the Eight, Edward the sixt, Quene Marie, Quene Elizabethes picture in a less table, The King of Fraunce, Henry, King of Scottes, James, King of Scottes, The picture of Our Ladie the Virgin Marie, Quene Anne, Henry, the third King of Fraunce in a little table, The Duke of Bullen, Phillip, King of Spayne, Twoo twynns, Quene Katherin, The Erle of Southampton, Mathewe, Erle of Lenox, Charles, Erle of Lenox, George, Erle of Shrouesbury, My Ladie [Bess herself], Lord Bacon, The Marquess of Winchester, the Ladie Arbella, Mr Henry Cavendishe, The Lord Straunge, The Lord Cromwell, Mrs Ann Cavendishe, The Duke of Sommerset, Sir Thomas Wyet, [and] The storie of Joseph.[49]

At Hardwick as elsewhere, copies of royal portraits filled the empty walls of the new Long Gallery. And when Henry Lord Arlington

109

(d.1685) furnished his post-Restoration gallery at Euston Hall, he continued to hang it "with pictures at length – on the one side the Royal family from K. Henry the 7th by the Scottish race his eldest daughter down to the present King William and his Queen Mary, the other side are forreign princes from the Emperour of Moroccoe the Northern and Southern princes and Emperour of Germany".[50] However, Lord Arlington had family portraits also in his private apartments at Euston, with some better pictures of Stuart royalty by Van Dyck. And portrait collections of this kind – commemorative likenesses of family and close friends – had begun to be formed from much earlier. In Thomas Howard's new gallery at Bindon House, for which he wrote to Cecil in 1609 for a portrait, would hang "the pictures of sundry of my honourable friends, whose presentation thereby to behold will greatly delight

43  The Long Gallery of c.1600 at Haddon Hall (Derbyshire), panelled in the Northern Renaissance classical taste.

me to walk often in that place where I may see so comfortable a sight".[51] It was a form of self-indulgence – combining exercise, gossip, and celebrity display – which many now felt they could afford.

At the great prodigy houses of this period – at Henry Griffith's Burton Agnes (1601–10) and Thomas Howard's Audley End (1605–14), at Robert Cecil's Hatfield (1607–12) and Henry Hobart's Blickling (1619–27), at Thomas Holte's Aston (1618–35) and Arthur Ingram's Temple Newsam (1622–37) – huge new exercise galleries continued to be built. And some of this, no doubt, was pure conservatism. Yet it is also true that the family portrait gallery was becoming a necessary part of noble life-styles. Thus the ancient Vernon pile at Haddon Hall, little changed since the late fourteenth century, was furnished with a new gallery in about 1600. Finely panelled in the developing classical taste, it was

*44  The pillared and pedimented Italianate front, with central "Venetian" window and prominent rustication below, with which Spencer Compton joined the two projecting ranges of the "vast stone pile" at Castle Ashby (Northamptonshire), shortly after he inherited the house in 1630.*

the "only good room" (Horace Walpole later thought) in what "can never have been a tolerable House".[52] Walpole also liked the classical front ("in better taste" than the rest) which Spencer Compton added to his "vast stone pile" at Castle Ashby. Built in the mid-1630s, the range shows the influence of the earl's youthful travels with Prince Charles, and is in the style of Inigo Jones. It carried a gallery on the first floor, "narrow & low, but long", where "between every window is a portrait".[53]

Castle Ashby, unlike Haddon, was not an old house. Begun only in 1574, it had already been modernized by William Compton (Spencer's father) in the 1620s, when the two stair turrets were heightened, a third storey was added, and the whole was crowned by a lettered balustrade, modifying Psalm 127 (*Nisi Dominus*) as its text: "Except the Lord build the house, they labour in vain that build it; except the Lord keep the house [city], the watchman waketh but in vain." Such inscribed parapets, of which there was another at Sir Arthur Ingram's Temple Newsam, probably originated in France.[54] And French influence was again paramount at contemporary Ham House, a great Jacobean mansion originally built for Sir Thomas Vavasour in *c*.1610, but almost immediately "done over" in the latest Paris fashions, first for William Murray (1637–39) and then for the Lauderdales (1672–77), Elizabeth and John – Murray's daughter and her second husband, the duke.

William Murray, an intimate of Charles I and Henrietta Maria, was exceptionally well placed to know what in France was *de rigueur*. He entirely re-built Vavasour's great staircase in a much grander manner, redecorated the first-floor family rooms in new colour co-ordinated schemes, and dismantled and remade the panelling of the Long Gallery in a stately parade of Ionic pilasters. It was for this same Long Gallery at Ham House that the Duke and Duchess of Lauderdale commissioned the expensive "Carved Guilt Frames" for the "Two and Twenty Pictures" of their acquaintance. As inventoried in 1677, these large portraits commemorated the noble personages (past and present) with whom the Lauderdales felt it politic to be linked – John Leslie, Duke of Rothes, Chancellor of Scotland; John Lord Thirlestane (d.1595), an earlier Scottish chancellor and grandfather of the duke; Thomas Lord Clifford, admiral and treasurer; Charles I (studio of Van Dyck) and Charles II (school of Lely); and many more.[55]

Horace Walpole, who visited Ham House on 10 June 1770, almost a century after the Lauderdales' improvements, liked their Long Gallery,

*William Murray's open-well staircase of 1637–38 at Ham House (Surrey) anticipated the new fashion French-style processional stairs, rarely seen in England before the Civil War but everywhere in demand from 1660s.*

46  In the Long Gallery at Ham House, the classical panelling was installed in 1639; the portraits, still
their original gilt frames, date to a second costly refurbishing of the family apartments, completed in the 16'
for the Lauderdales.

in which he found "many Vandycks or after him, & Lelys". But the
other rooms at Ham, much increased in number by the Lauderdales,
were "small & low" and while "magnificently furnished for that time
with velvet & embroidered beds, tapestry, pictures, rich cabinets & great
quantities of China", were "in a bad & barbarous taste".[56] More exact
contemporaries were kinder. John Evelyn was among the first to inspect
the Lauderdales' works, visiting Ham on 27 August 1678. "After din-
ner", he records, "I walked to Ham, to see the House & Garden of the
Duke of Laderdaile, which is indeede inferiour to few of the best Villas
in Italy itselfe, The House furnishd like a greate Princes; the Parterrs,
flo[wer] Gardens, Orangeries, Groves, Avenues, Courts, Statues, Per-
spectives, fountaines, Aviaries . . . must needes be surprizing &c".[57]
Evelyn, the botanist, gave most of his attention to Ham's gardens. And

this also was the emphasis of Ralph Thoresby of Leeds, another Fellow of the Royal Society. Thoresby found Ham "a very noble palace, though, to be free, the spacious court before the more ancient front of the hall pleased me best, having a vast number of the bustos and the Roman Emperors, &c. in marble, each in his distinct niche in the wall".[58] Roger North, in contrast, was more interested in what had happened to the house. Although a believer in conversions, he had seen some bad ones in his day, including Henry Lord Arlington's Euston Hall, where "it had bin much better to have bin contented with the plainess of the old designe, than to vamp it to no porpose". However,

An other repaired and reformed old house is Ham, upon Thames, done by the Duke and Duchess of Lauderdale, and is the best of the kind I have seen. It was what vulgarly is called an H, but the wings not long, being rather pavilion fashion, the midle single [one room thick], and the windoes large, as the use of the time was when built. The house is, in its time, esteemed one of the most beautyfull and compleat seats in the kingdome, and all ariseth out of the skill and dexterity in managing the alterations, which in my opinion are the best I have seen. For I doe not perceive any part of the old fabrick is taken downe, but the wings stand as they were first sett, onely behind next the garden they are joyned with a strait range intirely new.[59]

At Euston, it had been Arlington's mistake to be "frugally profuse". While intending (like the Lauderdales) to make his house "fitt to enter-tein his master the King", Arlington had not built it anew, but "would compass his designe by altering and vamping the old". His conversion had "produc't a *grand sale*, staircase, and royall apartment, in the cheif part of the house". But Arlington's windows were too small and his rooms either too high or too low, "and all the decoration bestowed upon them [including costly frescoes by Antonio Verrio], was but smoothing of wrinkles, or painting on a bad draught".[60] The Lauderdales avoided the worst of such excesses. They had kept the Great Hall of Vavasour's house, and left Murray's Long Gallery and Grand Staircase substantially intact. But they then doubled the width of the Jacobean H-plan house by inserting a new range of "rooms of parade" – ducal apartments below, royal above – between the two projecting wings of the garden front.

William Samwell, the Lauderdales' architect, was of the school of Roger Pratt. And what he gave them was a double-pile house.[61]

Samwell made another significant improvement for the Lauderdales. He equipped their state apartments with the new sash windows which, in their earliest Ham House form (with central mullion still in place), had only just made their first appearance in English building.[62] The word "sash" – from *chassis* (frame) – is of French origin. But it was English joiners who developed the larger counterbalanced sash, even before Christopher Wren (from the late 1680s) used it in his remodelling of the royal palaces. "The English are very skilful", observed a French visitor to London in 1685. "In the newly built houses I noticed one very convenient thing. That is the big glass windows with sliding sashes which one lifts without needing a notch to hold them in place. There is a counterweight which one cannot see at all, as heavy as the sash, which holds it back in any position in which one leaves it, and without fear that it will fall on the head of those who look out of the window, which I thought very convenient and agreeable."[63]

Such native ingenuity in the invention of the counterbalanced sash is a useful warning against assuming foreign influence in every novelty. And in much the same way, East Anglia's curvilinear brick gables, while almost always labelled "Dutch", developed characteristics of their own in that new setting.[64] Nevertheless, there are few significant words in the vocabulary of the Rebuilding which are not either French or Italian. The *galerie* and the *salon*, the *loggia* and the *visto*, are the most obvious of these borrowings from abroad. But as Vanbrugh told his patron, Sarah Duchess of Marlborough: "The word Corridore Madam is foreign, and signifys in plain English, no more than a Passage, it is now however generally us'd as an English word".[65] And Richard Lassels's popular *The voyage of Italy* (1670) opens with the vigorous disclaimer:

> [Some] will say I affect a world of exotick words not yet naturalized in England. No, I affect them not; I cannot avoid them; for who can speak of Statues, but he must speak of *Niches*; or of Churches, Wrought Tombes, or inlayd Tables; but he must speak of *Coupolas*; of *bassi rilievi*; and of *pietre commesse*? If any man understand them not, its his fault, not mine.[66]

Lassels affected reservations also about publishing yet another guide to Italy, "seeing two others have written of this Subject in English". He meant John Raymond (1648) – who "writes little and leaveth out much" – and Edmund Warcupp (1660) – who "writes much of Italy and saies little". Accordingly, he asked, "if these ingenious gentlemen have painted out Italy in *busto* only, and profile; why may not I paint her out at full face, and at her full length?" And he would have agreed, in any event, with both earlier authors that the general "excellency" of things Italian – in "Statuary, Limning [painting], Architecture, Gardning, Sceanes, Musick" – "gives them the precedency" over all Europe.[67] Northern architects and their patrons, often travellers themselves, found this chorus impossible to resist. As Maximilian Misson reported in 1691, from the rare perspective of one who preferred France over Italy:

> I have observ'd, that those who speak of Italy are usually full of Prejudices, in favour of that Country. Most Young Travellers being persuaded, that they shall find there an infinite Number of surprizing Rarities, go thither with a Resolution to admire every thing they see. And all the Relations we have of it, seem to be design'd for Panegyricks. The Fame of that part of the World has been rais'd so high, and so strongly establish'd, that 'tis esteem'd an unpardonable Crime to lessen its Reputation.[68]

Qualifying that reputation was nevertheless Misson's purpose. Back in 1648, John Raymond had made the claim: "For their Gardens, I dare confidently avow all Christendom affords none so voluptuous, as those within the Walls and Territory of Rome."[69] And Italian gardens, Misson himself concedes, are indeed "very *pleasant* places, and rather than give offence, I will e'en adventure to call 'em *fine* places". But "if we compare Frascati [the Villas Aldobrandini and Mondragone] to Versailles, or even to several other plesant Seats in France, that are not Royal Houses, I am perswaded, and dare positively affirm, that the celebrated Wonders not only of Frascati, but also of Tivoli [the Villa d'Este], and all the most beautiful places about Rome, I mean as to Gardens and Waterworks, deserve no higher Title than that of petty Toys".[70]

One of Misson's tests of excellence was cost. Of the Villa d'Este, an anonymous "English Gentleman" had written in 1675 that it "is larger, has better Prospect, more Fountains, greater Variety of Water-works, Grotta's, &c. than any other Villa whatsoever".[71] But Misson had since

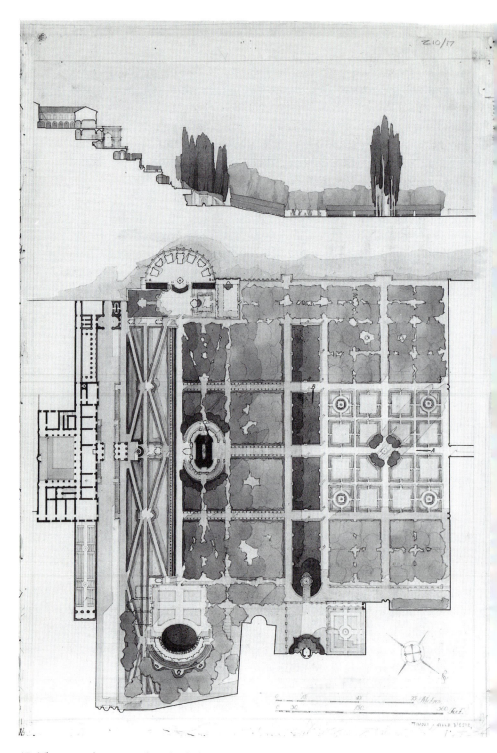

47 The terraced water-gardens (with fountains achieving different musical effects) at the Villa d'Este Tivoli, made for Cardinal Ippolito II d'Este between 1560 and 1575. This architect's drawing was prepared with other similar plans and sections of the great Italian gardens, for Italian Gardens of the Renaissance J. G. Shepherd and G. A. Jellicoe, first published in 1925.

visited Versailles. "I will not strive to refute the Opinion of those who believe that the Gardens and Water-works of Italy did formerly surpass those of France", he writes, "but since the Face of Affairs is alter'd, we ought also to change our Language . . . They tell us that the Palace and Gardens of Este cost Three Millions, and I will not pretend to contradict 'em; but I must beg leave to assure them, that Versailles has incomparable Beauties; that the Water-works of that Place exceed a Million of such as those that are at Tivoli; that the very Lead of the Canals at Versailles cost ten times more than all Tivoli".[72]

Competition at this high level could not fail to have had its influence on English palace-building – at Euston for the Arlingtons and at Chatsworth for the Devonshires, at Castle Howard for the Carlisles and at Blenheim for the Marlboroughs. And for each of these great houses, as for their innumerable lesser imitators, a necessary beginning was foreign travel. What could best be learnt abroad was now obvious. Italians, wrote that same anonymous "English Gentleman" (no friend of the French), "are of such a happy temper, that they can be excellent in any thing they please to undertake, even in Buffonnerie and Fooling, outdoing Monsieur [the Frenchman] himself, in whom 'tis natural; and besides their being the greatest Souldiers and Generals of all Ages, and excelling too in Politicks, the Mathematicks and solid Learning for Architecture, Sculpture, Music, and Painting, are as much admired by the wisest of the World, as France is by others, for their Modes of Habit, Speaking, Dancing, Riding, &c."[73] Richard Lassels, while in general agreement concerning the Italians, nevertheless gave the French the final word:

My opinion is, that its better for a young man to go first into Italy, and returning by Germany, Holland and Flanders, come into France, to give himself there the last hand in breeding . . . I would therefore have my Young Noblemans Governour [tutor] to carry him immediately into Italy at fifteen or sixteen, and there season his minde with the gravity, and wise Maximes of that Nation, which hath civilized the whole world, and taught Man Manhood. Having spent two or three years in Italy in learning the Language, viewing the several courts, studying their Maximes, imitating their Gentile Conversation, and following the sweet Exercises of Musick, Painting, Architecture, and Mathematicks, he will at his return know what true use to make of France. And having spent three years more there, in learning to Fence, Dance, Ride, Vault, Handle his Pike, Musket, Colours, &c. The Map, History, and Books of Policy; he will be ready to come home at twenty or one and twenty, a Man most compleat both in Body and Mind, and fit to fill the place of his Calling.[74]

Another purpose of the Englishman's *giro*, not unlike his public school, was to toughen him for Life after Mother. "Travelling", says Lassels, "preserves my young nobleman from surfeiting of his parents, and weans him from dangerous fondness of his Mother. It teacheth him wholesome hardship; to lye in beds that are none of his acquaintance; to speak to men he never saw before." Even so, he cautions, "I would not have my young Traveller imitate all things he sees done in France, or other Foreign Countreys". In Italy, "I would have him learn to make a fine house; but I would not have him learn of the Italians to keep a good house." In Holland, "I would have him learn to keep his house and hearth neat, but I would not have him adore his house, and stand in such awe of his hearth, as not to dare to make a fire in it, as they do." And in France, while he must learn of the French to "become any clothes well" and "get a good grace in walking and saluting", he must not "follow them in all their Phantastical and fanfaron clothings" or "dance as he walks, as many of them do".[75]

Those who learn to build like the Italians, to keep house like the Dutch, to parade and salute like the French, will borrow something costly from them all. The Arlingtons, John Evelyn noticed while staying with them at Euston Hall, "love fine things, & to live easily, pompously, but very hospitable; but with so vast expense as plunges my Lord into debt exceedingly". Countess Isabella, daughter of Louis of Nassau, "is a good natured, & obliging woman". Earl Henry himself, addicted to building, would "have all things rich, polite, & Princely". Abroad for many years, first for his education and then as a Royalist exile, Arlington "reades much, having both the Latine, French & Spanish tongues in perfection: has traveled much, & is absolutely the best bred & Courtly person his Majestie has about him". Evelyn, skilled in such things, had previously advised the earl on the planting of his walks ("a mile in length") and other woodlands. And as the Arlingtons' close friend, he was less critical than Roger North of their extravagance. In 1677, "the

Kings appartment [at Euston Hall] is both painted a fresca, & magnificently furnish'd: There are many excellent Pictures in the roomes of the greate Masters: The Gallery is a pleasant noble roome . . . The Chapell is pretty . . . The Orange-Garden is very fine, and leads into the Greene-house, at the end whereoff is a sall [salle] to eate in, & the Conservatory very long (some hundred feete) adorn'd with Mapps, as the other side is with the heads of Caesars ill cut in alabaster . . . The out offices make two large quadrangles, so as never servants liv'd with more ease & convenience, never Master more Civil: strangers are attended & accomodated as at their home in pretty apartments furnish'd with all manner of Conveniences & privacy: There are bathing roomes, Elaboratorie [laboratory], Dispensatorie, what not."[76] Four years earlier, while calling on Lady Arlington at her London home, Evelyn had been taken to see her "new dressing roome at Goring house, where was a bed, 2 glasses [mirrors], silver jarrs & Vasas, Cabinets & other so rich furniture, as I had seldom seene the like". Here, Evelyn muses, "to this excesse of superfluity were we now arriv'd, & that not onely at Court, but almost universaly, even to wantonesse, & profusion".[77]

Excess of superfluity, wantonness and profusion were still more obviously on show at the Whitehall apartment of Louise Renée de Kérouaille, Duchess of Portsmouth. One autumn morning in 1683, Evelyn followed the king to his mistress's quarters in the palace. There he observed Louise "in her morning loose garment, her maides Combing her, newly out of her bed: his Majestie & the Gallants standing about her":

> But that which [particularly] ingag'd my curiositie, was the rich & splendid furniture of this woman's Appartment, now twice or thrice puld downe & rebuilt, to satisfie her prodigal & expensive pleasures . . . Here I saw the new fabrique of French Tapissry, for designe, tendernesse of worke, & incomparable imitation of the best paintings, beyond any thing I had ever beheld: some pieces had Versailles, St Germans & other Palaces of the French King with Huntings, figures, & Landscips, Exotique fowle & all to the life rarely don: Then for Japon Cabinets, Skreenes, Pendule Clocks, huge Vasas of wrought plate, Tables, Stands, Chimny furniture, Sconces, branches, Braseras &c they were all of massive silver, & without number, besides of his Majesties best paintings: Surfeiting of this, I din'd yet at Sir Steph: Foxes [at Chelsea], & went con-

48 *"Excess of superfluity" in the Venetian Ambassador's Room at Knole (Kent). This carved and gilded bed and its accompanying furnishings, including the armchair, were commissioned by James II in 1688 (just before his flight) for the royal palace at Whitehall. In the King's Room, also at Knole, there is a rare set of silver toiletry, candlestands, sconces (wall-lights and glasses), and other "rich furniture", such as John Evelyn deplored in the private apartments of Lady Arlington and the Duchess of Portsmouth.*

*A state bedroom in the French style, designed by Daniel Marot in c.1690. Marot, a French*
*stant, fled Paris in 1684 and subsequently worked for William of Orange (William III of*
*and from 1689) both in Holland and in England.*

tentedly home to my poore, but quiet Villa [Sayes Court]. Lord
what contentment can there be in the riches & splendor of this
world, purchas'd with vice & dishonor?[78]

Evelyn could have had many excellent reasons for disliking Duchess
Louise, including that "perfect aversion for the French, as all Wise men
naturally have".[79] But the Frenchness of her furniture was not among
them. A well known francophile in Evelyn's London was Ralph Lord
Montagu of Boughton, twice ambassador to Louis XIV's court. "Mr
Montagues new Palace neere Bloomesbery" was built, Evelyn noted,
"after the French pavilion way". And most particularly to be admired
were its Versailles-inspired interiors, "than which for Painting & furniture, there was nothing more glorious in England". Prominent were the
frescoes of the Italian decorative painter Antonio Verrio, "especialy the
funeral Pile of Dido, on the Stayre Case, & Labours of Hercules, fight

50 *Ralph Lord Montagu's palace in Bloomsbury, finished in 1683, was built in the contemporary Par* *manner, with a formal forecourt and corner pavilions, like a grand hôtel particulier. Although badly damag* *the fire of 1686, when Verrio's prodigious frescoes were destroyed, Montagu House was almost immediate* *built in the French style as before, eventually giving way to the British Museum. This engraving of c.17* *by Sutton Nicholls.*

with the Centaures, Effeminacy with Dejanira, & Apotheosis or reception amongst the Gods, on the walls & roofe of the Greate roome above, [which] I think exceedes any thing he has yet don, both for designe, Colouring, & exuberance of Invention, comparable certainely to the greatest of the old Masters, or what they so celebrate at Rome".[80]

Verrio, who had been a history-painter in France before settling in England at the invitation of Charles II, also worked at Euston (for the Arlingtons), at Ham (for the Lauderdales), at Powis (for the Herberts), at Burghley (for the Cecils), and at Chatsworth (for the Cavendishes). Charles himself employed Verrio, in 1675–82, on his palatial refurbishment of Windsor Castle. It was from William III that Verrio accepted, towards the end of a long working life, his last great commission at Hampton Court. There, until his death in 1707, he was engaged on the

124

In the Chapel at Chatsworth (Derbyshire), the big Doubting Thomas (1693) over the altar is by
nio Verrio; the contemporary frescoes are by Louis Laguerre.

walls and ceilings of Christopher Wren's state apartments, for which he furnished mighty allegories in his most flamboyant style: for the King's Staircase, an *Apollo and the Muses* (the benefits of William's rule) and a *Satire on the Caesars* (the disgraced later Stuarts); for William III's State Bedchamber, an *Endymion Asleep in the Arms of Morpheus*.[81]

That mixture, as at Hampton Court, of Franco-Italian palace planning, of voluptuous history-painting in the tradition of Versailles, and of fine Dutch wood-carving (Grinling Gibbons and his school) was entirely characteristic of Grand Tour architecture. Much-admired Roman buildings had set the fashion. "This", reported Richard Lassels in 1670 of the already ageing Palazzo Borghese, built fully a century before, "is one of the noblest Pallaces in Rome. It gives you a fair broadside of windows, three stories one over another; and its length is prodigious . . . I saw a row of ten or twelve great chambers through which I looked at

52  *Petworth House (Sussex) was built in the 1690s for Charles Seymour, Duke of Somerset. This French-style garden front, originally domed at the centre, allowed the lining-up behind it of Seymour's apartments, to create a visto of formidable length.*

once".[82] Twenty years later, the Palazzo Borghese's "sweet Visto through thirteen several Rooms, terminated by a Water-work always playing" could still cause Robert Midgley to catch his breath.[83]

The full title of Midgley's book, in which he defers to Mr Lassels for a description of Rome "sufficient to supersede the Endeavours of any coming after him", is *Remarks in the Grand Tour of France and Italy. Perform'd by a person of quality, in the year, 1691.* And France, still more than Italy, was England's mentor. In France, from the mid-century, the connecting doorways of all suites of state apartments had been routinely aligned *en enfilade.* And Christopher Wren's new royal apartments at Hampton Court, begun in 1689 for William and Mary, predictably adopted the *enfilade* plan, creating two of the longest *vistos* ever seen. That same plan at Petworth, setting out the rooms of state *en enfilade*,

*Ralph Lord Montagu, created Earl of Montagu in 1689 and Duke in 1705, had been four times ambas- to France before he added this entirely French north front to Boughton House (Northamptonshire). ng the designers of Boughton's lush francophile interiors was the Huguenot Daniel Marot.*

127

was the entire rationale of Somerset's costly rebuilding of 1688–96. It was for Petworth's "proud duke", enriched by Percy gold, that Grinling Gibbons carved "the large chamber" (now the Grinling Gibbons Room) which Horace Walpole judged "the most superb monument to [his] skill".[84] Contemporaneously at Burghley House (where Grinling Gibbons also worked), Antonio Verrio rose to the challenge of another expensive francophile refurbishment, attaining a fresco-painter's apotheosis in Cecil's *Heaven Room*.[85]

Petworth's austere but elegantly proportioned garden front is already French enough. However, there is nothing more French in England than the north facade of Boughton House, built for Ralph, Earl of Montagu (the ex-ambassador), in the 1690s. Boughton – "a vast house", Walpole calls it, "in the French Style of Architecture" – has the rusticated ground-floor loggia and dormered mansard roof of the grandest contemporary French *hôtels*. And one of its characteristics, which was also very French, was the prominence accorded to the staircase. Montagu's Stone Staircase at Boughton, with frescoes by Louis Chéron, provided a stately ascent to rooms of great magnificence: "most of the ceilings painted, & richly furnished in the taste of that age".[86] Like the "handsome spacious Staircase" of the Spencers' neighbouring Althorp (after 1666), or the Herberts' Great Staircase at Powis (a decade later), Boughton's "spectacular" Stone Stair prepared the stranger for the etiquette-bound apartments of a courtly *piano nobile*, furnished as for the Sun King at Versailles.[87]

Today, the most intact of those apartments is Charles II's State Bedroom at Powis Castle, where the royal bed (hung about with tapestries depicting *Suleiman the Magnificent*) is placed deep in an alcove behind a proscenium arch, and railed-off like a box in the theatre. That sense of theatre, second nature to a Restoration courtier often raised abroad, gave fresh meaning to the processional stair. Elizabethan great stairs, while certainly grander than ever before, had typically risen in short straight flights, around a solid rectangular core. But the open-well staircase, dispensing with that core, was to set new standards of spaciousness at Thomas Sackville's Knole (1603–1608) and Robert Cecil's Hatfield (1607–12), immediately copied at Blickling and elsewhere. Moreover, it would be no more than a generation – and much less than that in France – before the supporting newel would vanish altogether in the triumph of the *escalier suspendu*.[88]

Even more spectacular than Montagu's Stone Stair at Boughton was his other Great Staircase at the now-
lished Montagu House, in Bloomsbury, seen here (with visitors admiring the frescoes) in a watercolour
ing by John Buckler (1770–1851).

55  The State Bedroom at Powis Castle, with the bed alcove railed off as at Versailles. The late seventee
century Brussels tapestries, showing to full advantage with the bed removed, depict scenes from the li
Suleiman the Magnificent, Sultan of Turkey (1520–66).

"To make a compleate Stairecase", warns Sir Henry Wotton in his *Elements* (1624), "is a curious peece of Architecture". First:

The vulgar Cautions are these. That it have a very liberall Light, against all Casualtie of Slippes, and Falles. That the space above the Head, bee large and Airy, which the Italians use to call *Un bel-sfogolo*, as it were good Ventilation, because a man doth spend much breath in mounting. That the Halfe-paces [landings] bee well distributed, at competent distances, for reposing on the way. That to avoyd Encounters, and besides to gratifie the beholder, the whole Staire-case have no nigard Latitude, that is, for the principall Ascent, at least ten foot in Royall Buildings.[89]

*The great cantilevered formal staircase at Roger Pratt's Coleshill House, built for his cousin Sir George, completed in the spring of 1662. It was a pioneering English essay in grand-stair construction, in the Italian manner of Inigo Jones. Like the rest of Coleshill, this important early stair was destroyed by fire in 1952; photograph is of 1919.*

Wotton continued with other practical counsels: individual stairs should be not less than a foot, nor more than 18 inches, in breadth; they should "exceede by no meanes halfe a foot in their height or thicknesse; for our Legges doe labour more in Elevation, then in Distention". But what truly awoke the scholar in Wotton and clearly interested him most was the geometry of the great stair, reducing "this doctrine to some Naturall, or at least Mathematicall ground", with references to Vitruvius and Palladio.[90] Just 10 years later, there would be the extraordinary engineering achievement of Inigo Jones's Tulip Stair at the Queen's House, Greenwich. Then, in little more than two decades and probably from the same source, came the great double staircase of Pratt's Coleshill.

Roger Pratt, comprehensive though his notebooks usually were, wrote surprisingly little about staircases. One of the few things he says is that "it is much easier ascending 12 steps on the outside of your house, than 22 within".[91] Nevertheless, Pratt had seen many fine stairs (both outside and in) during his travels through France and in Italy. And the huge cantilevered staircase of the house he built at Coleshill ranked at once among the grandest of his century. There is no hideaway quality in a staircase of this kind. Unlike the narrow defensible spaces of the medieval newel (or spiral) stair, the seventeenth-century geometrical staircase is of generously open plan: the context for grand descents and fine salutes. "All rising to great place is by a winding stair", wrote Francis Bacon in one of the more famous of his *Essays*.[92] Metaphorically, Bacon's apothegm remains as true today. But those stairs, since Bacon's time, have all been straight.

CHAPTER 5

# The Second Great Rebuilding
# in town and country

R oger Pratt's Coleshill, burnt down in 1952, has left at least some
record of its splendours. But Clarendon House, Pratt's acknowledged masterpiece, was in use just 16 years, before being sold to "rich
bankers & Mechanics" for redevelopment. "See the Viccissitude of
earthly things", moralized John Evelyn in 1683: "I was plainely aston-
ish'd as at this demolition, so noe lesse, at the little armie of Labourers,
& Artificers in levelling ground, laying foundations, & contriving greate
buildings at an expense of 200,000 pounds, if they perfect their
designe".[1]

What those "inferior people" intended, just north of Piccadilly, was
"a new Towne as it were, & the most magnificent *Piazza* in Europ". It
was not the first such speculation, nor the most successful. Inigo Jones's
Covent Garden *piazza* (for Francis Russell, Earl of Bedford) had led the
way. But whereas Inigo Jones, before the Civil War, had looked to the
Continent for his models – to the Place des Vosges in Paris and the
*piazza* at Livorno – there were already several London squares by 1680.
It was Restoration London's speculative builders, more than any others,
who developed the city square, with related streets and central garden,
to make the plan peculiarly their own.[2] Until that time, there had been
nothing uniform about an English street facade. Each house was a reflection of its owner. But the later seventeenth-century townhouse, as
Roger North complained in 1698, told less of its occupant than of its
builder. "Here I cannot but digress in complaint of this age", North
grumbled, "for laying aside the care of building for themselves, and

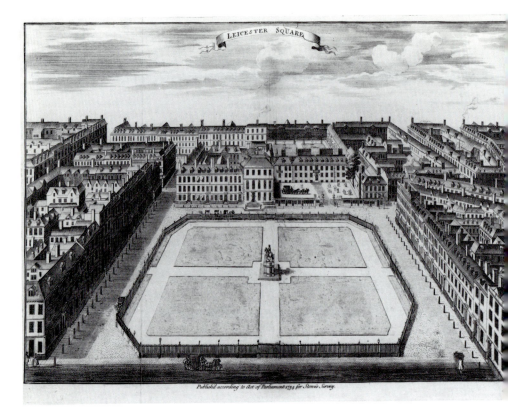

57 *Leicester Square, shown here fully developed in about 1725, was one of the earliest of Restoration London's new Continental-style piazzas, first laid out by Robert Sidney, Earl of Leicester, in 1670. Sid was a man of culture – "very conversant in books and much addicted to the mathematics" – who had b Charles I's ambassador to France between 1636 and 1641. He lost his taste for politics in the Civil War, retired in 1644 to his Kentish estates at Penshurst, to spend more time with his family and follow country suits until his death in 1677.*

familys; but leaving it to workmen such as bricklayers, carpenters, glaziers, &c. It is scarce knowne that a person of quality hath built in or neer London for himself; but all is done by profest builders, and the gentry hire or buy of them". Consequently "one may, in the face of most houses, discerne the calling of some builder or other most conspicuously . . . As some being set out with fine brick-work rubb'd and gaged, were the issue of a master bricklayer; if stone coyned, jamb'd, and fascia'd, of a stone mason; if full of windoe, with much glass in compass, and relieve, a glazier; if full of balcone and balustring, a carpenter; and so others."[3]

Lacking in individuality though they may have been, these earliest London squares and terraces met a growing demand for exclusive private spaces, carefully tailored to family needs, in reassuring association with other professionals. Already, each of these family units – for which lawyers and civil servants, merchants and visiting gentry all competed – had more in common with today's executive home on its purpose-built estate than with any medieval tenement that preceded them. These were not houses fit for communal living. Comparatively small, they were suited only to the most genteel of entertainment. When the tradition spread outwards (as it very quickly did) to the more important provincial capitals such as Bristol, it aided the development of a new code of living, setting a high premium on personal privacy and inimical to old-style hospitality.

Just how that code might operate, in a grand provincial townhouse, is very clearly shown in the "Explanation of the Draughts of a House Proposed for a Merchant", prepared by a Bristol architect in 1724. The elevation and plans (to which his notes attach) show a symmetrical house of classical design, on three floors over a basement. "At the Entrance", he explains, "you find a Vestibule for the Conveniency of Common people attending till they can be spoken to, or Strangers Servants to wait in and is therefore separated from the Stairs that they may not be at liberty to walk about and that the Family may pass privately about their affairs. . . . On the right hand of the Vestibule you find a handsome Withdrawing Room for the Mistress of the House to entertain Company in, with a Private door to the Staircase for her Servants to bring any thing (without exposing it to people who may be waiting in the Vestibule), with a Parlour behind of the same dimensions (and open to it for the greater Magnificence by a double door of Six foot wide when they want to entertain more Freinds than one Room will conveniently hold, or they are inclind to make a Shew)." Across the Vestibule from the withdrawing room is the business room or compter: "As this is the Support of the Family I have designd it large . . . It has a private door by the Back stairs to retreat without being seen by people that are visiting, and the conveying away anything that should not be exposed to view: And by it is the Back Stairs, to the Chambers that the Young Men [of the Compter] may at night go to their Beds and in the morning come to their business without disturbing or dirtying the best part of the House". Then "beyond the Back stairs is a Private Parlour where the Master may treat with any Dealer, or drink a glass with a Friend without disturbing the Family", or "where the Family when alone may eat". Behind the Vestibule, "You will find the Great Stairs with a door under the Middle Flight which opens to the Back Court in which the Kitchen and other Offices are proposd". Upstairs are the bed-chambers, four on each level: family exclusively on the "Best Chamber Floor"; both family and clerks on the next. "There being Eight good Chambers on two Floors, tis supposed those, with low Rooms [for servants] over the Kitchens, may be sufficient for any moderate Family, and to entertain a Friend or two who shall come out of the Countrey to visset or about business, And therefore no Garrets are intended."[4]

These are modest aspirations for a townsman of real wealth: to house a *moderate* family; to entertain *a friend or two*. And they match the "pinch-ing spirit" (as North saw it) of the speculative builder and his client, which "will infect all their works" and in which "there is allwais some scantyness that spoyles all".[5] "Pinching for room to increase the sale of houses", says North of these same builders, "is the first and greatest point with them, next to deck a dining room, withdrawing room, and perhaps a closet with some new fingle fangle, to tempt her gay ladyship".[6] And so, in the Bristol townhouse, on the Best Chamber Floor, the master bedroom must have its own "Niche for the Bed to stand in which is open to the Room by a large Arch if you please, or a Square Entablature supported by a Pillar at each end for the greater Ornament".[7] And "because there must be the parade", even on a nar-row London site:

This litle room [space] must be broke into dining room, bedcham-ber and closet; which the lady is content with being small, and so furnish't rich (or seeming so) with less cost, that is with cabbinetts, china, sconces &c., meer trifles. And this hath added to the mode, round stools like small drumms they call taburets; and many other ways, aggreable to litleness, whereby all the grandure proper to quality is layd aside; large rooms, great tables and glasses, capacious chimnys, spacious hangings, are not to be found, as when the no-bility built their owne houses. Nay the evil spreads, so that coun-try gentlemen of value and fortune, in their new erected seats, creep after the meanness of these town builders and order their houses in squares [i.e. double-pile] like suburb dwellings, than

*58  The elevation and ground-floor plan of a proposed merchant's house at Bristol, drawn by a local architect in 1724. The business room (compter) is to the left of the main entrance; pro-vision is made for two stairs (great and back); there is a family dining room (private parlour) behind the compter; and a double door may be opened between the withdrawing room and formal dining room (parlour) when the merchant and his lady have company.*

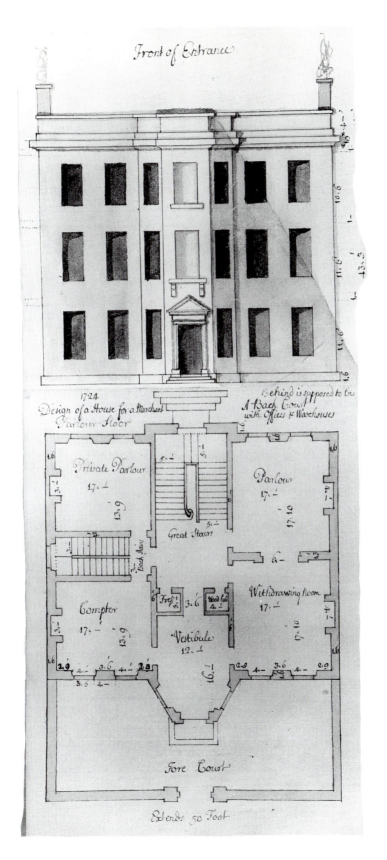

Front of Entrance.

1724
Design of a House for a Merchant
Parlour Floor

Behind is supposed to be
A Back Court
with Offices & Warehouses

Private Parlour
17. ⌐
13. 9

Great Stairs

Parlour
17. ⌐
17. 10

Back Stairs

Compter
17. ⌐
13. 9

Pref:
3. 6

Wood hold

Vestibule
12. ⌐

Withdrawing Room
17. ⌐
17. 10

Fore Court

Extends 50 Foot

which nothing is more unfitt for a country seat . . . which requires somewhat more like a court.[8]

North wrote at a time of growing assurance in English building, when the much-travelled Charles Talbot, Duke of Shrewsbury, could report from firsthand knowledge that "there is not in Italy so fine a house as [William Cavendish's] Chattesworth"; when "My Lord Carlisle [Charles Howard] has got his whole Garden Front up [at Castle Howard] And is fonder of his Work every day than Other"; when "My Lord Bindon [Henry Howard] is busy to the Utmost of his Force in New Moulding Audley end, And All the World are running Mad after Building, as far as they can reach".[9] Sir John Vanbrugh – soldier, drama-tist, and architect-extraordinary – was already busy on Blenheim Palace when he wrote thus in 1708 to Charles Montagu, Earl of Manchester. And Montagu, lately returned from Venice, was just then engaged (with Vanbrugh's help) on another costly rebuilding of his own Kimbolton Castle, remodelled in the 1690s but now made double-pile, with grand staircase and Rococo frescoes by Pellegrini.[10] That furious pursuit of fashion – Pellegrini's Venetian Rococo would have been new even at Versailles – had gripped both town and country by 1700. Even in the absence of the surplus wealth that had supported the First Rebuilding, it gave context and inspiration to the Second.

What separated the two Rebuildings, in many (if not most) towns, was the move from limited refurbishment to reconstruction.[11] Late-medieval English townhouses, typically rebuilt for greater comfort, had offered accommodation of good quality. They "do not seem very large from the outside", said an Italian visitor, describing London's "very many mansions" in 1497, "but inside they contain a great number of rooms and garrets and are quite considerable".[12] And as long as tradi-tional life-styles remained intact, there was very little reason for plan changes. Individuals showed their wealth in other ways, by unprec-edented accumulations of household goods. "My house within the city", Shakespeare makes the dotard Gremio say, in *The Taming of the Shrew*, "is richly furnished with plate and gold;/Basins and ewers to lave her dainty hands;/My hangings all of Tyrian tapestry;/In ivory coffers I have stuff'd my crowns;/In cypress chests my arras counterpoints,/Costly apparel, tents and canopies,/Fine linen, Turkey cushions boss'd with pearl,/Valance of Venice gold in needle-work;/Pewter and brass, and all things that belongs/To house or housekeeping."[13]

If the furnishings were rich and noble in Gremio's house, the proper place for him to live was still the city. Before the development of the Italianate square and terrace, and unprepared (as yet) for the suburban villa, most pre-Restoration city folk remained with their trades, living (as they always had done) over the shop. Wealthy Londoners – and prominent Bristolians were the same – were not over-eager to leave their city habitats for the slow ascent in social status as country gentry.[14] And one inevitable result of their conservatism was that urban house-plans stayed unaltered, such changes as occurred being mainly verbal. The "frame of three fayre houses" built by Roger Oldfield in London's Leadenhall Street in 1590 retained all the characteristics – the high narrow frontages and multi-chambered interiors – of those "quite con-

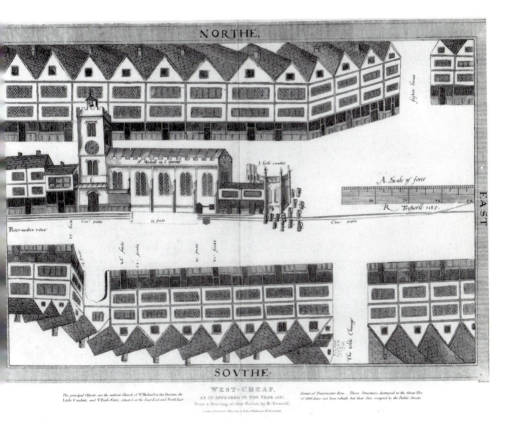

*Houses and shops in Elizabethan London's Cheapside (West Cheap), engraved in 1814 from Treswell's p of 1585.*

siderable" London mansions of 1497. When inventoried some two generations later, in the 1650s, their street-front first-floor rooms (the best in each house) were variously described as "the *Hall* next the Streete" and "the *Chamber* next the Streete over the Shopp".[15] While the emphasis, no doubt, was shifting as the common hall lost its centrality, the accommodation remained essentially the same. There was no record of modern improvements such as framed staircases.

Stairs are mentioned, but no more, in the 1629 inventory of the deceased John Whitson's Bristol tenement, among the very grandest in the city. Whitson, who died that March, had been Bristol's most eminent citizen. "He lived nobly; kept a plentifull table", memorialized his godson, John Aubrey, "and was the most popular magistrate in the city, alwaies chosen a member of Parliament. He kept a noble house, and did entertain and treat the peers and great persons that came to the city."[16] But for all the sophistication of Whitson's London contacts at Westminster and Whitehall, his house and its routines were a world away from Bristol's similar-status merchant-house of the following century. Whitson's tenement, with his shop and warehouse incorporated, was still his workplace. Traditional in plan, its updated elements were the floored-over Hall (creating two dining chambers, above and below); "Mistress Whitsons Closet" (furnished only with "a little Table bord with some purslane [porcelain] dishes and glasses and other small trifles"); and the Long Gallery. But Whitson's Gallery was less the formal parade space of the great noblemen of his acquaintance than the full-to-bursting linen store of the bourgeois citizen, packed with huge numbers (far more than he could need) of "fine holland sheets", "fine pillowbeers [cases]", "fine diaper napkins", and "fine damaske Table clothes". His best pictures, instead, were hung in the Great Parlour, among them a full-length portrait of his beautiful second wife, curtained-over (very probably) by his third.[17]

Whitson was a man of many parts: successful merchant venturer, assiduous politician, amorous three-time husband, and sardonic author of that pious meditation, *The aged Christians final farewell to the world and its vanities*, which ends with an affectionate leave-taking of his third beloved spouse ("the joy of my heart, the stay and comfort of mine old age") and of his many devoted friends ("the solace of prosperity, the comfort of adversity"), qualified by the reflection: "Whether this respect sprung from the love of my fortune or myself, it is no time now to enquire".[18] But he was 76 when he died, his godson tells us. And his views were as conservative as his house. In particular, Whitson had no time for the "insatiable thirst of science" of men younger than himself, who heap "question upon questions, never ceasing to make doubts and distinctions, to make knots and undo them, whereby they ensnare themselves, and mar others".[19] What he saw – and loved it not – was the beginning of the scientific revolution of William Harvey, Isaac Newton, John Evelyn and their friends: another stage in the crystallization of a new professional class, no longer committed to life above the shop, or to view the house as anything but dwelling-space.

In the event, street-front shops and common halls were to be the most notable absentees from the regular houses of "lobby-entrance plan" which, from the mid-century, launched another era of reconstruction in the towns.[20] These chimney-based houses, with their symmetrical facades, their centrally placed doorways, their diminutive vestibules with identical chambers to right and left, were the earliest

*60  A central chimney, between equal-sized chambers to right and left, determined the plan of the new "lobby-entrance" houses which became widely popular from about 1650. In this cottage at Mapledurham (Oxfordshire), dated 1691, the old-style common hall has gone; the front door is in the middle, with a small vestibule behind; an axial chimney-stack heats both front rooms; and there is a third room (with straight stair up) at the rear.*

purpose-built dwellings of a new "polite" society – not lordly, not rustic, not over-preoccupied with trade – in need of a dedicated architecture. It was an imitative society, for "every Englishman constantly holds a pair of scales wherein he exactly weighs the birth, the rank and especially the fortune of those he is in company with, in order to regulate his behaviour accordingly".[21] And it learnt swiftly from the example of the better-travelled nobleman, coming (as he did) to love regularity, to compare feature staircases, to parade in the garden and build gazebos.

These were the values of a moneyed leisured class. Their hold was the more secure on the "middling sort of people" – the clergy, the lawyers, the apothecaries and physicians – as country gentry took up residence alongside them. Bored with rural life, squires and their ladies came to the towns for their entertainment: for the balls, plays and races, and for the general "sociableness of the place". But they could also expect to live more cheaply than at home, with fewer obligations to their tenantry. "The plenty and cheapness of this city", said John Macky about York in 1714, "brings abundance of strangers hither for the conveniency of boarding, which is very cheap, and the apartments and diet good."[22] "Ah, what an excellent thing is an English Pudding!" apostrophized Maximilian Misson, thinking no doubt of that good diet: "Blessed be he that invented pudding, for it is a manna that hits the palates of all sorts of people . . . To come in [Yorkshire] Pudding time, is as much to say, to come in the most lucky moment in the world".[23]

Truly York (we may assume) had more puddings to the square foot than any other city in the kingdom. And cheap, varied and plentiful food was an obvious advantage of urban living. But attractive though many towns were fast becoming in post-Civil War England, there is little to suggest that the *proportion* of town-dwellers increased dramatically in this period, more significant being their rise in real wealth.[24] London, larger than any other European city by 1700, was the pioneering centre of a new money market – in government debt, company stocks and bonds – which had displaced, at last, the age-old primacy of rural rents. And the City's many investors, now more able to spread their risks, had less reason than ever to go rustic.[25] Meeting their growing demand for suitable accommodation, London's earliest terraced houses (unlike their counterparts abroad) were single-family units, private and exclusive from the start. Merchants who thus abandoned their street-front shops – doctors their surgeries, lawyers their chambers – were

*61 The entrance hall and stair of a typical terraced house in Great Ormond Street (London), developed in about 1700.*

leaving more than businesses behind. Agreeably settled in their fashionable urban terraces, between neighbours they could trust but need not see, entertaining was reduced to *the friend or two*; the family, once *extended*, became *nuclear*.[26]

London's squares and terraces, more consistently developed than those of any other city, have always had a quality of their own. They were at once – and have remained – very popular. However, one result of their success was that the capital's limitations – its miserly sites and the excessive regularity of its continuous-row developments – came to set the standard for the kingdom. "I will not exaggerate this which is so plain", said Roger North of the penny-pinching practices of London developers, "but onely observe that this humour hath vitiated all our modes, as well of furniture as of houses".[27] And so indeed it might have been, if economies alone were all that London's terraces could offer. In practice, that was far from being the case. Socially, the terraced house, hardly varying in plan, brought families of different backgrounds side-

62 Soho Square (originally King's Square, from the statue of Charles II in the middle
its adjoining streets in Soho Fields, was laid out in 1681 by Gregory King, the v•
genealogist, surveyor and statistician. This engraving of Soho Square in c.1725 (by

RE

Highgate

Sutton Str.

*...ds) shows the steady terraced development of eighteenth-century London northwards*
*... Hampstead and Highgate. It was reproduced in Strype's much enlarged sixth edition*
*... of John Stow's* Survey of London *(1598).*

by-side and taught them an identical life-style. Aesthetically, too, the continuous-row arrangement appealed to the sensibilities of literate men already persuaded of the superior virtues of regularity. What worried Sir John Lowther (d.1706), the urban developer and entrepreneur, was that the detached houses preferred by his tenants at Whitehaven (Cumberland) would "defeat his Design of building a regular town". Accordingly,

*63 Sir John Lowther's declared intention at Whitehaven (Cumberland) from the late 16 was to build a 'regular' town. Originally developed for the family's coal and salt tra Whitehaven's harbour grew hugely in importance from the late seventeenth century, u*

his building covenants, from 1699, included the requirement to build continuously, observing a common street line and "takeing up the whole length of the front". All new occupiers, likewise, must build "at least three Stories high besides the Sellars and Garretts, and in all not under Twenty eight foot in hight from the Levell of the Street to the Square of the Side Walls".[28]

*...d increasingly by tobacco importers. This fine prospect of Whitehaven, painted by Matthias ...d in the 1730s, shows the town with vacant plots, while development still continues on ...y streets.*

Level frontages, continuous rows and standard heights were all essential to Sir John Lowther's grand design. The result was a grid-plan town of a kind not seen in England since the late thirteenth-century Edwardian plantations. But total uniformity was frustrated at Whitehaven by the unanticipated prosperity of its later householders. From the 1690s, as the colonial tobacco trade expanded, independent merchants settled in the port, ready to conform to the scale of Lowther's rows, but otherwise building largely as they chose. Whitehaven's merchant-houses, unlike London's terraces, were of individual (if regular) design. Varying street facades put these differences on show. However, it was in their staircases, in particular, that Whitehaven's wealthier householders demonstrated their modernity, introducing metropolitan values to the north. Within half a century, the sub-medieval *newel* (still common in the north-west)

*64  Whitehaven's new plotholders observed common street lines and built to standard heights, while otherwise pleasing themselves about detail. Here in Howgill Street, developed in the 1730s, wealthy tobacco merchants welcomed their guests at a pedimented portal, before escorting them upstairs to the best parlour.*

and the primitive Jacobean *dog-leg* (fit only for smaller houses) had given way to the costly *open-well*. Along with these changes, private dining rooms and best parlours went one floor up, as Whitehaven's polite society moved upstairs.[29]

One of Lowther's frustrations, in overseeing his new development, was the failure of his richer tenants to build appropriately. Thus he took the Addisons to court in 1701–1703 for having "erected a Line of mean, Low and Contemptible buildings not above three yards high in the side walls . . . to the great deforming of that part of the Town [the West Strand] where your Orator was most Desirous it should have been regular & beautifull towards the Harbour".[30] But already the single-storey townhouse, surviving only in the remoter counties, had almost vanished.[31] And other popular improvements, gathering momentum from the sixteenth century, had usually included the rebuilding of chimneys – "pulling down the chimneys, to build them more safely, conveniently, &c. of brick", reported Ralph Thoresby in 1678 of his Kirk Gate house at Leeds [32] – and the fitting of glazed windows, affordable now by almost everybody.

It was one criticism of contemporary Italy, voiced by John Ray in the 1670s, that "in many Cities the paper windows (which are for the most part tatter'd and broken) disgrace the buildings, being unsuitable to their magnificence".[33] And Robert Midgley, travelling through France in 1691, observed the same phenomenon in provincial Lyons ("one of the greatest and chiefest towns in the Kingdom"), where "the Windows are generally of oyl'd paper, which keeps out the Heat of the Sun better than Glas, but takes off from the Nobleness of the Buildings".[34] Both remarked on such survivals because, as John Aubrey said of England, while "heretofore glasse windowes were very rare, only used in churches and the best roomes of gentlemen's howses. Yea, in my remembrance, before the civill warres, copyholders and ordinary poore people had none. Now the poorest people, that are upon almes, have it. In Herefordshire, Monmouth, Salop, etc., it is so still. But now this yeare [1671] are goeing up no lesse than 3 glasse-howses between Glocester and about Worcester, so that glasse will be common over all England."[35]

Aubrey's optimistic vision was shared by many – glass-makers, politicians and scholars alike – in that "glad confident morning" of the Restoration. It was "a glorious day", Evelyn noted, when the fleet sailed by Dover on 16 May 1672: "such a gallant & formidable Navy never I think spread saile upon the seas". And not anticipating its defeat just three weeks later at Southwold Bay, he was still in the best of spirits when, on 20 May:

> I was carried [from Margate] to see a gallant Widow a Farmoresse, & I think of Gygantic race, rich, comely, & exceedingly Industrious: She put me in mind of Debora [the charismatic prophetess], and Abigal [the clever beauty]; her house was so plentifully stored with all manner of Countrie provisions, all of her own groth, & all her conveniences so substantiall, neate & well understood; She herself so jolly & hospitable, & her land, so trim, & rarely husbanded, that it struck me with a kind of admiration at her Oeconomie.[36]

To Evelyn and his contemporaries, the wealth of that genial widow was certainly less remarkable than her good management ("oeconomie"). She lived in a famously prosperous county. And "a Kentish yeoman", as Fuller said, "passeth [in common speech] for a plain man of a plentiful estate, yeomen in this county bearing away the bell for wealth from all of their rank in England". A second characteristic of these well-off farmers was security of tenure – "the tenure of villainage (so frequent elsewhere) being here utterly unknown". A third was self-esteem – for "such yeomen refuse to have the title of Master put upon them, contenting themselves without any addition of gentility".[37] These attributes were not unique to Kent. But if, through swathes of England, greater security of tenure encouraged the long view, making builders at that time of many yeomen, Kentish disregard of social class was more unusual. In other fertile counties – including Fuller's native Northamptonshire ("fruitful in corn and grass") – gentility was of the essence of the Rebuilding.

Yetminster (Dorset), in the last decades of the seventeenth century, was the quintessential village of that Rebuilding. Its wealthy householders, dairy-farmers for the most part, were comfortably secure on their village holdings. And among their immediate neighbours were the younger sons of country gentry, excluded from their rural inheritances by elder brothers. Both classes, brought together at Yetminster, built the same. Their costly new stone houses had ornamental gables and classicizing doorcases, decorative hoodmoulds over multi-light mul-

*65 Fine feature staircases, like this one at Much Hadham (Hertfordshire), are evidence of enhanced social status and of the increasing importance of first-floor family rooms in the larger village houses of late seventeenth-century England.*

lioned windows, separate kitchens, first-floor parlours and feature stairs. Not content to be "constantly called but Goodman" like the men of Kent, Yetminster's *parish* gentry were accorded prestigious titles like "gentleman" and "master" by their contemporaries. They rubbed shoulders with the *country* gentry every day of their lives, and built at least as grandly in emulation.[38]

It was these wealthy rural householders – gentle by local courtesy rather than by title or descent – who required (as in the towns) the dignity of a good staircase and first-floor dining room. They furnished their new houses with two-storeyed porches, and raised their roofs aloft on attic floors. The characteristics of a gentleman's residence, in Gloucestershire at this time, were its panelled chambers and carved doorcases, plaster ceilings and many chimneys, separate kitchen, second-floor bedchambers and handsome stairs. And while all of these together seldom coincided in a farmhouse, the houses of aspiring gentry might have several of them.[39] One such Gloucestershire farmhouse was Mill Farm, in Tytherington: 10-room home of James Pullin (d.1690), a wealthy yeoman. What little survives at Mill Farm of high-status work is restricted to an eight-light kitchen window and some fine plasterwork. Yet we know that Goodman Pullin, mature in years and fortune, was styled "Master" by his friends; he had a clock in his hall; his parlour was his dining chamber, seating 12; and (like a gentleman) he drank his coffee there.[40]

Inevitably, there comes a time when the yeoman's working farmhouse and the gentleman's exclusive residence will part company. But that point had yet to be reached in the Restoration countryside, where the wealthier farmers (like the shopkeepers in the towns) were increasingly mindful of home comforts. An obvious casualty of these changes was the traditional hospitality of rural England.[41] However, the welcoming at home of family and close friends – a private satisfaction rather than a public rite – made demands of its own on farmhouse architecture. Tytherington's James Pullin was not the only Gloucestershire farmer to have his separate dining room, furnished entirely for entertainment.[42] As rents fell and wages rose, reducing income differences between the classes, even husbandmen built more permanently than they had ever built before, and yeomen lived increasingly like gentlefolk.

The northern tip of Oxfordshire was one of many islands of prosperity.[43] From the 1660s, Banbury's substantial farmhouses, remodelled already just before the Civil War, entered a second phase of reconstruction.[44] Like their fathers and grandfathers (the rebuilders of 1600–1640), Oxfordshire's yeomen valued their privacy. They no longer needed a common hall, and so got rid of it. But the distinguishing mark of this Second Great Rebuilding was less the final disappearance of the long-redundant hall, than a fresh traveller-led emphasis on regularity. Traditional *three-unit* houses – of hall, parlour and kitchen – continued to be built in northern Oxfordshire until the 1650s. But parlour and hall, after the mid-century, more often came together in symmetrical houses of *two-unit* plan, of which the other ground-floor element was the kitchen. In Abraham ffinch's house at Shutford, said Warden Woodward in 1674, "there is a Kitchen & Hall, or Parlour, very handsome". What he saw was a modern farmhouse of two-unit plan, in which the hall had been reduced to entrance-passage.[45]

That reduction was no absolute loss. Banbury's farmhouses, formerly single-storeyed, were now usually of two floors plus an attic. And the peculiar advantage of a central hall (with landings over) was that each individual chamber had separate access. It was this significant advance in personal privacy which has caused the central stair-passage – with a front door at one end, and a framed stair at the other – to be rated "the most important contribution the seventeenth century had to make to the development of [farmhouse] architecture".[46] With the adoption at many farmhouses of the fashionable double-pile plan – allowing twice as many chambers as before – there would be private accommodation for every family member: a privilege unknown (and unwanted) in medieval England but, in vernacular building, "the ultimate achievement of the Renaissance".[47]

Other preoccupations, no longer exclusive to the nobility, were shared by yeomen. Chief among them was an obsession with building "in the Italian and Greek manner" – with "uniform" facades and with "the bases, capitals and other ornaments of the orders so much pleaded for and so religiously executed" by travelled noblemen. "I cannot ascribe such necessity to them", wrote Roger North of the more ambitious of these ornaments, "but all the world must agree they are beautyfull".[48] In the yeoman's farmhouse also, that beauty would show better if his dwelling faced the road; if it were sited more handsomely, on a rise and on its own; if it were freed of the contagion of working buildings. The larger farmhouses of Georgian England were almost all of that description: symmetrical and double-pile, with attached pilasters, Tuscan porches, denticulated cornices and new-style sashes. Their model was the local rectory or lesser manor-house.[49]

In the countryside, accordingly, just as in the towns, architecture became the agent of social levelling. The yeoman who preferred to be called a "farmer" in late eighteenth-century England probably lived in a double-pile house. But so also did the nobleman at one end of the scale, and the wealthier artisan or husbandman at the other. While the final product was the same, dissolving regional styles in all but cottages, it was commonly reached at a most uneven pace. Yorkshire is a large county: so big and so diverse that a delay of 50 (or more) years separated the farmhouse rebuildings of the agricultural central plain from those of the industrial Pennines to the west. But differences could be much more localized than this. The villagers of remote Haworth, although Pennine clothworkers like their neighbours, had been left with the fag-end of their trade. They prospered far less obviously than Upper Calderdale's yeomen-clothiers, and lagged at least a generation in their Rebuilding.[50]

Upper Calderdale (like Evelyn's Kent) was a "dear dear land . . . a blessed plot . . . a demi-paradise . . . another Eden".[51] It caught even the worldly Londoner by surprise. One August day, early in the 1720s, Daniel Defoe crossed the Pennines from Rochdale. It was a bleak and lonely track, "both very troublesome and dangerous":

> [But] the nearer we came to Hallifax, we found the houses thicker, and the villages greater in every bottom; and not only so, but the sides of the hills, which were very steep every way, were spread with houses, and that very thick . . . We found the country, in

66  Upper Calderdale, seen here in the mid-nineteenth century, still kept its rugged character but was no longer "one continued village" of yeomen-clothiers. In this 1845 lithograph from Tait's Views on the Manchester and Leeds Railway, industrialization has come to Calderdale and big mills already line the valley floor.

THE SECOND GREAT REBUILDING IN TOWN AND COUNTRY

short, one continued village, tho' mountainous every way, as before; hardly a house standing out of a speaking distance from another, and (which soon told us their business) the day clearing up, and the sun shining, we could see that almost at every house there was a tenter [frame], and almost on every tenter a piece of cloth, or kersie, or shalloon, for they are the three articles of that country's labour; from which the sun glancing, and, as I may say, shining (the white reflecting its rays) to us, I thought it was the most agreeable sight that I ever saw . . . look which way we would, high to the tops and low to the bottoms, it was all the same; innumerable houses and tenters, and a white piece upon every tenter.[52]

Cloth is still being made in Upper Calderdale today. But the mills are in the valleys and the hillside clothiers are no more, with only the husk of their Rebuilding remaining. Immediately west of Halifax are the two big townships of Warley and Norland. There, at a recent count, between a third and a half of all working households had evidently found the means to rebuild before 1700. It was yeomen-clothiers, not gentry, who built four out of five of the largest farmhouses.[53]

While plainly not of gentry status, these yeomen learnt to live in genteel ways. Consumed by curiosity, Defoe knocked on the doors of some of Upper Calderdale's "master manufacturers". He found their houses "full of lusty fellows, some at the dye-fat, some dressing the cloths, some in the loom, some one thing, some another, all hard at work". But the manufacturer's "shop" or workplace was at the lower end of his house, carefully separated from his private quarters by a cross-passage. And his journeymen (like married farmhands) lived in cottages. "Among the manufacturers houses", Defoe reported also, "are likewise scattered an infinite number of cottages or small dwellings, in which dwell the workmen which are employed, the women and children of whom, are always busy carding, spinning, &c. so that no hands being unemploy'd, all can gain their bread, even from the youngest to the antient".[54]

Successive rebuildings, over the years, increased the segregation within farmhouses. Near Halifax again, the big clothier farmhouse called High Bentley, in Shelf, began life as a late-medieval aisled hall.[55] When first built in the fifteenth century, the only hearth at High Bentley was in the central "housebody", or common hall. At the upper end of the hall was a cross-wing with private chambers; at the lower was a

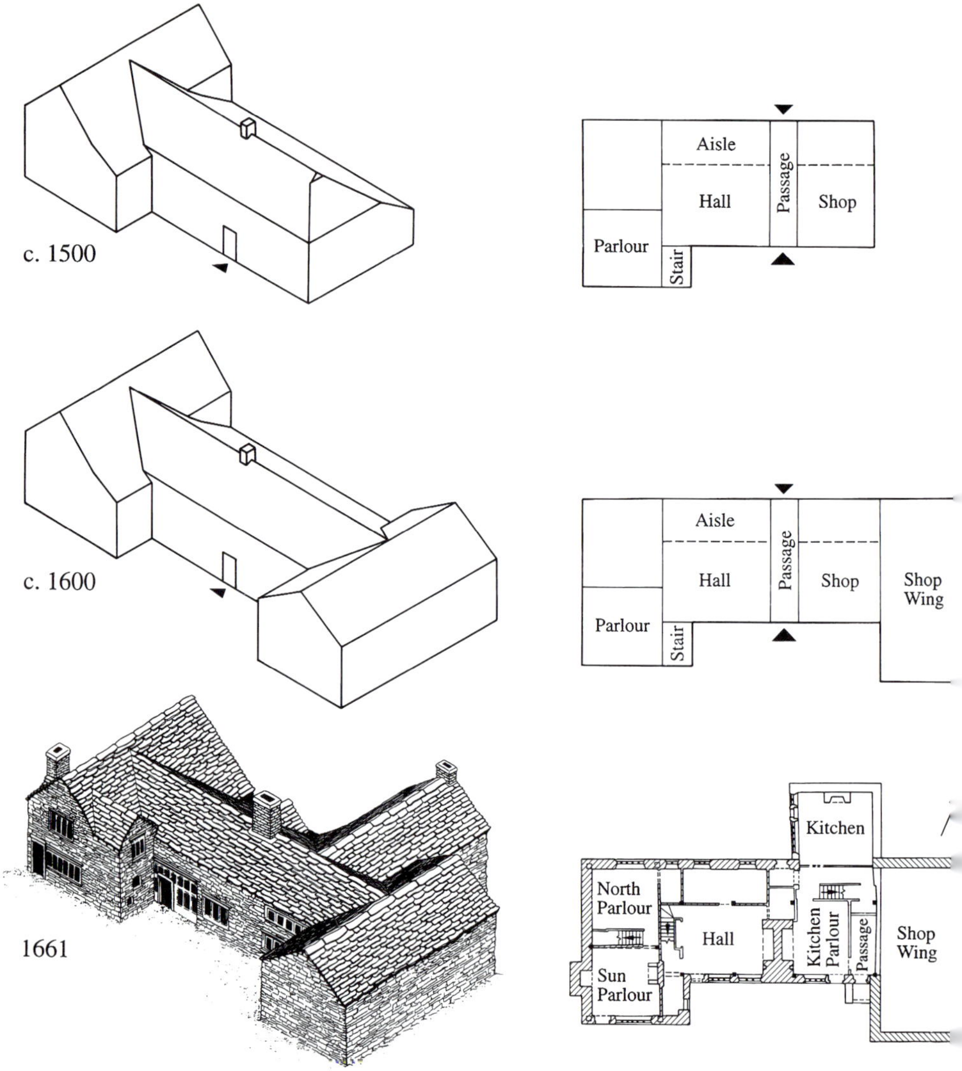
c. 1500
Aisle
Hall
Passage
Shop
Parlour
Stair
c. 1600
Aisle
Hall
Passage
Shop
Shop Wing
Parlour
Stair
1661
Kitchen
North Parlour
Hall
Kitchen Parlour
Passage
Shop Wing
Sun Parlour

*67 Three stages in the development of High Bentley in Shelf (West Yorkshire), from the comparatively m clothier's farmhouse of c.1500 to Richard Wade's rebuilding of 1661, in which his workshop and li quarters were kept well separate.*

"shop" below the passage. In about 1600, another big cross-wing was added to High Bentley, more than doubling its existing workshop space. But it was Richard Wade's second rebuilding, of 1661, which was the more radical. From that time, all cooking (and servants) would be banished to a new attached kitchen. The open hall was kept, but modernized for family use and entertainment – ceiled for warmth at tie-beam level, and fitted with a first-floor gallery and display fireplace. Richard resited his front door to give it a modern lobby-entrance; he moved the medieval cross-passage against the 1600 workshop wall; and raised a substantial chimneystack in its place.[56] Thirty years later, the Wades of High Bentley were still known locally as "yeomen". Samuel Wade, like Richard, was both farmer and clothier. However, he kept his workmen separate, at the far end of his house, and entertained like a gentleman in a galleried hall, furnished for at least a dozen guests.[57]

Almost alone among rebuilders, a significant minority of these Calderdale yeomen-clothiers preserved their open halls as party spaces. But the new purpose-built housebody, even in Calderdale at this time, was a rarity.[58] And the great majority of yeomen-builders, on starting afresh, would omit the hall entirely from their farmhouses. After the fashion of the gentry – and at almost the same period – yeomen everywhere began to opt for the central-entry house, as "regular" as their circumstances would allow. Adding another storey and going double-pile, they transformed the entrance passage from what had once been social barrier into unifying circulation space. There were similar-sized parlours on each side of this passage; at its end was a framed staircase, opposite the front door; above, off a central landing, were the separately entered bedchambers of the family. On both sides of the Pennines – in Lancashire as well as Yorkshire – these first symmetrical farmhouses date to the latter end of the seventeenth century. They were the equal of any in the South.[59]

Farmers' wives "who do nothing but drink tea", and their aspiring-gentry menfolk "who can now lay in their port wine by the pipe, and send their daughters to boarding school" are polemical fictions of the mid-eighteenth century.[60] Neither need be taken too seriously. But the rich yeoman's gentrification is not in doubt, its reverse side being alienation from his servants. Again architecture was to play a crucial role. It is an "inviolable rule", Roger North began his essay *On planning a country house* (1696), "to have the *entrata* in the midle":

But this must not be the common passage for all things, in regard your freinds and persons of esteem should pass without being annoyed with the sight of foull persons [i.e. the servants], and things, which must and will be moving in some part of a large and well inhabited dwelling. Therefore, for such occasions there must be a back-*entrata* . . . The like is to be sayd of stayres. For the cheif must not be annoyed with disagreeable objects, but be releived of them by a back-inferior staircase.[61]

While North's intended readership was gentry-builders like himself, what he prescribed was already practised in many farmhouses. Back entrances had long been standard in medieval houses of any size. And as early as 1627, when Philip Brome rebuilt his farmhouse at Isle Abbotts (Somerset), he allowed no access, whether on the first floor or in the attics, between his servants' low-grade quarters and his own.[62] Three years later, the much simpler Topham's Farm, at Conistone (North Yorkshire), was nevertheless furnished with a second, lesser staircase, provided only for the servants' bedchamber just above.[63] Almost identical arrangements, but with ladders in place of stairs, have survived at Burwains in Briercliffe (1642) and Lower Townhouse in Great Marsden (before 1650), two big farmhouses of the Lancashire Pennines.[64] And what all these houses shared was deliberate segregation, isolating the servants' quarters from the rest.

It was about the disaffection of such servants – "laid in some cold out-house, or meanest Loft, of a Poor Cottage, to have the leavings of coarse fare there" – that Richard Mayo wrote in 1693.[65] Once the yeoman's hearth-sharers, they had only lately become the victims of an increasingly polarized society, in which every fresh improvement thrust them lower. Cambridgeshire probate inventories of the 1660s, matched with their associated hearth-tax entries, have shown again the "incontrovertible association between wealth and house-size" which kept the poor labourer or lesser husbandman in his one-hearth cottage (of just two or three rooms) distinct in every way from the rich yeoman in his five-hearth farmhouse (of eight or more). John Mickelly, of West Wickham, was one of the more prosperous of those Cambridgeshire yeomen, worth almost £550 on his death. He had lived in a big farmhouse of 13 rooms and five hearths, of which only the kitchen hearth was shared.[66]

Of Goodman Mickelly and his like, it might truly be said that "his outside is an ancient yeoman of England, though his inside may give arms with the best gentleman and never see the herald".[67] Others were more overtly ambitious. Thomas Atcherley of Myddle, born in 1617 into a well-off family of Shropshire tanners, died a gentleman in 1681.

All four of his surviving daughters married gentry. Atcherley was "a great dealer in timber", the purchaser of much land, and the builder of "fair" houses upon it. He "did serve many offices with much care and faithfulness. He was three times high constable of the hundred of Pimhill; he was often churchwarden of this parish."[68]

Thus was Atcherley immortalized in Richard Gough's *The history of Myddle* (1706), an engaging parish-pump chronicle of his own village. But Gough was more interested in the personalities of his fellow villagers than in their works. He says nothing about the conversion, which certainly happened in his time, of the Atcherley family tannery (built by Thomas's father) into a residence. Nor does he mention the growing practice, reaching Myddle while he lived, of resiting the farmer's drawing-room on the first floor.[69] Gough was in his mid-60s when he began writing his *History*. And in his twilight years, wealthy Shropshire yeomen were still passably content with shows of pewter, brass and linen in their farmhouses. Only the gentry had silver forks and porcelain teawares, clocks and looking-glasses, upholstered chairs and couches, pictures, and divided curtains at their windows.[70] Yet even these distinctions were wearing down. In more go-ahead communities, including Tyneside's Whickham, they had all but disappeared by 1700.

Whickham, in the high-yield Durham coalfield, was one of England's first industrialized societies. Since the 1570s, it had shared the growing riches of the near-by port of Newcastle. And whereas Newcastle (Defoe conceded) was "not the pleasantest place in the world to live", it was yet "a place of very great business".[71] Most of that business was in "the great trade of coales", chiefly to London. And it was from London that new fashions came back north. In Gough's remote and rural Myddle, only the rector, William Holloway (d.1689), had been able to enjoy such upmarket effects as a looking-glass, a close-stool, and a couch.[72] But Whickham's enterprising copyholders fared much better. They had window curtains like gentlemen, desks and upholstered chairs, pictures and maps, wall mirrors, clocks and virginals; they had drinking-glasses, porcelain ("chieny") dishes, and silver cups; their kitchens were well provided with specialist cooking equipment – with spice boxes, scales and mortars, with chafing-dishes, fish-steamers and pudding-pans.[73]

Many of these comforts were new even to Whickham in the later seventeenth century. And there were special local circumstances to promote them. Nevertheless, what Whickham's yeoman inventories clearly establish by this date is a much wider demand than there had ever been before for the "frontstage" furnishings of the gentry. Only two Whickham inventories list clocks before the Civil War; after the Restoration, there were 10. And while only Whickham's gentry had owned silver plate before 1650, silver was listed in almost a third of the inventories from 1660 to the end of the century.[74] Social class might be defined by such possessions. Thus when Whickham's richer yeomen joined the parish gentry, one way they chose to show it was in their furnishings. In just the rank below, Whickham's only "modestly" prosperous copyholders lacked the clocks, curtains and carpets of their aspiring gentry neighbours; they had no pictures or mirrors to adorn their walls; they bought no silver; and on their buffets was neither porcelain nor glass.[75]

It has been suggested of mixed-economy Whickham that because of the impact of industrial and commercial development on traditional class loyalties and distinctions, "domestic living standards (and in particular the possession of specific novelties) may have acquired a significance of an altogether new order".[76] And that may well have been the case in County Durham. But similar consumer behaviour, with no such special cause, was already characteristic of many regions. Late seventeenth-century Writtle, west of Chelmsford (Essex), was a representative home counties parish, "peculiar" only in the technical sense of exemption from the jurisdiction of its bishop. Yet of three substantial Writtle yeomen who died within days of each other in midwinter 1689–90, not one lacked his share of those image-enhancing furnishings more usually associated with minor gentry. All three Writtle yeomen had clocks in their halls; they each had a looking-glass – Henry Bullen had two – and a quantity of silver plate. Window curtains were listed at two of their houses, with desks and chests of drawers, couches and upholstered chairs. John Clarke had "two littell carpettes" in his parlour; Henry Bullen had "one picture"; Joseph Bonnington had "some books" in his hall.[77]

William Bird, who lived at Horseley Park in the same parish, was one of Joseph Bonnington's appraisers. Bird was a well-off gentleman-farmer. And it is easy to reconstruct from his own probate inventory (dated 26 May 1691) the life-style to which his yeoman neighbours had aspired. Bird had a separate well-equipped kitchen. His former hall, no longer shared, had become a family living room, furnished with a couch and a "press cubbord", five "joyned" stools, four leather chairs and an "old elbow chaire", some fire-irons, and an extending ("drawing") table of the kind first encountered in Essex inventories of the 1670s. Other novelties occur in Bird's personal apartments, of which both the parlour (his dining room) and the parlour chamber (his bedroom) had their own fireplaces. There was a large looking-glass in Bird's parlour, with 12 cane chairs and two of the newly fashionable oval tables. In his bedchamber, along with his great curtained and canopied bed, Bird had a red damask couch, a chest of drawers of olive wood, a looking-glass also framed in olive, and a small private treasury of silver plate: "a large silver boll, a small silver cupp, nine silver spoones, a lignum vit[a]e cup tip't with silver". There was another "good feather bedd" in the adjoining pantry chamber, quilted and curtained in "gray searge", with six chairs upholstered in the same. In the pantry below were more upholstered chairs –

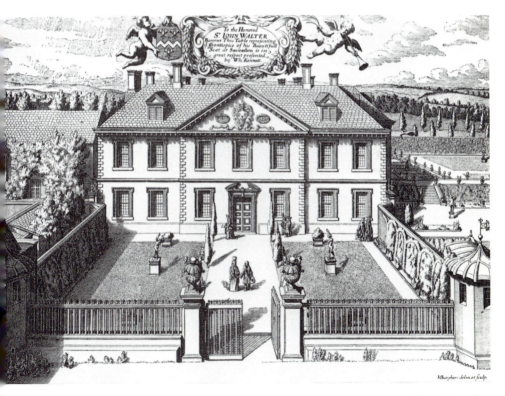

Sir John Walter's "beautiful seat" at Sarsden (Oxfordshire), rebuilt in the 1690s after a fire and seen here a contemporary engraving by Michael Burghers. Sarsden House exactly matches the complete gentleman's dition, there being "very few comforts among man-kind which such an estate could not give".

"five calves leather chaires, a cloath elbow chaire, [and] two cloath stooles" – with a quantity of pewter, a case of knives, and six dozen glass bottles. All the windows were curtained in these smaller private chambers, and there was a modern long-case clock on the stairs.[78]

William Bird had done well. But he was no richer overall than many yeomen of his day, and would almost certainly have aspired to greater things. "The Compleat English Gentleman", says Defoe (who was never one himself), is "the Glory of the Creation, the exalted Head of the whole Race . . . a Person of Merit and Worth; a Man of Honour, Virtue, Sense, Integrity, Honesty, and Religion".[79] Emulated by all, even the "great ones" called him lucky. Thus, relates Defoe:

> The late ever glorious King William [III] us'd frequently to say that, if he was not a king, and Providence had mercifully plac'd his station of life in his choice, he would be an English gentleman of two thousand pounds a year. His Majesty gave many very good reasons for the narrow compass of his desires, and one which I thought was very significant was this: that it was the stacion of life that gave the least room for disquiet and uneasyness in the world, and the greatest opportunity of calm and content; that there were very few comforts among man-kind which such an estate could not give.[80]

The king spoke thus, Defoe continues, "not from an empty speculation, but from a long experience in the manner of living publick and the state and pomp of a great household". "Call no man happy till he dies", warned Solon the Greek; "he is at best but fortunate." However, with "his time unengross't" (by petty business) and "his head unencumbr'd" (with great concerns), the fortunate English heir of "a little compact estate of £2,000 a year" – as Dutch William saw – was the happiest human creature to draw breath.[81]

CHAPTER 6

# Neat compact boxes

Higher rents and lower taxes, foreign travel and a new consumerism, the regulation of hospitality and the control of plague all contributed at different times and in separate ways to the long-term ascent of the English gentleman. From less than half the lands of England in the Late Middle Ages, the gentry's share had risen to more than two-thirds by 1700, and was still increasing.[1] But while no single explanation prevails today, the view of most contemporaries was more robust. "When one puts to them", writes Joan Thirsk, "the question how and at whose expense the gentry rose in the sixteenth and seventeenth centuries, their answer is unambiguous. They rose at the expense of their younger brothers".[2]

In England, reported the Pomeranian traveller Lupold von Wedel in 1584–85, "the value of the estates of the nobility cannot be reduced, for the eldest son inherits all; the others enter into some office or pursue highway robbery".[3] To many continentals like himself, primogeniture was unthinkable. And there were always those in England, led by the disinherited, who viewed this brutal custom with disfavour. A few of the bolder spirits found some comfort in it. "I have heard my father thank God many a time that he was a younger brother", Defoe makes one of them say, "because if he had not, he would have been a blockhead, an untaught lump of ignorance and pride, as his elder brother was and as most of the eldest sons of his acquaintance were."[4] However, Defoe wrote his *Compleat English gentleman* in 1728–29, when the role of younger brothers was already less oppressive as they discovered new employment in the professions. In von Wedel's generation – and even more so in the next – their plight had seemed more desperate by the hour.[5]

What had made their situation especially hard to bear was the changing composition of the noble household. It had long been argued, in defence of primogeniture, that the preservation of an estate allowed the sole heir to keep his entire family in decent comfort. And wherever more distant relatives did indeed live at home, this happened with most frequency in the upper classes.[6] But the long-term bias in English society was against it. There is diminishing evidence, in early-modern England, of the complex *extended* family households still habitual at this period on the Continent. Typically, the simple *nuclear* family – parents, children and servants – lived alone. "I doe not desire any more company in my house then my wife, children and servants", Henry Oxinden reminded his younger brother in 1636. But James had been sick, and "to doe you a curtesy I shall bee willing of your company during the time aforesaid [a month or six weeks]", for "I know by this time you have learnt there is a difference betweene Meum [mine] and Tuum [thine], not only amongst strangers but amongst friends and Brothers" like themselves.[7]

Squire Oxinden sounds less generous than in reality he was. James, then a student at Cambridge, was a profligate and a waster. And there were two other brothers (Richard and Adam) to set up in life, as well as two sisters (Kate and Bess). Coming early into his inheritance, while still only 21, Henry had the charge of his sibling's portions (each £300), yet had many money worries of his own.[8] One continuing cause of those anxieties was building. Henry, like his late father, was a builder. When Richard Oxinden, a second son, got Great Maydekin in Barham (Kent) as his portion, he had improved the house as soon as he could afford it, with brick chimneys and a new south range. Two decades later, it was Henry's turn to gentrify the "mansion house" at Great Maydekin. Henry's notebook records how, in 1633, he "went Squire wise to the brew house, and built it where it now standeth" on the hillside; he "tooke down the old malthouse adjoining to the [recently converted] withdrawing roome . . . [and] new builded the brewhouse, & Milkhouse & the roomes over them, which all fell down of their own accord, by reason of age, which brings all at last to the ground".[9] Henry was a dedicated tree-planter throughout his long life: oak and ash, pears and cherries, walnuts, hollies and yews. And 30 years later, when forced to sell Great Maydekin, he was still building and planting at the brick dower-house "called little Maydeken", to which he moved in 1663. Shortly afterwards, before "my long weakness began", Henry made that final summary of the works at Great Maydekin which is now one of the texts of the Rebuilding:

> My father Richard Oxinden Esq builded Great Maydeken in the yeare 1620, except the great staire case & the stone head at the west side of the with drawing roome & the brew house & the roomes as far as that head there reach, which I builded. I also wainscotted the great Parlour, the with drawing roome, the great chamber over the great Parlour the little closet beside it & both the studies & the closet within the Chamber over the little Parlour and Kitchin. I builded the portch and layd the purbeck stones from it to the gate & builded the gate, & walled the gardens as they now are. I builded the malt house & the barne & the rest of the roomes to the stables which stable my great Grandfather Mr James Brooker builded [in 1596].[10]

Many of those improvements had been completed by 1633. They followed Henry's marriage to Anne Peyton of Knowlton Park, and were associated with the nest-building of a typical young couple, without the resources to rebuild altogether, yet determined to modernize what they could. Not long afterwards, in correspondence with a new neighbour, Henry recalled those recent works. Sir Basil Dixwell, who had inherited land in Barham, had just started the building of Broome Park. And both Dixwell and Oxinden had been interested somewhat earlier in the purchase of a farm between their properties. During their discussions, Dixwell's final query had concerned the partition of the farmhouse. As Oxinden remembered in March 1635, "my answeare unto you [then] was, that you was a builder, and I had some occasione to build, and that wee might take it downe and you have the one part, I the other".[11] Dixwell (much the richer man) had neglected their agreement and bought the farm. And by the time his neighbour wrote in protest, he was already at work on the fine brick mansion that would cost him £8000.[12] Broome Park, although much altered internally, is still there. With its multiple giant pilasters and coronet of pedimented gables, all of the highest quality cut and moulded brickwork, it is a *tour de force* of Caroline Mannerism.[13]

Even with Inigo Jones at Court, a witty house like Broome could expect to attract much attention. Nobody looked harder than Dixwell's neighbour. In 1634, Oxinden relates, Sir Basil "diked & quicksetted the great pasture feilds beside the house viz. before it, & layd them to pasture which before had been errable ground time out of the memory of Man". Then in April 1635, Sir Basil "layd the foundation of the house at Broome, it was up by the middle of No[vember]". He built the stable in 1636 and his brewhouse the next year, and "there were used about the house, outhouses & walling, twentie and seaven hundred thousand brickes which hee made, besides thousands which hee bought: the sand

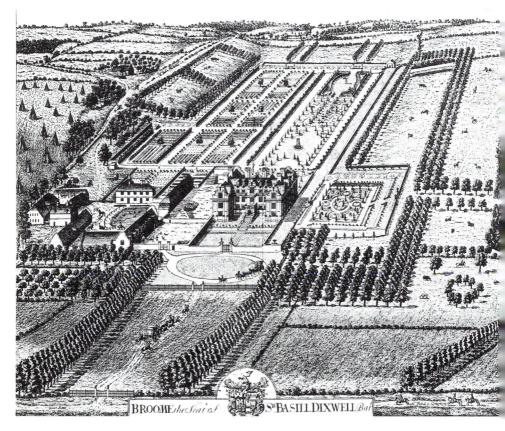

69  In Thomas Badeslade's early eighteenth-century drawing of Sir Basil Dixwell's Broome Park (Kent), bu in the 1630s just before the Civil War, particular attention is given to the orderly French-style plantations o big Restoration garden, soon afterwards swept away by new landscaping.

which hee bought come to 500*li* & the lead used about the house to 500*li*". But it was September 1637 "before the joiners had made any great progress in wainscotting the rooms, & it was St. Mich. 1638 before they & the painters had finished their work, and made the house ready for Sir Basil to come into it".[14] In the summer of that same year, while the workmen were still busy, Dixwell had arranged a neighbourly viewing. "I request you", he wrote to Squire Oxinden on 11 June 1638, "that you and your wife and the Capt that is with yow would be pleased to take the payne to walke downe on Thursday next about two of the clocke in the afternoone to Broome house wher yow shall meete myselfe and the Gentlemen and Gentlewomen which are of my house, that are very desirous to see yow all there and to eate a cake and drinke a bottle of wine together".[15]

That companionable picnic, in an almost finished house, is a last window on polite society before the wars. Four years later Sir Basil was dead, King Charles had raised his standard, and the neighbours were pitched against each other. The Kentish gentry, deeply divided by the struggle, included a good many who were ruined by it. But one of those who, through much hardship, survived its worst effects was Sir George Sondes of Lees Court, south of Faversham. Sondes, in happier times, had won "much reputation and esteem of the gentry" for his moderation and temper as sheriff of Kent in the "difficult business" of Ship Money.[16] He had continued a Royalist ("strictly loyal in his principles"), but was allowed after 1650 to return to Lees Court, where he busied himself immediately on completing the new range he may already have started some years earlier. Sondes had been a regular visitor to Whitehall before the war, and knew what the King's Surveyor was about. Accordingly, there is a Jonesian correctness in the garden front at Lees – Hasted describes it as "built after a design of Inigo Jones" – on which 14 identical Ionic pilasters march in giant order like tin soldiers.[17]

The rebuilding of Lees Court would probably have continued in that style, had it not been for a family calamity. On 7 August 1655, Freeman Sondes, Sir George's second son, murdered his sleeping elder brother with a cleaver.[18] That "horrid deed" at once became a *cause célèbre* of the contemporary debate on primogeniture. Stung by the accusations of "fanatic ministers", the distraught father wrote a narrative of the crime which attributed it (probably correctly) to innate character differences between his sons. But for almost everybody else at the time, the savage

*70 Sir George Sondes, when required after 1650 to retire to his estates, added this new south range to Lees Court (Kent), to create one of the best and most original facades of the Protectorate. It was in a bedchamber here that Freeman Sondes did his "horrid deed", murdering his elder brother, George, with a cleaver.*

fratricide in the bedroom at Lees Court was the clearest demonstration of the evils of sibling rivalry and sheltered idleness. Freeman, hanged after trial at Maidstone just two weeks later, confirmed the general verdict before he died. Gentlemen, he advised from his own bitter experience, should "not suffer their sons to live in idleness (which exposes a man to temptation) but to employ them in some honest public calling".[19]

Sir George had done his best to interest Freeman in the Law, or in a career (failing that) as city merchant. But the war had made men restless. And Freeman Sondes was not the only young blood to find himself frustrated: too early to take employment he believed below his rank, yet too late to stay perpetually at home. Old-style paternalism was also much to blame, for Sir George had contributed to keeping his sons at home by making them too welcome in his household. "I am sure no man's house in the country is more open to rich and poor than mine", he wrote in his *Plain narrative*; "there are twenty poor people at least weekly relieved, and that more than once. My lowest proportion in my house, whether I be there or not, is every week a bullock, of about fifty stone, a quarter of wheat, and a quarter of malt for drink, which makes about a barrel a day for my household".[20]

This was traditional hospitality in the grand old manner, and Sir George still saw it as obligation. But like the inflated baronial retinues of late-medieval England, such ceremonial largesse was now history. Royal governments, whose own centralization was a chief cause of those changes, nevertheless viewed the "decay" of hospitality with concern. One day, James predicted, "England will onely be London". And in 1616, when the king made that prophesy, his own nobility was bringing it to pass. "As every fish lives in his own place", moralized James, "some in the fresh, some in the salt, some in the mud: so let everyone live in his own place, some at Court, some in the Citie, some in the Countrey."[21] But he had had to order his gentry home for Christmas just the year, before; and that was neither the first nor the last time that he did it.

There were two long-standing reasons – external defence and local justice – why the gentry should "live and remaine at lest nine moneths of the yeere in the Shires".[22] But a third had now been added to the list. It was already the case that large country landowners, in times of dearth, would close up their households, lay off their servants, and save money by moving to the city – "with covetous minds to live in London and about the city privately and so also in other towns corporate without charge of company". Thus spoke Elizabeth in the great famine of 1596, requiring them to return to their estates.[23] However, saving money was rarely the only reason for moving to the towns, of which the particular attraction was good company. Out in the country, as Squire Vincent once explained, his associates necessarily were the "dwellers there about: as graziers, butchers, farmers, drovers, carpenters, carriers, tailors, and such like men", who he had found "very honest and good companions". So indeed they were, agreed Valentine (the Londoner), "but not for you being a gentleman". Rather than let their "bluntness and rusticity" infect Vincent's discourse, "if you did, for the most [part] live in court or city among the better sort, you should ever find company there, fit for your estate and condition: I mean noble[men] and gentlemen".[24]

The city's siren call, already clearly heard in this well known dialogue of the 1570s, became much more urgent after 1604 on the release of travel mania among the English. With Europe at peace, many English noblemen could at last experience for themselves the less formal urban life-styles of the Continent. They evidently liked what they saw, for as James acknowledged in 1615:

> The decay of Hospitalitie in all parts of this Our Kingdome, so much the more increaseth, by reason that Noblemen, Knights, and Gentlemen of qualitie, doe rather fall to a more private and deli-cate course of life, after the manner in forreine Countreys, by liv-ing in Cities and Townes, then continue the ancient and laudable custome of this Realme in house-keeping upon the principall Seates and Mansions in the Countrey.[25]

James was nobody's fool. He was right to lament the selfishness of his nobility in neglecting "to live in the steps and examples of their worthy Ancestours, by keeping and entertaining Hospitalitie, and charitable relieving of the poore according to their estate and meanes". But he must have been aware, each time he sent them home, that the values of the city travelled with them.

One product of the Grand Tour, even at its first appearance, was a growing appreciation of quality in building, along with the conviction that the "principles of architecture . . . [are] necessary also for a gentle-man to be known".[26] And soon there were young noblemen whose greatest passion was the practical application of those principles. Sir Roger Townshend, a rich Norfolk landowner, was among them. Raised for the most part in London, he had begun buying architectural treatises at an early age – "many Italian and French books of Architecture" was Roger Pratt's later comment on his library. And before building for himself at Raynham Hall, he had made a particular study of the work of Inigo Jones; had visited contemporary prodigy houses such as Henry Hobart's Blickling, Robert Cecil's Hatfield and Thomas Howard's

---

71 *It was much more economical for Henry Somerset, Duke of Beaufort (d. 1699), to live in his compact London lodgings than to maintain the huge household at Badminton (Gloucestershire), where he is said to have kept "nine original tables covered every day". These plans of c. 1685 show Beaufort's London house to have included a hall (A) on the ground floor, with kitchen under; over the hall was the duke's dining room (F), having a*

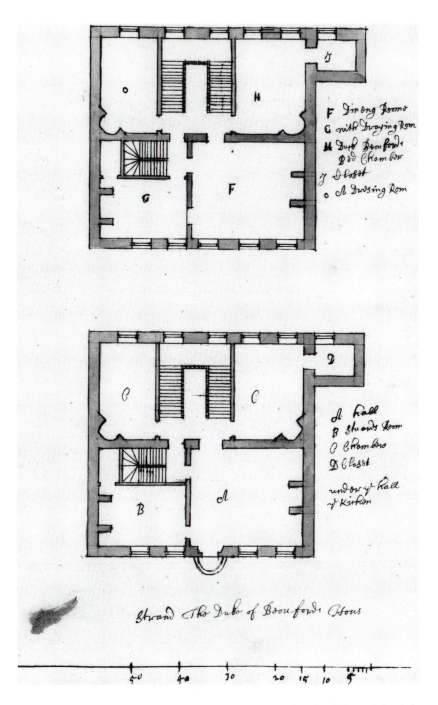

F Dining Roome
G with Draying Rom
H Duke Beaufords
Bed Chamber
J Closet
O A Dressing Rom

A Hall
B Stewards Room
C Chambers
D Closet

under ye hall
ye Kitchen

Strand The Duke of Beaufords House

50    40    30    20  15  10  5

smaller withdrawing room (G) alongside it; Beaufort's bedchamber (H) was behind the
dining room, with a dressing room (O) across the landing of the great stair; there was a
second smaller stair for service use; and there were two other bedchambers (C & C) and a
steward's room (B) on the ground floor.

Audley End; and had travelled frequently on the Continent – at least once with his builder, William Edge – to learn more. After a false start in 1619, work at Raynham began again in 1622 and was nearing completion in December 1636 when checked by Townshend's death. There was no shortage of funds on Sir Roger's part, and the most likely explanation of the leisurely pace of his works is that he regarded them at all times as his hobby.[27]

That devotion kept Townshend, who was only 40 when he died, at the leading edge of contemporary building practice. It caused him to change his mind several times at Raynham, and not all his decisions were the right ones. Nevertheless, what resulted was a house of such fine restraint and regular proportions that the well-informed Roger North, some six decades later, took Raynham to be of the "beginning of the reign of Charles II", at "the first entrance of the mode I have bin

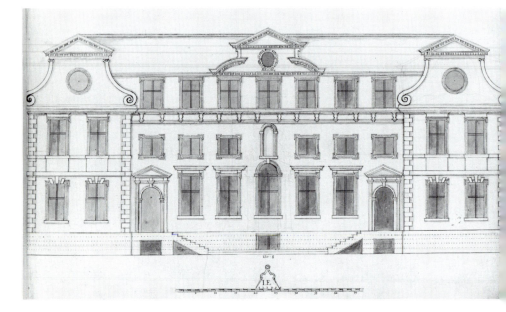

*72  Sir Roger Townshend's entrance facade at Raynham Hall (Norfolk), built in the late 1620s, is shown as originally planned with two front doors, leaving his hall uninterrupted in the middle. Such big common halls, if already declining in importance even while Townshend built, were still required in rural areas for hospitality. But households were much smaller and the tenantry less welcome guests by the time this drawing made in 1671. And Raynham's two front doors had been replaced before 1700 by the more impressive central portal of today. Another associated improvement, of some two decades later, was the re-use of former hall space for a stair.*

speaking of". North's reactions to Raynham were mixed. "Some things are singular in it", he wrote in the 1690s, "as the front hath no door in the midle, but on each side 2 principall doors." Also Raynham's great hall "hath [too] great prerogative of room, to the damage of the rest of the house". The lighting of its staircases was "neither fair nor pleasant", and some of its other details were "lumpish". But North particularly liked Raynham's garden front ("an Ionick order and frontone done much *alla regolare*"); he praised its situation ("promoted to the sumit of an hill, which makes an excellent avenue, all rising from the towne and valey, with a pomp I have not seen any where"); and he concluded that the house, for all its faults, "is noble and pleasant, and the greatest inconvenience is [only] that the stables are so far off".[28]

If Townshend had ever lived in his new house at Raynham, it would not have been in the manner of his ancestors. Even in his own day,

*It was the east (garden) front at Raynham – "an Ionick order and frontone done much alla regolare" – ...ch won special praise from Roger North in the 1690s.*

Raynham's great hall ("paved with marble") was far better suited to formal entrances than to the hospitable entertaining of rural tenantry. And that role would be confirmed, soon after North was there, by the insertion of a grand central portal.[29] Much earlier than this, when Townshend's house was almost ready, King Charles had complained (just as his predecessors had done) that "of late yeeres a greater number of the Nobilitie and Gentrie, and abler sort of His people with their Families, have resorted to the Cities of London and Westminster, and places adjoyning, and there made their residence, then in former times". And again he ordered them home in 1632 "to the severall Counties where they usually resided, and there [to] keepe their habitations and hospitalitie".[30] But increasingly there were those, like Townshend himself, who chose to hold such hospitality at arm's length. Rayham's main approaches, as replanned in 1621, were by a stately half-mile avenue from the nearest village.[31] And when Townshend and his successors kept Christmas at the Hall, it was less to preserve those "ancient English usages" regretted by all conservatives than to enjoy the feast in private with their families.

Such new exclusive life-styles, chiefly learnt abroad, were available for purchase off the peg. One of Daniel Defoe's more plausible stories in *The compleat English gentleman* of 1728–29 concerns an anonymous Hampshire gentleman "of a great estate and of a mighty antient family, belov'd in the country where he lives to an extravagance". Sir A. B. (as Defoe calls him) was a traditionalist. He liked to keep open house as his ancestors had done, so that "at Christmass, if he is oblig'd to be at Court or at the Parliament or both, he never fails to make a trip into the country on purpose to call all his poor neighbours and tennants together to make their hearts glad with his open house-keeping, and to see them all merry according to antient custome and the usage of his ancestors".[32] However, when he built himself a house, as both rank and wealth dictated, everything he ordered must be new.

"A few yeares ago", relates Defoe, "[Sir A. B.] built a noble mansion house for the family, enclos'd his park with a brick wall, enlarg'd his gardens and canals and fishponds". It was a "charming house and a seat fitt for a man of his quality". The furniture was "rich, new, and very well fitted". But before all was done, Sir A. B. had a friend over to inspect the works – "a particular friend . . . a man of letters, [who] had liv'd abroad, seen abundance of the fine pallaces in France, in Italy, in Germany and

*Joannes Kip drew Sir Robert Atkyns's "compact box" at Swell, along with other bird's-eye views of coun-*
*seats, for that historian's* The ancient and present state of Glostershire *(1712). It was of just such a*
*se that Sir A.B. (Defoe's noble buffoon) would have been proud.*

other places". This friend "acknowledg'd that all was admirably well here,
and even out-did the forreigners" in point of building. Yet, said he, "You
want [lack] some good paintings; pictures are a noble ornament to a
house. Nothing can set it off more." On the contrary, retorted Sir A. B.,
"you see my great staircase is tollerably full, and I have some more
a-comeing down [from London] for the hall". But "did you buy them
your self?" asked his friend, noting their poor quality. "To tell you the
truth, I did not", came the reply; "Nay, if I had, it might have been
worse; for I do not understand them at all. I love a good story in a picture
and a battle or a sea peace; but as for the performance, the painting, I
have no notion of it; anybody may impose upon me".[33] And so they had.

175

A second point of difference was Sir A. B.'s books. There was no library in the house when his friend came to visit. But "a gentleman of your figure should not be without a library . . . 'tis more in fashion now than ever it was". Persuaded to spend on books what he had set aside for pictures, Sir A. B. visited a large bookshop when next in London. And there, after making some pretence of reading for a while, he startled the bookseller by asking, "What shall I give you for all the books upon that side of your shop?" Those books, interposes Defoe, "look'd all fair and new, and were most of them or many of them guilded and lettered on the back". The bookseller, warning of duplicates, "hum'd and haw'd a little" about the price. But his objections were swept aside, and a deal was quickly made between the parties:

> The books were taken down, pack'd up in cases, and went down by sea to Southampton, and from thence by land to the gentleman's fine house; where a room haveing been appointed before hand for

75 *The working library, with glazed-front bookcases (presses), of the diarist Samuel Pepys (d. 1703),* a was set up in his London house in c. 1690.

that purpose, they were all in a very few days set up in their order in presses made on purpose with glass doores before them, that they might appear in all the extraordinary forms of a library.[34]

This noble buffoon was another eldest son: one of "our born gentry, as they call themselves . . . really scandalously ignorant and untaught". And Defoe's sympathy was clearly with the "man of letters" who, while abroad, had learnt so much more than his friend. Yet the house that scholar liked was very English. Its obvious advantage over Continental parallels was in "our manner of building in England, where neat compact boxes are the usage of the country, not vast pallaces to be finish'd in appartments by the heirs for fiv or six generacions to come and as the estate will allow the charge".[35] And those neat compact boxes – exclusive to the nuclear family in country as in town – had been the homes and castles of wealthy Englishmen for at least a century.

It was not just the rich who lived that way. In less developed societies more dependent on child labour and on the self-sustaining economies of extended families, the households of the poor are very large. In England, they were more likely to be small. This, for example, was plainly the case at Romford (Essex), where surviving communicant lists of 1562 have been used in recent calculations of household size. Elizabethan Romford's gentlemen had households which, with servants and dependent relatives, totalled 7.8 persons on average. But mean household sizes then fell very sharply, from innkeepers (5.6) to bakers (4.5), from cloth-workers (3.8) to leather-workers (3.2), bottoming-out at 2–2.7 among the poor.[36] There is nothing especially surprising in figures such as these, which have their parallels in the Late Middle Ages.[37] But with personal incomes rising and with new houses more affordable than they had ever been before, the scene was set in Late Tudor and Stuart England for a regime of exclusive family boxes. English children left home early and married late. When they began nest-building – at 25 on average – they had long since moved away from the parental home and had accumulated at least some savings of their own. "When thou art married", counselled William Whateley in 1624, "live of thy self with thy wife, in a family of thine own, and not with another, in one family, as it were, betwixt you both . . . [for] as the young bees do seek unto themselves another hive, so let the young couple another house".[38] It was precisely what young marrieds wished to hear.

William Whateley, vicar of Banbury (1610–39), was a Puritan divine of unorthodox opinions which, on divorce in particular, were proscribed.[39] But on housing he preached to the converted. What he recognized was the role of the compact family house in confirming a successful relationship. Love, Whateley claimed, "is the life and soule of marriage". It will "become such if some naturall meanes be used to confirme it . . . [and that] naturall means is cohabitation". Accordingly, let the young couple have "one house, one table, one chamber, one bed . . . let them be as much in each others presence, as businesses of their callings will permit; let them often talke together, and be sorry together, and be merry together, and communicate their joyes and griefes each with other; and this will surely knit them, if any thing will". Consider how the rich are disadvantaged. "Why should it bee wondred at", Whateley asks (perhaps thinking of a sprawling palace like the Suffolks' Audley End), "that great personages doe very often disagree in marriage . . . [when] for state and pompes sake, they accustome to divide themselves often in houses and table, commonly in chamber and bed? Doth not this their separation give the divell great advantage against them? Shall it not be easie for him to sunder their affections by degrees, that so sunder their bodies?"[40]

Whateley was no optimist about matrimony. "A thing of such difficultie should not be lightly undertaken", he warns. Without love, marriage "is a most miserable and uncomfortable societie, and no better than a very living death".[41] His remedy, characteristically English, was to close the door on the warm supportive circle of the extended family. Englishmen find it difficult to share. When the dying John Shaw, in 1573, provided for the partition of his Wensleydale farm between his widow and the nephew who would succeed him, he felt obliged to add: "so long as thay can so agree and when thay cannot agree & dwell together then I will that thay devide it equally betwene them".[42] And, in reality, there is very little material evidence in early-modern England of house-sharing on any major scale. Divided farmhouses have been recognized and listed in Wales and East Anglia, in Lancashire, in Cheshire, and in the south.[43] But such partitioning – for widows, for married heirs, or for partner-brothers – was usually only temporary. And what is surely most remarkable about these "unit-system" houses is not that they continued to occur in rural areas throughout the period, but that their numbers at any time were always small.

*76 Divided houses were never common in England, but Dairy Farmhouse at Tacolneston (Norfolk) was one of them. Built in the mid-seventeenth century, Dairy Farmhouse had owner's accommodation – a well-finished parlour with parlour chamber above – on one side of the front door, and family and service quarters on the other. Each separate unit had its own newel stair, the only passage between the two being provided at ground-floor level, behind the porch.*

In the Wensleydale wills, of which John Shaw's was one, these occasional divisions are spelled out. Michael Pratt's widow, in 1599, is to "keepe my mother during hir naturall liefe with meat, drinke and clothes"; she herself is to share the farmhouse with her son.[44] Then George Thwaites, in 1654, provides for his widow "to remayne and dwell in my mansion fyrehouse and have one convenient roome therein and free liberty to ioyne and lye in the hallstead of the sayd house and have sufficient use of the fyre at the only charges of him or them to whome I shall bequeath the remaynder of the sayd fyrehouse".[45] Elizabeth Thompson, in 1659, is to have "the midell roume" of her dying brother's farmhouse "during hir life".[46] And some 20 years later, in the most explicit of these arrangements, George Johnson of Skellgill ("being weak and sick of body") provides for his Ellen:

I will that my wife shall have all my houshold goods, monys and debts owing unto me, and that she shall have my now dwelling

179

house dureing the time and term of her life naturall, and after her decease I will that my brother Will Johnson shall have it during his life, and after his decease I give that part upon the west side of the chimney unto George Johnson, son of my said brother William, and that part on the east side of the entree I give to Gawen Johnson, [second] son of my said brother William.[47]

Ellen Johnson, left alone at Skellgill, probably continued in the farmhouse by herself. And with early-modern English households averaging less than five, there would have been nothing too exceptional in her sole occupancy.[48] In part, this was just the way the English liked to live. But it was also a reflection of the high mortalities of the time, never worse than in the third quarter of the century.[49] Children were the ones most at risk. "In the afternoon", records Samuel Pepys of a September day in 1660, "my wife went to the burial of a child of my cozen Scott's, and it is observable that within this month my Aunt Wight was brought to bed of two girls, my cozen Stradwick of a girl and a boy, and my cozen Scott of a boy, and all died".[50] Forty years later, with death still at the door, Ralph Thoresby reflected on a visitation of the smallpox – "now epidemical and very fatal" – to which his own children had calamitously succumbed. "It had pleased God", he wrote, "to give me four children, who were all sick at the same time, of the same distemper. We were now deprived of two of them, Elizabeth and Ruth . . . But I ought also to record the tender mercies of the Lord, who spared the lives of my son, Ralph, and daughter Grace, who yet survive, and I hope may be useful in their respective generations".[51]

This understated sorrow, hiding a greater pain, must be one of the reasons why the English of all periods have been thought to be incapable of love. And certainly it has been said of the upper-gentry Verneys and their circle that they were "less concerned with the need for providing affection or even continuity in their children's lives" than with educating them for their expected role in high society. For whatever reason, "parents could not make the kind of emotional investment [in their children] which would be considered appropriate today".[52] However, one inevitable consequence of the disappearance of the greater household was the concentration of parental feelings in smaller units. "We give hostages to Fortune when we bring children into the world", John Evelyn comforted his grieving brother George in 1656: "Children are such blossomes as every trifling wind deflowres, and to be disordered at their fall, were to be fond of certaine troubles, but the most uncertaine comforts."[53] Yet just two years later, Evelyn himself was hard to comfort on the loss of his own son Dick: "the prettiest, and dearest Child, that ever parents had . . . a prodigie for Witt, & understanding". And in March 1685, when their daughter Mary died, the Evelyns were bereft and inconsolable: "ô how desolate hast Thou left us, Sweete, obliging, happy Creature! To the grave shall we both carry thy memory".[54]

Evelyn's long lament was for a "deare child" reared at home, "most dutifull to her parents, whom she lov'd with an affection temper'd with greate esteeme, so as we were easy & free, & never were so well pleased, as when she was with us, nor needed we other Conversation".[55] And Evelyn, a younger son, was necessarily a parent of the more modern kind, raising his children not in the "large and antient" Wotton of his father (Richard) and elder brother (George), but in the comparatively modest ambience of a suburban villa. True, Sayes Court was no typical family house. Its gardens, especially, were of an enviable sophistication, covering at least 100 acres.[56] "Came his Majestie [Charles II] to honor my poore Villa with his presence", boasted Evelyn on 30 April 1663, "viewing the Gardens & even every roome of the house; & was then pleased to take a small refreshment".[57] Even so, there would be a world of difference between the Italianate villa at Deptford by the Thames, where the king took his collation, and the old-style roast-beef mansion of Evelyn's youth. There, at Wotton, Richard Evelyn had been "a lover of hospitality". His "Mansion house" – "left him by my Grandfather, and now my Eldest Brothers" – was a "Building after the antient fashion of our Ancestors . . . not onely very Capacious, but exceedingly Commodious . . . suitable to those hospitable times".[58]

Evelyn, at the Restoration, wrote of a world almost lost. And even Wotton, the family home, had been much changed. Large-scale improvements began at Wotton soon after Richard's death, when Evelyn spent the summer there in 1643, "balancing whether I should go immediatly abroad . . . in a tyme of so great jealosy". It was then, while armies fought, that Evelyn built ("by my Brothers permission") a little alfresco study over a cascade at Wotton, "to passe my Malencholy houres shaded there with Trees":

This trifle, however despicable, was the Occasion of my Bro[ther

George's] vast Expence, when some yeares after, he Inlarged the Gardens, built the [temple] Portico, & Cutt the Mount into the present shape it now is of, with the fountaines in the Parterr, which were amenitys not frequent in the best Noble mens Gardens in England: This being finished whilst I was abroad, was conducted by a Relation of ours, George Evelyn who had ben in Italy, but was mistaken in the Architecture of the Portico, which tho' making a magnificent shew, has greate faults in the Colonade, both as to the Order, which [is Doric and] should have ben Corinthian & the Ornaments, the rest is very tollerable.[59]

Evelyn thought little of Captain George, who "believed himself a better Architect than realy he was . . . and over built everything" he did.[60] But like him or not, George was reputed a "greate Travellor". And it was that qualification, in an architect of the mid-century, which had come to be increasingly important. Among those who left England in 1643, after the bitter fighting of that summer, was the gentleman-architect Roger Pratt. And it was Pratt's maxim, following his own six years abroad, that "no man deserves the name of an Architect" who has not studied ancient Rome or has made himself familiar with "the more modern [forms of building] of Italy and France etc".[61] Roger Pratt was back in England in August 1649; and Sir George Pratt's Coleshill (reduced to ashes just before) rose again by his advice as compact villa.[62] Three years later, John Evelyn came home, "no more intending to go out of England . . . there being now so little appearance of any change for the better".[63] While abroad, one of Evelyn's first and most memorable experiences had been the visit he paid, on 1 April 1644, to Marie de' Medici's Parisian gardens at the Luxembourg. Laid out by Jacques Boyceau, they were famous especially for a huge box parterre, "so rarely designd, and accurately kept cut; that the embrodery makes a stupendious effect". It was this formal parterre which Evelyn reproduced, early in 1653, in his new "Ovall Garden" at Sayes Court.[64]

In John Evelyn's circle, as in that of Roger Pratt, of John Aubrey, Roger North and many more, to see a house as foreign was to praise it. John Aubrey, for example, admired the Jonesian garden front at the Earl of Pembroke's Wilton House, with "two stately pavilions at each end, all al Italiano".[65] And Evelyn also, at Wilton in 1654, found much to applaud in that same "modern built part towards the Garden", with its "magnificent chimny-pieces, after the French best manner".[66] Over 20 years later, Evelyn's highest praise for the Lauderdales' conversion of the already recently remodelled Ham House was that they had rendered it "inferiour to few of the best Villas in Italy itselfe".[67] And in 1683, when eventually complete, Evelyn liked the "stately & ample Palace" of Ambassador Montagu in Bloomsbury, not merely for the "designe, Colouring, & exuberance of Invention" of "Signor Virios fresca Paintings", but for being built (by Robert Hooke) "after the French pavilion way".[68]

It was of the next Montagu House, rebuilt *sans* Verrios after the fire of 1686, that Roger North sang the praises a decade later, welcoming its spacious layout and service court. "I should be glad", North said, "to see the like imitated by others who build with full and luxurious purses, because it is the true way of composing the conveniences of a family in severall orders without fraction and indecorum."[69] However, most of North's contemporaries were building differently at that time, and generosity of scale was hard to find. It had been usual in the past, North reminds us, to build a *spreading* house: for the central hall to be furnished at one end with "a great parlor, and a pair of stairs, called also great, and a door into the garden, and at the other end, buttery pantry kitchen, and a litle parlor for every day eating". But important changes had taken place within his lifetime:

It is but late that servants have left their eating in the hall. This in my time was done in my father's house. But since [then] it hath bin usuall, to find a room elswhere for them; and the master, in summer especially, leaves his litle parlor to eat there. Thus the hall is kept clean, which is not to be done when it is the refectory of the whole family. Here ended the antique order of housing, and since the reigne of Charles II scarce any of that intention hath bin built.[70]

What had then followed was the opposite extreme. "It was an old fault", North conceded, "to spread the housing too much, and a very commendable conduct [now] to compose it more orderly together." But "that hath ledd to such compaction, that an house is lay'd on an heap like a wasps-nest, and much of greatness as well as conveniences lost by it".[71] Writing in the 1690s, when the new fashion was general, North listed the disadvantages of compaction: *first*, that "all the noises of an house are heard every where"; *secondly*, "which is worse, all smells that offend, are a nusance to all the rooms, and there is no retiring from them"; *thirdly*, that "it is hard to gaine closets and interior rooms . . . without sacrifising as good room as the best to purchase them"; *fourthly*, that "you cannot modell rooms to the use, but some will be too high and some too low . . . the great and small rooms are all of a pitch"; and *lastly*, that "all cold and heat are more offensive in a pile than in a spread house, being double; because the proximity of the rooms gives a tinct of the same air throuot, which I could scarce have beleeved if I had not proved it [for myself]".[72]

That proof he would have found at Chevening, in West Kent, for six decades the home of his aunt. Lady Dacre's Chevening – of "an Italian designe" by Inigo Jones (*c*.1630) or John Webb (*c*.1650) – exhibited every one of those faults. Moreover, North knew Chevening best in his aunt's decline (she died aged 93), when she probably never opened a window:

> The designe is a room of *entrata*, where the great staires rise to the sumitt of the house, and so open to the midle room above also. On each side a room, the right hand is the withdrawing room, and the left, passing a stair downe to the kitchen, for servants. And from that by the end wall passing a litle back stair, to the comon parlor. The midle backward is a large dining room sett off with pilaster and arcuated [arched] wanscote, on the right the great, and on the left the comon parlor. The staires are too steep and height is wanting in the greater rooms below.[73]

Lady Dacre died in 1698. Her death was quickly followed by a costly programme of refurbishment, in which French-style service pavilions and a grand circular staircase (by Dubois) remedied the worst of the deficiencies.[74]

When James Stanhope bought Chevening in 1715, he was already seriously rich. And for those like himself with "full and luxurious purses", there was no cause to refrain from the kind of *spreading* building which had reached its apotheosis at Blenheim Palace. However, "superfluous spreading" presented problems of its own. Communication ("long passages") and high cost ("great charge") were the most obvious of these. But North adds another powerful indictment. "It is hard", he

77 *The compact house at Chevening (Kent), as it was in 1679 when Lady Dacre still lived there. Such dense, piled-up plans had their obvious disadvantages, for "all the noises of an house are heard everywhere" and "which is worse, all smells that offend, are a nusance to all the rooms, and there is no retiring from them" (Roger North).*

writes, "upon this rambling foundation to project any elegance of disposition within or without".[75] Some 60 years later, Horace Walpole – Grand Tour traveller, *literato*, wit, and connoisseur – would undoubtedly have concurred with this assessment. In one energetic day, on 17 July 1760, Walpole visited three great Oxfordshire houses: Rousham, Ditchley and Blenheim. He liked Rousham's theatrical gardens ("the best thing I have seen of Kent"); declared James Gibbs's compact Ditchley a "very good house"; but thought Vanbrugh's sprawling Blenheim "execrable within, without, & almost all round".[76]

Of the three different architects assessed that day, only Vanbrugh (who knew France well) had never served an Italian apprenticeship. James Gibbs, in Rome for six years from 1703, had studied under the celebrated Roman architect, Carlo Fontana. And William Kent, subse-

78 *This arcaded terrace at Rousham Park, in Oxfordshire, is one of the principal orna-*
*ments of the great Romantic garden ("the best thing I have seen of Kent", wrote Horace*
*Walpole) laid out in 1738–40 for General James Dormer by the Roman-trained painter*
*and architect William Kent (d.1748), who also remodelled Dormer's house.*

quently known as "the Signior" by his acquaintance, had passed a decade in Rome from 1709, learning the art of fresco-painting.[77] It was
Lord Burlington, the dedicated Palladian, who met Kent in Rome in
1714–15 and later brought him home as long-term protégé. Nor was

there any shortage of noble patrons of that quality, similarly exposed to "the most famous buildings" on their *giros*. Once it had been the belief of William Harrison and many of his contemporaries that "the usual sending of noblemen's and mean [middle] gentlemen's sons into Italy . . . in short time will turn to the great ruin of our country", for they commonly "bring home nothing but mere atheism, infidelity, vicious conversation, and ambitious and proud behaviour, whereby it cometh to pass that they return far worse men than they went out".[78] And that had remained the Late Elizabethan view, as long as fear of popery stayed uppermost. But in just two generations, all had changed. Successive Great Rebuildings, separated by Charles I's confrontational policies and the tragedy of civil war, show the difference. During the *First* – of which Harrison was one of the earliest interpreters – building was by pattern-book, the best mason-architects only rarely went abroad, and the influence of returned travellers was minimal. In the *Second*, the Roman-trained artist and Grand Tour nobleman reigned supreme.

If "elegance of disposition" was now the characteristic quality of the century, another necessary consideration was building cost. The almost universal prosperity which had characterized English landowners before the Civil War was no more. And although well connected noblemen continued building actively, very few escaped the downturn altogether. Thus while the post-war financial difficulties of the Cecil earls of Salisbury were indeed much increased by "the excessive family affection of the third Earl [James] and the excessive folly and imprudence of the fourth", the crisis in Cecil fortunes had begun earlier. Between 1642 and 1650, Earl William (d.1668) met almost £30,000 in wartime charges. Yet it had been that same Earl William, son of Robert Cecil (builder of Hatfield House), who had made such a success of the pre-war management of his estates that he had raised the family revenues by over a third.[79]

That success is the more remarkable because of the huge building debts inherited by Earl William in 1612. However, great landowners like himself were still able, before the war, to take advantage of a tax regime especially favourable to their class. They could expect to profit from the rising prices, falling wages and renegotiable leases consequent on an increasing population. And there were costly traditional charges – in the support of a great household or in the maintenance of hospitality – which they no longer felt obliged to meet in full. From the Restoration at latest, only the last of those many benefits still obtained.

Most important overall was the slowing down and then cessation of that "strong and sustained" population growth which, for almost a century, had supported the extravagant life-styles of many landowners. Growth was already weakening in the early 1620s. It had halted altogether by 1656, and was followed by three decades of decline. A slow recovery began again in the late 1680s. But mortalities stayed high and birth rates low, and the population of England in 1750 was barely larger than in 1656.[80] Not everybody did badly in these circumstances. Wages rose and rents fell; many foodstuffs were cheaper than before. However, those worst affected included the former great consumers, whose disposable wealth, already reduced by fines and confiscations, was eroded still further by the direct taxation which was a permanent legacy of civil war.[81] Some landowners such as the Verneys, almost ruined by the struggle, turned successfully to enclosure for a remedy.[82] Others, such as the Russells, with estates on London's rim, made huge fortunes as suburban developers.[83] But for the majority of landed gentry, over a generation or more, rising contemporary standards of family comfort and personal privacy coincided with the erosion of real incomes.

The "neat compact boxes" of Restoration England were in part a response to that reduction. But the "new order of housing" that replaced the old was not primarily poverty led. When John Evelyn lamented the "excess of superfluity not onely at Court, but almost universaly" in his day, he was speaking of the straitened 1670s.[84] And two decades later, the parade of corrupting "fasshion" observed by Roger North in London's modish terraces was again the stuff of egregious consumerism.[85] If these had been the values only of the corrupt "boufoones & Ladys of Pleasure" who kept Charles II company at Whitehall, they might have been forgotten with the *braggadocio* of the Stuarts. In reality, as Evelyn saw, they were much more widely shared, setting a new agenda for the Second Great Rebuilding, less dominated than the First by surplus profits.

There are two dictionary definitions of the adjective "egregious". One, in the good sense, is "excellent" or "remarkable"; the other is "outrageous" or "gross". And to each Great Rebuilding of Tudor and Stuart England, both of those meanings might apply. Yet to subsume one Rebuilding in the next – bracketing First and Second as though they were identical – is to make a serious category mistake. Trend-setting rebuilders of both periods had objectives in common: in particular, for the extension of private space. They sited their great houses where everybody could see them; planted their huge gardens; and shared a taste for conspicuous display. However, the differences between them were at least as significant, promoted by new levels of understanding.

Never was change more rapid, nor politicking more extreme, than in the Restoration London of returned exiles. When Edward Hyde began building Clarendon House in 1664, on a prominent site near the Palace of St James, he was already the butt of the king's intimates: of Barbara Palmer, Lady Castlemaine, who "set herself most violently against him", and of George Villiers, Duke of Buckingham, who "as oft as he was admitted to any familiarities with the king, studied with all his wit and humour to make lord Clarendon and all his counsels appear ridiculous". At first, said Bishop Burnet, the lord chancellor had intended "a good ordinary house", but then "not understanding those matters himself, he put the managing of that into the hands of others [including his architect Roger Pratt], who ran him into a vast charge of about £50,000, three times as much as he had designed to lay out upon it".[86] It was a fatal mistake, for Hyde's profligacy coincided with reverses overseas and catastrophes at home, including the Great Plague (1665–66), and Fire of London (1666), so that "it was [too] visible that in a time of public calamity he was building a very noble palace".[87] Finally cornered by his accusers, Clarendon resigned the chancellorship on 30 August 1667, and was banished and impeached not long afterwards. But the notoriety of his works and the *schadenfreude* of his enemies had made his palace the most famous in the kingdom.[88]

Much the most obvious comparisons at the time – voiced both by Pepys and by Evelyn – were between Edward Hyde's new Clarendon House (1664–67) and Thomas Howard's as yet unchallenged private palace at Audley End (1605–14). But whereas Jacobean Audley End was a *spreading* house – a huge double-courtyard mansion in the long-familiar English style – Restoration Clarendon was *compact* and very French. Moreover, although the gross extravagance of Hyde's *hôtel* was condemned by every critic, it had cost him only a quarter of what the former Lord Treasurer, before the Civil War, was alleged to have spent on Audley End.[89] By the time Evelyn saw Clarendon House in 1666 – declaring it then "the most magnificent house in England, I except not Audly-end" – size and cost had ceased to be his criteria. And it must be evident already that in so valuing the "solidity & beauty most symetrically combin'd together" of classical Clarendon House, over the "gaudy and barbarous ornaments" of mixed-Gothic Audley End, a new post-*giro* generation had found its voice.[90] The Second Great Rebuilding, in complete contrast to the First, saw the triumph of taste over riches.

# Notes

**Abbreviations**

Aubrey     Andrew Clark, ed., *"Brief lives", chiefly of contemporaries, set down by John Aubrey, between the years 1669 & 1696* (Oxford, Clarendon Press, 1898).

Bacon     John Pitcher, ed., *Francis Bacon. The essays* (Harmondsworth, Penguin Books Ltd, 1985).

Defoe     Daniel Defoe, *A tour through the whole island of Great Britain* (London, Dent, 1974), revised edn.

Evelyn     E. S. de Beer, ed., *The diary of John Evelyn* (London, Oxford University Press, 1959).

Fiennes     Christopher Morris, ed., *The journeys of Celia Fiennes* (London, Cresset Press, 1949).

*Galateo*     J. E. Spingarn, ed., *Galateo. Of manners & behaviour, by Giovanni della Casa* (Boston, The Humanists' Library, 1914).

Harrison     Georges Edelen, ed., *The description of England by William Harrison* (Ithaca, Cornell University Press, 1968).

North     Howard Colvin & John Newman, eds, *Of building. Roger North's writings on architecture* (Oxford, Clarendon Press, 1981).

Pratt     R. T. Gunther, ed., *The architecture of Sir Roger Pratt* (Oxford, Oxford University Press, 1928).

*The courtier*     W. H. D. Rouse, ed., *The book of the courtier by Count Baldassare Castiglione, done into English by Sir Thomas Hoby. Anno 1561* (London, Everyman, undated).

Walpole     Paget Toynbee, ed., *Horace Walpole's journals of visits to country seats, &c.*, Walpole Society 16, 1927–28, pp. 9–80.

Wotton     Frederick Hard, ed., *The elements of architecture by Sir Henry Wotton* (Charlottesville, University Press of Virginia, for Folger Shakespeare Library, 1968).

Note: Individual volumes in Nikolaus Pevsner's *The buildings of England* series (Harmondsworth, Penguin Books Ltd) – not always the current edition – are given thus: *Berkshire*, 1966; *Dorset*, 1972 etc.

## Chapter 1
## The First Great Rebuilding

1. R. H. Tawney, The rise of the gentry, 1558–1640, *Economic History Review*, **11**, 1941, pp. 1–38.
2. W. G. Hoskins, The rebuilding of rural England, 1570–1640, *Past & Present*, **4**, 1953, p. 48.
3. Peter Smith, *Houses of the Welsh countryside. A study in historical geography* (London, Her Majesty's Stationery Office, 1975), *passim*; and see also *An inventory of the ancient monuments in Glamorgan. Volume IV: Domestic architecture from the Reformation to the Industrial Revolution. Part II: Farmhouses and cottages* (Royal Commission on Historical Monuments, 1988).
4. R. T. Mason, *Framed buildings of the Weald* (Horsham, Coach Publishing, 1964); John Warren, ed., *Wealden buildings. Studies in the timber-framed tradition of building in Kent, Sussex and Surrey* (Horsham, Coach Publishing, 1990); Eric Mercer, *English vernacular houses. A study of traditional farmhouses and cottages* (London, Her Majesty's Stationery Office, 1975), pp. 11–19 and *passim*; Frank Atkinson & R. W. McDowall, Aisled houses in the Halifax area, *Antiquaries Journal*, **47**, 1967, pp. 77–94; N. W. Alcock & Michael Laithwaite, Medieval houses in Devon and their modernization, *Medieval Archaeology*, **17**, 1973, pp. 100-125.
5. Raymond Wood-Jones, *Traditional domestic architecture of the Banbury region* (Manchester, Manchester University Press, 1963), p. 209 and *passim*; Derek Portman, Vernacular building in the Oxford region in the sixteenth and seventeenth centuries, in *Rural change and urban growth 1500–1800,* eds C. W. Chalklin & M. A. Havinden (London, Longman, 1974), p. 163.
6. Linda J. Hall, *The rural houses of North Avon and South Gloucestershire 1400–1720* (Bristol, Museum and Art Gallery, 1983), pp. 88–92.
7. *Rural houses of West Yorkshire, 1400–1830* (Royal Commission on Historical Monuments, 1986), ch. 4: The yeoman rebuilding of the 17th and 18th centuries; *Glamorgan* (Royal Commission on Historical Monuments, 1986), pp. 28–9.
8. R. Machin, The Great Rebuilding: a reassessment, *Past & Present*, **77**, 1977, p. 55; and see also the same author's *The houses of Yetminster* (Bristol, University of Bristol, Department of Extra-Mural Studies, 1978), part II: Historical problems. For a very different and less historical approach which omits the inventory evidence, starts with the premise that "apparent waves of rebuilding may be illusory", and then places greater emphasis on subdivision and normal attrition rates in different regions and classes of rural housing, see the important papers by C. R. J. Currie, Time and change: modelling the attrition of old houses, in *Vernacular Architecture*, **19**, 1988, pp. 1–9, and Robert Taylor, Population explosions and housing, 1550–1850, *ibid.*, **23**, 1992, pp. 24–9.
9. Public Record Office SP12/156; quoted in my *Medieval Southampton. The port and trading community, AD 1000–1600* (London, Routledge & Kegan Paul, 1973), p. 217.
10. The title of Harrison's first edition was *An historical description of the island of Britain* (1577). In the second edition (1587), Harrison used *The description of England* as a running title, and it is as this that his treatise has since become known (Georges Edelen, ed., *The description of England by William Harrison* (Ithaca, Cornell University Press, 1968), p. xv (footnote)).
11. Mary Dewar, ed., *A discourse of the commonweal of this realm of England, attributed to Sir*

*Thomas Smith* (Charlottesville, University Press of Virginia, 1969), pp. 63–4, 83–4; for Smith as a builder, see Mary Dewar's *Sir Thomas Smith. A Tudor intellectual in office* (London, Athlone Press, 1964), ch. 17: Hill Hall.

12. Harrison, p. 200.
13. *Ibid.*, pp. 200–201; for coal-burning, the fireplace and the farmhouse chimney, see John Hatcher, *The history of the British coal industry. Volume one. Before 1700: Towards the age of coal* (Oxford, Clarendon Press, 1993), pp. 409–18: Domestic heating and cooking. Hatcher quotes William Harrison and also the less well known comment of John Aubrey (1626–97): "Anciently, before the Reformation, ordinary men's houses, as copyholders and the like, had no chimneys but flues like louver holes; some of them were in being when I was a boy" (*ibid.*, p. 411).
14. For this, see especially John Russell's *Boke of nurture*, edited by Frederick J. Furnivall, *Manners and meals in olden time* (London, Early English Text Society, 1868), pp. 115–228.
15. For a full account of these developments, see my *The architecture of medieval Britain. A social history* (New Haven & London, Yale University Press, 1990), *passim*.
16. This English rendering of Levinus Lemnius's Latin text was published in 1581 (William Brenchley Rye, ed., *England as seen by foreigners in the days of Elizabeth and James the First* (London, John Russell Smith, 1865), pp. 77–9).
17. Paul Slack, Mortality crises and epidemic disease in England 1485–1610, in *Health, medicine and mortality in the sixteenth century*, ed. Charles Webster (Cambridge, Cambridge University Press, 1979), p. 32 and *passim*; D. M. Palliser, Tawney's century: Brave new world or Malthusian trap, *Economic History Review*, **35**, 1982, pp. 346–7; and see also the same author's Dearth and disease in Staffordshire, 1540–1670, in *Rural change and urban growth*, eds C. W. Chalklin & M. A. Havinden (London, Longman, 1974), pp. 57–9. The suggestion that influenza caused the crisis was originally made by F. J. Fisher in 1965; for recent support of Fisher's suggestion, see John S. Moore, Jack Fisher's 'flu: a visitation revisited, *Economic History Review*, **46**, 1993, pp. 280–307.
18. E. A. Wrigley & R. S. Schofield, *The population history of England 1541–1871* (London, Edward Arnold, 1981), pp. 210–11.
19. Joan Thirsk, *Economic policy and projects. The development of a consumer society in early modern England* (Oxford, Clarendon Press, 1978), pp. 4–7, 12–13 and *passim*.
20. Harrison, p. 126.
21. The dialogue on a *Cyvile and uncyvile life* (1579) was printed by W. C. Hazlitt, ed., *Inedited tracts: illustrating the manners, opinions and occupations of Englishmen during the sixteenth and seventeenth centuries* (London, Chiswick Press, for Roxburghe Library, 1868), pp. 33–4.
22. *Ibid.*, p. 40.
23. For the argument that during the sixteenth century "the food of the rich became increasingly luxurious while the food eaten by the poor became more heavily weighted towards cheap bread grains", see Andrew B. Appleby, Diet in sixteenth-century England: sources, problems, possibilities, in *Health, medicine and mortality in the sixteenth century*, ed. Charles Webster (Cambridge, Cambridge University Press, 1979), p. 115.
24. Hazlitt, *Inedited tracts*, p. 20.
25. F. J. Fisher, ed., *The state of England anno dom. 1600 by Thomas Wilson*, Camden Miscellany, Royal Historical Society, **16**, 1936, p. 24; for the plight of younger sons, see

Joan Thirsk, Younger sons in the seventeenth century, *History*, **54**, 1969, pp. 358–77; also Jack Goody *et al.*, eds, *Family and inheritance. Rural society in Western Europe, 1200–1800* (Cambridge, Cambridge University Press, 1976), particularly chs 7–8.

26. For a useful sketch of Francis Hastings's career, see Claire Cross, ed., *The letters of Sir Francis Hastings 1574–1609*, Somerset Record Society **69**, 1969, pp. xiii–xxxiii.

27. For some recent cautions, see R. B. Outhwaite, Progress and backwardness in English agriculture, 1500–1650, *Economic History Review*, **39**, 1986, pp. 1–18, and Roger Burt, The international diffusion of technology in the early modern period: the case of the British non-ferrous mining industry, *ibid.*, **44**, 1991, pp. 249–71.

28. Hazlitt, *Inedited tracts*, p. 26.

29. Edward Surtz & J. H. Hexter, eds, *The complete works of St Thomas More. Volume 4* (New Haven & London, Yale University Press, 1965), p. 67.

30. Mary E. Finch, *The wealth of five Northamptonshire families 1540–1640*, Northamptonshire Record Society **19**, 1956, p. 16.

31. *Ibid.*, ch. 3: Spencer of Althorp; and see also H. Thorpe, The lord and the landscape illustrated through the changing fortunes of a Warwickshire parish, Wormleighton, *Transactions and Proceedings of the Birmingham Archaeological Society*, **80**, 1962, pp. 38–77.

32. Finch, *The wealth of five Northamptonshire families*, p. 66.

33. *Ibid.*, p. 74 and *passim*; ch. 4: Tresham of Rushton.

34. Eric Kerridge, *Agrarian problems in the sixteenth century and after* (London, Allen & Unwin, 1969), ch. 4: Enclosures.

35. J. R. Wordie, The chronology of English enclosure, 1500–1914, *Economic History Review*, **36**, 1983, p. 505 and *passim*.

36. Lawrence Stone, *Family and fortune. Studies in aristocratic finance in the sixteenth and seventeenth centuries* (Oxford, Clarendon Press, 1973), pp. 181, 216–17.

37. *Ibid.*, pp. 190–94, 226–8.

38. For recent surveys of research on iron-working, see Henry Cleere & David Crossley, *The iron industry of the Weald* (Leicester, Leicester University Press, 1985), especially ch. 7: The mature industry; and David Crossley, *Post-medieval archaeology in Britain* (Leicester, Leicester University Press, 1990), ch. 7: The archaeology of ferrous metals.

39. Rosamond Meredith, The Eyres of Hassop, 1470–1640, *Derbyshire Archaeological Journal*, **85**, 1965, p. 69 and *passim*.

40. D. W. Crossley, The performance of the glass industry in sixteenth-century England, *Economic History Review*, **25**, 1972, pp. 430–33; for the cloth industry, see the useful summaries in D. C. Coleman's An innovation and its diffusion: the "new draperies", *Economic History Review*, **22**, 1969, pp. 417–29, and the same author's *The economy of England 1450–1750* (Oxford, Oxford University Press, 1977), pp. 75–82.

41. R. S. Smith, Glass-making at Wollaton in the early seventeenth century, *Transactions of the Thoroton Society*, **66**, 1962, pp. 24–34; Eleanor S. Godfrey, *The development of English glassmaking 1560–1640* (Oxford, Clarendon Press, 1975), pp. 59–74, 173–4.

42. For Charnock and the early industry, see Crossley, *Post-medieval archaeology in Britain*, pp. 226–8.

43. Godfrey, *The development of English glassmaking*, pp. 212–13.

44. As given on an inscription, now lost but formerly at Warwick Church (M. W. Farr, ed., Nicholas Eyffeler of Warwick, glazier. Executors' accounts and other documents concerning the foundation of his almshouse charity, 1592–1621, in *Miscellany I*, ed. Robert Bearman, Dugdale Society **31**, 1977, p. 29).

45. *Ibid.*, pp. 34–5; for Gilling Castle, see *Yorkshire. North Riding*, pp. 167–8 and plate 31.

46. Farr, Nicholas Eyffeler of Warwick, glazier, p. 52; the quotations are from the Southampton *Description* of 1582, already given at the beginning of this chapter.

47. *Ibid.*

48. *Ibid.*, pp. 108–10.

49. *Ibid.*, p. 50.

50. *Ibid.*, pp. 109–10.

51. Harrison, pp. 197–9.

52. A. D. Dyer, ed., Probate inventories of Worcester tradesmen, 1545–1614, in *Miscellany II*, Worcestershire Historical Society **5**, 1967, p. 16.

53. M. A. Havinden, ed., *Household and farm inventories in Oxfordshire, 1550–1590* (London, HMSO for Historical Manuscripts Commission, 1965), pp. 21, 26, 245–6, 265–7, 272.

54. D. G. Vaisey, ed., *Probate inventories of Lichfield and District 1568–1680*, Staffordshire Record Society **5**, 1969, pp. 33, 47, 48–9, 56, 59.

55. D. Portman, *Exeter houses 1400–1700* (Exeter, Exeter University Press, 1966), p. 48.

56. Margaret Cash, ed., *Devon inventories of the sixteenth and seventeenth centuries*, Devon and Cornwall Record Society **11**, 1966, p. xviii.

57. Rye, *England as seen by foreigners*, p. 110.

58. Cash, *Devon inventories*, pp. 29–31.

59. *Ibid.*, pp. 31–3.

60. Farr, Nicholas Eyffeler of Warwick, glazier, pp. 71–3.

61. For some recent serious reservations concerning their use, see Margaret Spufford, The limitations of the probate inventory, in *English rural society, 1500–1800. Essays in honour of Joan Thirsk*, eds John Chartres & David Hey (Cambridge, Cambridge University Press, 1990), pp. 139–74.

62. Harrison, p. 199.

63. Alan Dyer, Urban housing: a documentary study of four Midland towns 1530–1700, *Post-medieval archaeology*, **15**, 1981, p. 213; for useful confirmation of Dr Dyer's early dating of the Worcester rebuilding and for other datable rebuildings in the same city, see Pat Hughes, Property and prosperity: the relationship of the buildings and fortunes of Worcester, 1500–1660, *Midland History*, **17**, 1992, pp. 39–58.

64. Eric Kerridge, *Textile manufactures in early modern England* (Manchester, Manchester University Press, 1985), p. 21.

65. Dyer, Probate inventories of Worcester tradesmen, pp. 15–18.

66. Havinden, *Household and farm inventories in Oxfordshire*, pp. 303–7.

67. Dyer, Probate inventories of Worcester tradesmen, pp. 29–30, 46–8.

68. William Reed, ed., *The Ipswich probate inventories 1583–1631*, Suffolk Records Society **22**, 1981, p. 28.

69. *Ibid.*, pp. 108–10; the very high figure for Ann Goodeere's plate reflects the common belief, conveyed by Elizabeth Smythe to her son in the 1630s, that "money spent on strong substantial plate will doe you more service and credit than in your purse" (Philippa Glanville, *Silver in Tudor and early Stuart England. A social history and catalogue of the national collection 1480–1660* (London, Victoria & Albert Museum, 1990), p. 47 and ch. 2: The new consumers, *passim*).

70. Havinden, *Household and farm inventories in Oxfordshire*, pp. 248–9.

71. Gottfried von Bülow, Journey through England and Scotland made by Lupold von Wedel in the years 1584 and 1585, *Transactions of the Royal Historical Society*, new series, **9**, 1895, p. 268. What von Wedel meant by "peasant", as Philippa Glanville (*Sil-*

*ver in Tudor and early Stuart England*, p. 47) points out, citing the same passage but in a slightly different translation, was "yeoman".

72. Rye, *England as seen by foreigners*, p. 110.
73. Havinden, *Household and farm inventories in Oxfordshire*, p. 30.
74. *Ibid.*, pp. 48–9, 248–9.
75. E. R. C. Brinkworth *et al.*, *Banbury wills and inventories. Part one. 1591–1620*, Banbury Historical Society **13**, 1985, pp. 68–9.
76. Raymond B. Wood-Jones, *Traditional domestic architecture of the Banbury region* (Manchester, Manchester University Press, 1963), ch. 4: The yeoman house in the 16th century. For a valuable study of the datestone evidence in northern Lancashire, pointing to a much later concentration of building activity there in the three decades 1670–1700, see M. E. Garnett, The Great Rebuilding and economic change in South Lonsdale 1600–1730, *Transactions of the Historic Society of Lancashire and Cheshire*, **137**, 1987, pp. 55–75.

## Chapter 2
## Of building

1. North, p. 7.
2. Evelyn, p. 640. Henry Bennet, Earl of Arlington, built most prodigiously at Euston Hall, south of Thetford.
3. North, pp. 5–6.
4. *Ibid.*, p. 89.
5. F. J. Furnivall, ed., *Andrew Boorde's introduction and dyetary* (London, Early English Text Society, Extra Series **10**, 1870), p. 238.
6. Robert Burton, *The anatomy of melancholy* (London, Chatto & Windus, 1891), new edn, p. 334.
7. Wotton, pp. 7–8. The domestic arrangements to which Sir Henry Wotton would have become accustomed during his embassies in Italy are discussed by Peter Thornton, *The Italian Renaissance interior 1400–1600* (London, Weidenfeld & Nicolson, 1991), pp. 283–320 (Part three: Architectural planning).
8. Wotton, pp. 9–10.
9. *ibid,* p. 6.
10. Furnivall, *Andrew Boorde's introduction and dyetary*, pp. 233–4, 236.
11. Burton, *The anatomy of melancholy*, pp. 332–3.
12. North, p. 89.
13. Pratt, p. 55.
14. Stuart Piggott, Sir John Clark and "The country seat", in *The country seat. Studies in the history of the British country house presented to Sir John Summerson*, eds Howard Colvin & John Harris (London, Allen Lane The Penguin Press, 1970), p. 112.
15. Bacon, p. 193.
16. *Ibid*, pp. 193–4; Burton, *The anatomy of melancholy*, p. 331.
17. James Spedding, ed., *The works of Francis Bacon. Vol. VIII: The letters and life I* (London, Longman, 1861), pp. 332–7.
18. Bacon, p. 194.
19. Felicity Heal, *Hospitality in early modern England* (Oxford, Clarendon Press, 1990), ch. 3: The changing vision of hospitality.

20. P. S. Donaldson, ed., George Rainsford's *Ritratto d'Ingliterra* (1556), Camden Miscellany, Royal Historical Society, vol. 27, 1979, pp. 94–5.
21. Harrison, pp. 126–7.
22. Quoted by Heal, *Hospitality in early modern England*, p. 101.
23. Jonathan Powis, *Aristocracy* (Oxford, Blackwell, 1984), p. 27.
24. John Weaver, ed., The building accounts of Harrold Hall, in *Miscellanea*, Publications of the Bedfordshire Historical Society **49**, 1970, pp. 56–80.
25. Peter C. D. Brears, ed., *Yorkshire probate inventories 1542–1689*, Yorkshire Archaeological Society Record Series, **134**, 1972, pp. xi, 101, 125.
26. Owen Ashmore, Household inventories of the Lancashire gentry, 1550–1700, *Transactions of the Historic Society of Lancashire and Cheshire*, **110**, 1958, p. 75. For a useful comment on these changes in the context of the Great Rebuilding debate, see N. W. Alcock, The Great Rebuilding and its later stages, *Vernacular Architecture*, **14**, 1983, pp. 45–8.
27. North, pp. 125–6.
28. Fiennes, pp. 63–4. The prodigious Audley End clearly lent itself to such statistics. "The house has 140 fireplaces", noted William Schellinks on 3 October 1662, "and very curious and decorative chimneys, standing like pillars in an orderly manner on the house, sometimes 2, 3, 4, and 5 gathered together." (Maurice Exwood & H. L. Lehmann, eds, *The journal of William Schellinks' travels in England 1661–1663*, Camden Fifth Series, Royal Historical Society, **1**, 1993, p. 149.)
29. Pratt, pp. 24, 61–2. The debate about who designed Coleshill is not yet over; for a recent restatement of the Inigo Jones claim, see Timothy Mowl and Brian Earnshaw, Inigo Jones restored, *Country Life*, 30 January 1992, pp. 46–9.
30. Pratt, pp. 29–30.
31. Fiennes, pp. 24–5.
32. Evelyn, pp. 753–4.
33. John Summerson, *Architecture in Britain 1530 to 1830* (Harmondsworth, Penguin Books Ltd, 1953), p. 95.
34. Wotton, pp. 70–71.
35. W. C. Hazlitt, ed., *Inedited tracts: illustrating the manners, opinions and occupations of Englishmen during the sixteenth and seventeenth centuries* (London, Chiswick Press, for Roxburghe Library, 1868), pp. 56–7; North, p. 138.
36. Pratt, pp. 27–8, 64.
37. North, pp. xiv–xv.
38. Fiennes, p. 26.
39. *Ibid.*, p. 27; sadly, the house when visited in November 1991 was in poor repair, though little altered externally since first built.
40. Defoe, vol. 2, pp. 174–5, 179.
41. *Ibid.*, p. 175; for England's primary role in developing the counterbalanced sliding window, see H. J. Louw, The origin of the sash window, *Architectural History*, **26**, 1983, pp. 49–72.
42. Fiennes, pp. 99–100; for the State Rooms at Chatsworth and their decorators, see Francis Thompson, *A history of Chatsworth* (London, Country Life, 1949), pp. 148–59.
43. Fiennes, p. 100; Thompson, *A history of Chatsworth*, pp. 121–3.
44. Daniel Parsons, ed., *The diary of Sir Henry Slingsby, of Scriven, Bart.* (London, Longman, 1836), pp. 51–2.

45. *Ibid.*, p. 52. Of these great houses, Temple Newsam and Audley End survive in whole or part; Lord Burghley's Theobalds and John Lord Savile's Howley have both gone; William Lord Eure's Malton has left a lodge and other fragments. Of Slingsby's own Red House (near Moor Monkton), only his father's chapel (p. 3) remains.
46. Wotton, p. 72.
47. Pratt, p. 28.
48. North, p. 144.
49. Fiennes, p. 99.
50. Wotton, pp. 72–3.
51. John Dixon Hunt & Peter Willis, eds, *The genius of the place. The English landscape garden 1620–1820* (London, Paul Elek, 1975), p. 95.
52. Fiennes, p. 97.
53. Hunt & Willis, *The genius of the place*, p. 95.
54. Defoe, vol. 2, pp. 175–6.
55. Quoted by Colin Thubron in his description of Suzhou, "city of gardens" (*Behind the wall* (London, Penguin Books Ltd, 1988), p. 137). For a useful and well illustrated modern account of Chinese gardens, their meaning and context, see Maggie Keswick, *The Chinese garden. History, art and architecture* (London, Academy Editions, 1978).
56. For a reconstruction of the Pratolino gardens, see Paul van der Ree, Gerrit Smienk and Clemens Steenbergen, *Italian villas and gardens* (London, Prestel/Thames & Hudson, 1992), pp. 75–82.
57. The mature works of André le Nôtre at Versailles and elsewhere are described and abundantly illustrated by F. Hamilton Hazlehurst, *Gardens of illusion. The genius of André Le Nostre* (Nashville, Vanderbilt University Press, 1980); but see also William Howard Adams, *The French garden 1500–1800* (London, Scolar Press, 1979), pp. 79–101, and the fine illustrations in Torsten Olaf Enge & Carl Friedrich Schröer, *Garden architecture in Europe 1450–1800* (Cologne, Benedikt Taschen, 1990), part 2: Baroque and Rococo gardens.
58. Dorothy Stroud, *Capability Brown* (London, Faber & Faber, 1975), new edn, pp. 104–5.
59. Furnivall, *Andrew Boorde's introduction and dyetary*, p. 239.
60. Harrison, p. 265.
61. Furnivall, *Andrew Boorde's introduction and dyetary*, pp. 281–2; for a more complete Elizabethan alphabetical table "briefly shewing the Physical operations of every hearb and plant therein contained", see Thomas Hill's *The gardener's labyrinth*, ed. Richard Mabey (Oxford, Oxford University Press, 1988), pp. 200–217.
62. Harrison, pp. 270–71.
63. *Ibid.*, p. 270.
64. As said by Francis Thynne and quoted by Roy Strong, *The Renaissance garden in England* (London, Thames & Hudson, 1979), p. 69.
65. Clare Williams, trans., *Thomas Platter's travels in England 1599* (London, Jonathan Cape, 1937), p. 200.
66. Strong, *The Renaissance garden in England*, p. 53.
67. *Ibid.*, pp. 63–9; Williams, *Thomas Platter's travels in England*, pp. 195–7; and for Lumley's Italian models, see David Coffin, *Gardens and gardening in papal Rome* (Princeton, Princeton University Press, 1991), especially chs 2: Statuary gardens and 3: Waterworks: Fountains, nymphaea, and grottoes.

68. Wotton, p. 109.
69. *Ibid.*, pp. 110–11.
70. Strong, *The Renaissance garden in England*, pp. 123–4.
71. Wotton, pp. 111–12.
72. Bacon, p. 201.
73. Hunt & Willis, *The genius of the place*, p. 141.
74. *Ibid.*, p. 145.
75. *Ibid.*, pp. 96–9.
76. Evelyn, pp. 877–8.
77. *Ibid.*, pp. 327–8.
78. K. G. Ponting, ed., *Aubrey's natural history of Wiltshire* (Newton Abbott, David & Charles, 1969), p. 93.
79. Hunt & Willis, *The genius of the place*, pp. 8, 205.
80. *Ibid.*, p. 212.
81. H. F. Clark, *The English landscape garden* (Gloucester, Allen Sutton, 1980), p. 41; and see also David C. Stuart, *Georgian gardens* (London, Robert Hale, 1979), ch. 6: China.
82. Hunt & Willis, *The genius of the place*, p. 322.

## Chapter 3
## Social space

1. F. J. Furnivall, ed., *Andrew Boorde's introduction and dyetary* (London, Early English Text Society, Extra Series **10**, 1870), p. 239 (also quoted in ch. 2).
2. *The courtier*, pp. 98–101.
3. Foster Watson, ed., *The boke named The governour, devised by Sir Thomas Elyot, knight* (London, Everyman, undated), pp. 85, 95.
4. R. W. Chapman, ed., *Johnson's journey to the western islands of Scotland and Boswell's journal of a tour to the Hebrides with Samuel Johnson Ll. D.* (London, Oxford University Press, 1930), p. 345.
5. *Galateo*, p. 19. For a recent discussion of the profound influence on contemporary manners of such widely read books as Castiglione's *The courtier* and della Casa's *Galateo*, see John Hale, *The civilization of Europe in the Renaissance* (London, Harper Collins, 1993), pp. 488–94 and *passim*.
6. *Galateo*, p. 39.
7. *Ibid.*, pp. 37, 40, 44, 87.
8. *Ibid.*, p. 86.
9. *Ibid.*, p. 92.
10. *The courtier*, p. 20.
11. *Ibid.*, pp. 308–10; and see J. R. Woodhouse, *Baldesar Castiglione. A reassessment of The courtier* (Edinburgh, Edinburgh University Press, 1978), pp. 176–7.
12. *Galateo*, p. 99.
13. Wotton, pp. 20–21. Palladio begins *The four books of architecture* with the same general principle, rather more succinctly expressed: "Beauty will result from the form and correspondence of the whole, with respect to the several parts, of the parts with regard to each other, and of these again to the whole." (quoted by Denis Cosgrove, *The Palladian landscape* (Leicester, Leicester University Press, 1993), p. 100).

14. J. Alfred Gotch, *Inigo Jones* (London, Methuen, 1928), pp. 81–2. Inigo Jones's spelling raises such a barrier to understanding that I have modernized the orthography of these two extracts.

15. Quoted by John Stoye, *English travellers abroad 1604–1667* (New Haven & London, Yale University Press, 1989), new edn, p. 6.

16. William Aldis Wright, ed., *English works of Roger Ascham* (Cambridge, Cambridge University Press, 1904), pp. 218, 234.

17. Bacon, p. 113.

18. Joan Simon, *Education and society in Tudor England* (Cambridge, Cambridge University Press, 1967), pp. 347–8.

19. George Saintsbury, ed., *Isaak Walton. The lives of John Donne, Sir Henry Wotton, Richard Hooker, George Herbert and Robert Sanderson* (London, Humphrey Milford, 1927), p. 106.

20. Bacon, pp. 113–14; Pratt, p. 24.

21. Pratt, pp. 3–6, 23–4, 60.

22. Kenneth Charlton, *Education in Renaissance England* (London, Routledge & Kegan Paul, 1965), p. 223.

23. Evelyn, pp. 116–207.

24. William Bray, ed., *Diary of John Evelyn Esq., FRS to which are added a selection from his familiar letters* (London, Bickers & Son, 1879), vol. 3, pp. 340–41.

25. Evelyn, pp. 353, 543.

26. Henry B. Wheatley, ed., *The diary of Samuel Pepys* (London, G. Bell & Sons, 1928), vol. 1, p. 68.

27. *Ibid.*, vol. 6, p. 292.

28. *Ibid.*, vol. 7, pp. 130–31.

29. Fiennes, pp. 63–4; P. J. Drury, *No other place in the kingdom will compare with it*: The evolution of Audley End, 1605–1745, *Architectural History*, **23**, 1980, pp. 4–5.

30. North, pp. 62–3.

31. *Ibid.*, p. 63.

32. The advice is Fregoso's to the Prince in *The courtier* (p. 293).

33. Drury, *No other place in the kingdom will compare with it*, pp. 5, 24, 27.

34. William Brenchley Rye, ed., *England as seen by foreigners in the days of Elizabeth and James the First* (London, John Russell Smith, 1865), p. 64.

35. *Ibid.*, pp. 132–5. Half a century later, William Schellinks still considered Audley End a "splendid house or palace . . . a wonderful building, of many halls, rooms, chambers, and cellars, the like of which we had not seen in England apart from Hampton Court" (Maurice Exwood & H. L. Lehmann, eds, *The journal of William Schellinks' travels in England 1661–1663*, Camden Fifth Series, Royal Historical Society, **1**, 1993, p. 148).

36. Drury, *No other place in the kingdom will compare with it*, p. 4.

37. John Summerson, ed., *The book of architecture of John Thorpe in Sir John Soane's Museum* (Walpole Society; printed for the Society by the University Press, Glasgow, 1966), p. 97 and plate 93; Winstanley's perspective view is reproduced in Russell Chamberlin's *Audley End* (London, English Heritage, 1986), pp. 28–9.

38. Summerson, *The book of architecture of John Thorpe*, p. 10.

39. John Florio, *The essayes of Michael Lord of Montaigne (1603)* (London, George Routledge & Sons, 1885), new edn, p. 66.

40. *Kirby Hall, Northamptonshire*, 1980, p. 17.

41. Drury, *No other place in the kingdom will compare with it*, pp. 19–20; Anthony Blunt, *Art and architecture in France, 1500 to 1700* (Harmondsworth, Penguin Books Ltd, 1957), p. 81.

42. Joseph Hunter, ed., *The diary of Ralph Thoresby, FRS* (London, Henry Colburn & Richard Bentley, 1830), vol. 1, p. 65.

43. North, pp. 123–4.

44. *Ibid.*, p. 135.

45. *Ibid.*, p. 137.

46. *Ibid.*, pp. 129–30; for the *loggia* as dining-space in Italy, see Peter Thornton, *The Italian Renaissance interior 1400–1600* (London, Weidenfeld & Nicolson, 1991), p. 291.

47. Wright, *English works of Roger Ascham*, p. 236.

48. J. H. Hexter, *Reappraisals in History* (London, Longman, 1961), p. 54; Rosemary O'Day, *Education and society 1500–1800* (London, Longman, 1982), ch. 5: The role of the ancient universities to 1640.

49. W. C. Hazlitt, ed., *Inedited tracts: illustrating the manners, opinions and occupations of Englishmen during the sixteenth and seventeenth centuries* (London, Chiswick Press, for Roxburghe Library, 1868), pp. 82, 87–8.

50. *Galateo*, p. 18.

51. Hazlitt, *Inedited tracts*, p. 38.

52. G. S. Gordon, ed., *Peacham's compleat gentleman 1634* (Oxford, Clarendon Press, 1906), p. 231.

53. *Ibid.*, pp. 239, 242.

54. *Ibid.*, p. 231.

55. *Ibid.*, p. 104.

56. *Ibid.*, p. 107.

57. *Ibid.*, pp. 107–8.

58. John Keats, *Ode to a Nightingale*.

59. Aubrey, vol. 1, p. 311.

60. *Ibid.*, vol. 1, p. 312.

61. Victor Skretkowicz, ed., *Sir Philip Sidney. The Countess of Pembroke's Arcadia (The new Arcadia)* (Oxford, Clarendon Press, 1987), pp. 85–6.

62. *Bedfordshire*, 1968, pp. 40–41.

63. K. G. Ponting, ed., *Aubrey's natural history of Wiltshire* (Newton Abbott, David & Charles, 1969), pp. 83–4.

64. John Bold, *Wilton House and English Palladianism* (London, HMSO, 1988), pp. 33–5; Timothy Mowl & Brian Earnshaw, Inigo Jones restored, *Country Life*, 30 January 1992, pp. 46–9.

65. Ponting, *Aubrey's natural history of Wiltshire*, p. 86; for a discussion of this garden, see Roy Strong, *The Renaissance garden in England* (London, Thames & Hudson, 1979), pp. 147–64. William Schellinks, who visited Wilton in September 1662, also describes its "extremely elegant, interesting and pleasant" gardens at some length, noting the bronze gladiator, the pavilion "in Italian style", and Isaac de Caus's "very splendid" bird-song water works in the grotto (Exwood & Lehmann, *The journal of William Schellinks' travels in England*, p. 133).

66. L. C. Wickham Legg, ed., *A relation of a short survey of the western counties made by a Lieutenant of the Military Company in Norwich in 1635*, Camden Miscellany, Royal Historical Society, **16**, 1936, p. 66.

67. *Ibid.*, p. 67.

68. Margaret Whinney, *Sculpture in Britain 1530 to 1830* (Harmondsworth, Penguin Books Ltd, 1964), p. 36; and see also Francis Haskell & Nicholas Penny, *Taste and the Antique* (New Haven and London, Yale University Press, 1982), ch. 5: Casts and copies in seventeenth-century courts and pp. 221–4: Borghese Gladiator.
69. *Ibid.*, p. 26 and plate 17.
70. *Ibid.*, pp. 29–30; *North-East Norfolk and Norwich*, 1962, p. 297.
71. *Kirby Hall, Northamptonshire*, 1980, pp. 12–13.
72. *Diary of Nicholas Stone, Junior*, Walpole Society **7**, 1919, p. 197; Stoye, *English travellers abroad*, p. 141.
73. Evelyn, pp. 342–3, 351.
74. Bold, *Wilton House and English Palladianism*, pp. 40, 43–6; see also Peter Thornton, *Seventeenth-century interior decoration in England, France and Holland* (New Haven & London, Yale University Press, 1978), ch. 2: The spread of the French ideal.
75. Fiennes, p. 8.
76. Defoe, vol. 1, pp. 193–4.

## Chapter 4
## The Grand Tour house

1. K. G. Ponting, ed., *Aubrey's natural history of Wiltshire* (Newton Abbott, David & Charles, 1969), p. 102.
2. Mark Girouard, *Robert Smythson and the Elizabethan country house* (New Haven and London, Yale University Press, 1983), revised edn, p. 204.
3. Victor Skretkowicz, ed., *Sir Philip Sidney. The Countess of Pembroke's Arcadia (The new Arcadia)* (Oxford, Clarendon Press, 1987), p. 85.
4. Girouard, *Robert Smythson and the Elizabethan country house*, p. 204.
5. Roger Schofield, Taxation and the political limits of the Tudor state, in *Law and government under the Tudors. Essays presented to Sir Geoffrey Elton,* eds Claire Cross, David Loades & J. J. Scarisbrick (Cambridge, Cambridge University Press, 1988), pp. 238–9.
6. Aubrey, vol. 2, p. 183.
7. John Florio, trans., *The essayes of Michael Lord of Montaigne (1603)* (London, George Routledge & Sons, 1885), new edn, pp. 110–11; for critical studies of this growing desire for privacy, see Roger Chartier, ed., *A history of private life. III. Passions of the Renaissance* (Cambridge, Mass., Belknap, 1989), particularly ch. 2: Forms of privatization; and James Casey, *The history of the family* (Oxford, Blackwell, 1989), ch. 7: The rise of domesticity.
8. John Freeman, ed., *Thomas Fuller. The worthies of England* (London, George Allen & Unwin, 1952), p. 381.
9. James Spedding *et al.*, eds, *The works of Francis Bacon. Vol. VII: Literary and professional works II* (London, Longman, 1859), p. 169.
10. Aubrey, vol. 1, pp. 78–9.
11. *Ibid.*, vol. 1, p. 82.
12. Walpole, p. 21.
13. *Ibid.*, p. 72.
14. *Ibid.*, p. 46.
15. *Ibid.*, p. 69.

16. For the Revival, see particularly Girouard, *Robert Smythson and the English country house*, ch. 6: Bolsover Castle and the revival of chivalry; and Arthur B. Ferguson, *The chivalric tradition in Renaissance England* (Washington, Folger Books, 1986), pp. 66–82: The Elizabethan revival and 126–38: The chivalric revival and the sense of history; also for the antiquaries, see May McKisack, *Medieval history in the Tudor age* (Oxford, Clarendon Press, 1971), ch. 3: Patrons and collectors; and Elizabeth K. Berry, *Henry Ferrers, an early Warwickshire antiquary 1550–1633*, Dugdale Society Occasional Papers **16**, 1965, *passim*.

17. Jean Manco, David Greenhalf and Mark Girouard, Lulworth Castle in the seventeenth century, *Architectural History*, **33**, 1990, pp. 30, 46.

18. L. C. Wickham Legg, ed., *A relation of a short survey of the western counties made by a Lieutenant of the Military Company in Norwich in 1635*, Camden Miscellany, Royal Historical Society, **16**, 1936, p. 71.

19. Manco *et al.*, Lulworth Castle in the seventeenth century, pp. 31, 45.

20. Richard Lassels, *The voyage of Italy, or a compleat journey through Italy* (London, 1670), preface.

21. Florio, *The essayes of Michael Lord of Montaigne*, p. 110.

22. Lassels, *The voyage of Italy*, preface.

23. William Bray, ed., *Diary of John Evelyn Esq., FRS* (London, Bickers & Sons, 1879), vol. 3, p. 262.

24. *Ibid.*, pp. 263–4.

25. Rosalys Coope, The "Long Gallery": its origins, development, use and decoration, *Architectural History*, **29**, 1986, pp. 44–5.

26. H. M. Colvin, ed., *The history of the King's Works* (London, HMSO, 1982), vol. 4, pp. 18–19; Rosalys Coope, The gallery in England: names and meanings, *Architectural History*, **27**, 1984, pp. 446–7; for the late arrival of the gallery in Italy, see Peter Thornton, *The Italian Renaissance interior 1400–1600* (London, Weidenfeld & Nicolson, 1991), pp. 313–15.

27. Colvin, *The history of the King's Works*, p. 199; Simon Thurley, Henry VIII and the building of Hampton Court: a reconstruction of the Tudor Palace, *Architectural History*, **31**, 1988, pp. 16–21.

28. Colvin, *The history of the King's Works*, p. 200. Nonsuch is discussed and illustrated by Simon Thurley, *The royal palaces of Tudor England. Architecture and court life 1460–1547* (New Haven & London, Yale University Press, 1993), pp. 60–65 and *passim*.

29. W. K. Jordan, ed., *The chronicle and political papers of King Edward VI* (London, George Allen & Unwin, 1966), pp. 3, 165.

30. Maurice Howard, Self-fashioning and the classical moment in mid-sixteenth-century English architecture, in *Renaissance bodies. The human figure in English culture c.1540–1660*, eds Lucy Gent & Nigel Llewellyn (London, Reaktion Books, 1990), pp. 198–217.

31. John Summerson, *Architecture in Britain 1530 to 1830* (Harmondsworth, Penguin Books Ltd, 1953), p. 18.

32. *Ibid.*, p. 19; *The first & chief groundes of architecture. By John Shute, paynter and archytecte. First printed in 1563* (London, Country Life, facsimile edition with introduction by Lawrence Weaver, 1912), dedication.

33. Girouard, *Robert Smythson and the Elizabethan country house*, p. 15; P. J. Drury, "A fayre house, buylt by Sir Thomas Smith": the development of Hill Hall, Essex, 1557–81, *Journal of the British Archaeological Association*, **136**, 1983, p. 120.

34. Freeman, *Thomas Fuller*, p. 175.

35. B. W. Beckingsale, *Burghley. Tudor statesman 1520–1598* (London, Macmillan, 1967), pp. 61, 286.

36. Summerson, *Architecture in Britain*, p. 24.

37. Hugh Trevor-Roper, *The plunder of the arts in the seventeenth century*, Walter Neurath Lecture (London, Thames & Hudson, 1970), p. 16.

38. R. Malcolm Smuts, *Court culture and the origins of the Royalist tradition in early Stuart England* (Philadelphia, University of Pennsylvania Press, 1987), pp. 118–20: The great aristocratic collections.

39. *Diary of Nicholas Stone, Junior*, Walpole Society **7**, 1919, pp. 162–3.

40. H. J. Louw, Some royal and other great houses in England. Extracts from the journal of Abram Booth, *Architectural History*, **17**, 1984, p. 507.

41. John Summerson, The building of Theobalds, 1564–1585, *Archaeologia*, **97**, 1959, pp. 117, 124.

42. Richard Simpson, Sir Thomas Smith and the wall paintings at Hill Hall, Essex: scholarly theory and design in the sixteenth century, *Journal of the British Archaeological Association*, **130**, 1977, pp. 1–20.

43. Wotton, p. 98.

44. *Ibid.*, pp. 99–100.

45. Quoted by Peter Thornton, *Seventeenth-century interior decoration in England, France and Holland* (New Haven & London, Yale University Press, 1978), p. 254.

46. Evelyn, p. 1006.

47. *The First Part of Henry the Sixth*, ii: iii: 36–7.

48. Charles Lethbridge Kingsford, Essex House, formerly Leicester House and Exeter Inn, *Archaeologia*, **73**, 1922–3, p. 49.

49. Lindsay Boynton, ed., *The Hardwick Hall inventories of 1601* (London, Furniture History Society, 1971), p. 29; and see also David N. Durant, *Bess of Hardwick. Portrait of an Elizabethan dynast* (London, Weidenfeld & Nicolson, 1977), pp. 172–3.

50. Fiennes, p. 150.

51. David Piper, Some portraits by Marcus Gheeraerts II and John de Critz reconsidered, *Proceedings of the Huguenot Society*, **20**, 1958–64, pp. 213–14; at Audley End, the Long Gallery was still furnished, when William Schellinks saw it in October 1662, with Howard's original "portraits of the ancestors of the Earls of Suffolk, and of many kings, of Henry VII, Henry VIII, James, Charles I, Henry IV of France, Queen Elizabeth and many other kings and nobles" (Maurice Exwood & H. L. Lehmann, eds, *The journal of William Schellinks' travels in England 1661–1663*, Camden Fifth Series, Royal Historical Society, **1**, 1993, p. 149). For the origins of the gallery as picture-space, see Susan Foister, Paintings and other works of art in sixteenth-century English inventories, *The Burlington Magazine*, **123**, 1981, pp. 273–82.

52. Walpole, p. 29.

53. *Ibid.*, p. 53.

54. *Northamptonshire*, 1973, p. 141; *West Yorkshire*, 1959, p. 349.

55. Peter Thornton & Maurice Tomlin, *The furnishings and decoration of Ham House* (London, Furniture History Society, 1980), pp. 136–7.

56. Walpole, p. 67.

57. Evelyn, p. 653.

58. Joseph Hunter, ed., *The diary of Ralph Thoresby, FRS* (London, Henry Colburn & Richard Bentley, 1830), vol. 2, p. 134.

59. North, p. 144.
60. *Ibid.*, pp. 142–3.
61. John Dunbar, The building-activities of the Duke and Duchess of Lauderdale, 1670–82, *Archaeological Journal*, **132**, 1975, pp. 222–3, 229.
62. *Ibid.*, pp. 224–5 and plates XXVIA and XXVIIA; H. J. Louw, The origin of the sash-window, *Architectural History*, **26**, 1983, p. 64.
63. Quoted by Louw, The origin of the sash-window, p. 69.
64. H. J. Louw, Anglo-Netherlandish architectural interchange *c.*1600–*c.*1660, *Architectural History*, **24**, 1981, pp. 5–6.
65. In a letter dated 10 July 1716 (Geoffrey Webb, ed., *The complete works of Sir John Vanbrugh* (London, Nonesuch Press, 1928), vol. 4, p. 71; also quoted by Lawrence Stone & Jeanne C. Fawtier Stone, *An open elite? England 1540–1880* (Oxford, Clarendon Press, 1984), pp. 345–6).
66. Lassels, *The voyage of Italy*, preface.
67. John Raymond, *An itinerary contayning a voyage, made through Italy, in the yeare 1646, and 1647* (London, 1648); Edmund Warcupp, *Italy, in its original glory, ruine and revival, being an exact survey of the whole geography, and history of that famous country . . . and what ever is remarkable in Rome* (London, 1660).
68. Maximilian Misson, *A new voyage to Italy: with curious observations on several other countries, as, Germany, Switzerland, Savoy, Geneva, Flanders, and Holland*, 2 vols (London, 1699), 2nd edn, preface.
69. Raymond, *An itinerary contayning a voyage*, introduction.
70. Misson, *A new voyage to Italy*, p. 41.
71. Anon., *A tour in France & Italy, made by an English gentleman, 1675* (London, 1676), p. 91.
72. Misson, *A new voyage to Italy*, p. 43.
73. Anon, *A tour in France & Italy*, pp. 122–3.
74. Lassels, *The voyage of Italy*, preface.
75. *Ibid.*; Aubrey had heard another reason for foreign travel: "Sir John Danvers [1588–1655] told me that when he was a young man, the principall reason for sending their sons to Travell, was to weane them from their acquaintance and familiarity with the Servingmen: for then Parents were so austere and grave, that the Sonnes must not be company for their father, and some company men must have: so they contracted a familiarity with the Serving men, who got a hank upon them they could hardly after clawe off." (Oliver Lawson Dick, ed., *Aubrey's Brief lives* (London, Secker & Warburg, 1949), pp. 80–81).
76. Evelyn, pp. 639–40.
77. *Ibid.*, p. 585.
78. *Ibid.*, pp. 756–7.
79. As said by the English Gentleman about the Grand Duke of Tuscany (*A tour in France & Italy*, p. 39).
80. Evelyn, pp. 625, 674, 757, 839.
81. *Hampton Court Palace*, 1982, pp. 10–12.
82. Lassels, *The voyage of Italy*, p. 238.
83. Robert Midgley, *Remarks in the Grand Tour of France and Italy. Perform'd by a person of quality in the year, 1691* (London, 1705), 2nd edn, p. 167.
84. *Petworth House*, 1954, p. 20.
85. *Bedfordshire*, 1968, pp. 223–4.

86. Walpole, p. 54; for a full discussion of "the French style" at Boughton, see Gervase Jackson-Stops, French and Dutch influence on architecture and interiors, in *Boughton House. The English Versailles*, ed. Tessa Murdoch (London, Faber & Faber, 1992), pp. 56–65.
87. Murdoch, *Boughton House*, pp. 63–4 and plate 21; *Powis Castle, Powys*, 1980, pp. 13, 15.
88. André Chastel & Jean Guillaume, eds, *L'Escalier dans l'architecture de la Renaissance* (Paris, Picard, 1985), pp. 60–61, 176.
89. Wotton, p. 57.
90. *Ibid.*, pp. 58–9.
91. Pratt, p. 57.
92. Bacon, pp. 92–3.

## Chapter 5
## The Second Great Rebuilding in town and country

1. Evelyn, p. 754.
2. Mark Girouard, *The English Town* (New Haven & London, Yale University Press, 1990), p. 157.
3. North, p. 25.
4. John Bold, The design of a house for a merchant, 1724, *Architectural History*, **33**, 1990, pp. 75–82.
5. North, p. 25.
6. *Ibid.*, p. 26 (footnote).
7. Bold, The design of a house for a merchant, p. 80.
8. North, pp. 25–6.
9. Geoffrey Webb, ed., *The complete works of Sir John Vanbrugh* (London, Nonesuch Press, 1928), vol. 4, pp. 24–5.
10. *Bedfordshire*, 1968, p. 280.
11. For a recent summary of the urban evidence, see Peter Borsay, *The English urban Renaissance. Culture and society in the provincial town 1660–1770* (Oxford, Clarendon Press, 1989), pp. 47–9 and *passim*; and see also Alan Dyer, Urban housing: a documentary study of four Midland towns 1530–1700, *Post-Medieval Archaeology*, **15**, 1981, p. 217 and *passim*.
12. C. H. Williams, ed., *English historical documents 1485–1558* (London, Eyre & Spottiswoode, 1967), p. 189.
13. *The Taming of the Shrew*, ii: i: 338–48; as quoted by Jeremy Lake, *The great fire of Nantwich* (Nantwich, Shiva Publishing, 1983), p. 113.
14. R. G. Lang, Social origins and social aspirations of Jacobean London merchants, *Economic History Review*, **27**, 1974, pp. 28–47; and see also Patrick McGrath, ed., *Merchants and merchandise in seventeenth-century Bristol*, Bristol Record Society **19**, 1955, pp. xxxi–xxxii, for the same reluctance to retreat to the country in later life.
15. Priscilla Metcalf, Living over the shop in the City of London, *Architectural History*, **27**, 1984, pp. 96–103.
16. Aubrey, vol. 2, p. 298.
17. Patrick McGrath, *John Whitson and the merchant community of Bristol*, Bristol Historical Association Pamphlets **25**, 1970, pp. 13–14; and the same author's *Merchants and*

*merchandise in seventeenth-centry Bristol*, pp. 80–89.

18. McGrath, *John Whitson and the merchant community of Bristol*, pp. 18–19.

19. *Ibid.*, p. 18.

20. Eric Mercer, *English vernacular houses. A study of traditional farmhouses and cottages* (London, HMSO, 1975), pp. 61–6; J. T. Smith, *English houses 1200–1800. The Hertfordshire evidence* (London, Her Majesty's Stationery Office, 1992), pp. 162–3; for the plan's sixteenth-century rural origins, see Anthony Quiney, The lobby-entrance house: its origin and distribution, *Architectural History*, **27**, 1984, pp. 456–66.

21. Said by a Swiss visitor and quoted by Peter Earle, *The making of the English middle class. Business, society and family life in London, 1660–1730* (London, Methuen, 1989), p. 331.

22. Quoted by Borsay, *The English urban renaissance*, p. 223.

23. Quoted by Earle (*The making of the English middle class*, p. 275) from Misson's *Mémoires et observations faites par un voyageur en Angleterre* (The Hague, 1698).

24. C. W. Chalklin, *The provincial towns of Georgian England. A study of the building process 1740–1820* (London, Edward Arnold, 1974), p. 17.

25. Earle, *The making of the English middle class*, ch. 5: Investment.

26. Stefan Muthesius, *The English terraced house* (New Haven & London, Yale University Press, 1982), p. 3. Representative plans of London's terraced houses, including a house in Bloomsbury Square, are usefully described and illustrated by A. F. Kelsall, The London house plan in the later 17th century, *Post-Medieval Archaeology*, **8**, 1974, pp. 80–91.

27. North, p. 25.

28. Sylvia Collier, *Whitehaven 1660–1800* (London, HMSO, 1991), p. 41.

29. *Ibid.*, pp. 80–81.

30. *Ibid.*, p. 41.

31. For the case of the Midlands, see Dyer, Urban housing, p. 209.

32. Joseph Hunter, ed., *The diary of Ralph Thoresby FRS* (London, Henry Colburn & Richard Bentley, 1830), vol. 1, p. 14.

33. John Ray, *Observations. Topographical, moral, & physiological; made in a journey through part of the Low-Countries, Germany, Italy, and France* (London, 1673), p. 397.

34. Robert Midgley, *Remarks in the grand tour of France and Italy. Perform'd by a person of quality, in the year, 1691* (London, 1705), 2nd edn, p. 10.

35. Aubrey, vol. 2, p. 329.

36. Evelyn, p. 573.

37. John Freeman, ed., *Thomas Fuller. The worthies of England* (London, George Allen & Unwin, 1952), p. 258.

38. R. Machin, *The houses of Yetminster* (Bristol, University of Bristol, Department of Extra-Mural Studies, 1978), especially pp. 156–7.

39. Linda Hall, Yeoman or gentleman? Problems in defining social status in seventeenth- and eighteenth-century Gloucestershire, *Vernacular Architecture*, **22**, 1991, pp. 2–19; and for the houses, see the same author's *The rural houses of North Avon and South Gloucestershire 1400–1720* (Bristol, Museum and Art Gallery, 1983), *passim*.

40. Hall, Yeoman or gentleman?, p. 16.

41. Felicity Heal, *Hospitality in early modern England* (Oxford, Clarendon Press, 1990), pp. 385–8.

42. Hall, Yeoman or gentleman?, p. 6.

43. R. C. Allen, Inferring yields from probate inventories, *Journal of Economic History*,

48, 1988, pp. 117–25; for the country as a whole, see R.V. Jackson, Growth and deceleration in English agriculture, 1660–1790, *Economic History Review*, **38**, 1985, pp. 333–51.

44. Derek Portman, Vernacular building in the Oxford region, in *Rural change and urban growth 1500–1800*, eds C. W. Chalklin & M. A. Havinden (London, Longman, 1974), p. 163; Raymond B. Wood-Jones, *Traditional domestic architecture of the Banbury region* (Manchester, Manchester University Press, 1963), ch. 6: Later developments of the regional house 1646–1700.

45. Wood-Jones, *Traditional domestic architecture of the Banbury region*, p. 109.

46. Peter Smith, Some reflections on the development of the centrally-planned house, in *Collectanea historica. Essays in memory of Stuart Rigold*, ed. Alec Detsicas (Maidstone, Kent Archaeological Society, 1981), pp. 193, 197.

47. Peter Smith, *Houses of the Welsh countryside. A study in historical geography* (London, HMSO, 1975), pp. 233–6.

48. North, p. 116.

49. Smith, Some reflections on the development of the centrally-planned house, p. 193.

50. *Rural houses of West Yorkshire, 1400–1830* (Royal Commission on Historical Monuments, 1986), p. 130.

51. As the dying John of Gaunt's vision of England, in Shakespeare's *King Richard the Second*, II: i: 40–68.

52. Defoe, vol. 2, pp. 193–4.

53. *Rural houses of West Yorkshire*, pp. 112, 124.

54. Defoe, vol. 2, p. 195.

55. For this house-type, characteristic of the Halifax region, see Mercer, *English vernacular houses*, pp. 14–16.

56. *Rural houses of West Yorkshire*, p. 213.

57. *Ibid.*, p. 136.

58. Christopher Nettleton, of Ryecroft in Tong (1669), was the exception (*ibid.*, pp. 136, 219).

59. *Ibid.*, pp. 166–7; *Rural houses of the Lancashire Pennines, 1560–1760* (Royal Commission on Historical Monuments, 1985), pp. 69–74. Rebuilding his house in Restoration Lancashire, it has recently been calculated, would have cost the yeoman farmer about £100: "for his money he would get a house, parlour, kitchen and buttery, an inside staircase, one good hearth and chimney on the end wall, or possibly a double hearth on the inside wall, three divided rooms or a long loft upstairs, and a barn attached." (M. E. Garnett, The Great Rebuilding and economic change in South Lonsdale 1600–1730, *Transactions of the Historic Society of Lancashire and Cheshire*, **137**, 1987, p. 70).

60. Both quoted by J. A. Sharpe, *Early modern England, A social history 1550–1760* (London, Edward Arnold, 1987), p. 201.

61. North, pp. 122–3.

62. Cary Carson, Segregation in vernacular buildings, *Vernacular Architecture*, **7**, 1976, pp. 24–5, 27.

63. Barry Harrison & Barbara Hutton, *Vernacular houses in North Yorkshire and Cleveland* (Edinburgh, John Donald, 1984), pp. 77–8.

64. *Rural houses of the Lancashire Pennines*, 1985, pp. 98–100, 134–5, 157.

65. Quoted by Ann Kussmaul, *Servants in husbandry in early modern England* (Cambridge, Cambridge University Press, 1981), p. 40.

66. Margaret Spufford, *Contrasting communities. English villagers in the sixteenth and seventeenth centuries* (Cambridge, Cambridge University Press, 1974), pp. 36–41.

67. As quoted by Eric Kerridge, *The farmers of Old England* (London, Allen & Unwin, 1973), pp. 137–8.

68. David G. Hey, *An English rural community. Myddle under the Tudors and Stuarts* (Leicester, Leicester University Press, 1974), pp. 97–102; Richard Gough, *The history of Myddle* (1700–1706) (Firle, Sussex, Caliban Books, 1979), pp. 32–3.

69. Hey, *An English rural community*, p. 124.

70. Lorna Weatherill, *Consumer behaviour and material culture in Britain, 1660–1760* (London, Routledge, 1988), p. 172.

71. Defoe, vol. 2, p. 251; for post-Civil War Whickham and the north-east coalfield, see John Hatcher, *The history of the British coal industry. Volume I. Before 1700: Towards the age of coal* (Oxford, Clarendon Press, 1993), pp. 88–96.

72. Hey, *An English rural community*, p. 126.

73. David Levine & Keith Wrightson, *The making of an industrial society. Whickham 1560–1765* (Oxford, Clarendon Press, 1991), pp. 231–41: Goods.

74. *Ibid.*, p. 233.

75. *Ibid.*, p. 235.

76. *Ibid.*, p. 239.

77. Francis W. Steer, ed., *Farm and cottage inventories of mid-Essex 1635–1749* (London and Chichester, Phillimore, 1969), 2nd edn, pp. 198–202.

78. *Ibid.*, pp. 207–9; Bird is styled "gentleman" in an earlier inventory of 1684, when appraising the goods of John Taverner (pp. 172–3).

79. Karl D. Bülbring, ed., *The compleat English gentleman by Daniel Defoe* (London, David Nutt, 1890), pp. 20–21.

80. *Ibid.*, p. 102.

81. *Ibid.*, p. 104.

## Chapter 6
## Neat compact boxes

1. Barry Coward, *Social change and continuity in early modern England 1550–1750* (London, Longman, 1988), pp. 43, 48.

2. Joan Thirsk, Younger sons in the seventeenth century, *History*, **54**, 1969, p. 359; and see also the same author's The European debate on customs of inheritance, 1500–1700, in *Family and inheritance. Rural society in Western Europe, 1200–1800,* eds Jack Goody, Joan Thirsk and E. P. Thompson (Cambridge, Cambridge University Press, 1976), pp. 177–91.

3. Gottfried von Bülow, ed., Journey through England and Scotland made by Leopold von Wedel in the years 1584 and 1585, *Transactions of the Royal Historical Society*, **9**, 1895, p. 268.

4. Karl D. Bülbring, ed., *The compleat English gentleman by Daniel Defoe* (London, David Nutt, 1890), pp. 50–51.

5. Thirsk, Younger sons in the seventeenth century, pp. 361, 374–5.

6. Ralph Houlbrooke, *The English family 1450–1700* (London, Longman, 1984), pp. 52–3.

7. *Ibid.*, p. 42; Dorothy Gardiner, ed., *The Oxinden letters 1607–1642* (London, Con-

stable, 1933), pp. 114–15.

8. Gardiner, *The Oxinden letters*, pp. xxiv–xxix; for Richard Oxinden's will (1629), see *The Genealogist*, **37**, 1921, p. 148.

9. *The Genealogist*, **8**, 1893, p. 152.

10. *Ibid.*, **38**, 1922, pp. 251–2.

11. Gardiner, *The Oxinden letters*, p. 98.

12. *The Genealogist*, **8**, 1898, p. 151; for this and some comparisons, see Malcolm Airs, *The making of the English country house 1500–1640* (London, Architectural Press, 1975), pp. 86–90.

13. *North East and East Kent*, 1983, pp. 165–7 and plate 81.

14. *The Genealogist*, **8**, 1893, pp. 150–51.

15. Gardiner, *The Oxinden letters*, pp. 139–40. It would be nice to think that the little poem which ends Henry Oxinden's notebook relates to this same occasion, though the reference to Oxinden's illness makes this less likely:

> Thrice wellcome Noble Sr you be
> Unto your Mansion House, & mee,
> Which joyes with mee to see you there
> With glory shine in your own sphere:
> Where if you stay I shall be well
> Although how soon I can not tell,
> But certain tis I shall not die
> Whilst you at Broome I may espie,
> Nor underground shall ever sink
> Whilst I your Mallago can drink.
>     (*The Genealogist*, **38**, 1922, p. 253)

16. Edward Hasted, *The history and topographical survey of the county of Kent* (Wakefield, EP Publishing, 1972), reprint of 2nd edn (1797–1801), vol. 6, p. 484; and see also Sir Roger Twysden's comment in Kevin Sharpe's *The personal rule of Charles I* (New Haven and London, Yale University Press, 1992), p. 566.

17. *North-East and East Kent*, 1983, pp. 370–71 and plate 82; Hasted, *The history and topographical survey*, vol. 6, p. 484.

18. Oxinden gives the date as 6 October, and another hand has noted against this entry: "The two brothers Sondes quarrelled about a Scarlet Coat" (*The Genealogist*, **8**, 1893, p. 103).

19. Quoted by Thirsk, Younger sons in the seventeenth century, p. 372.

20. Quoted by Alan Everitt, *The community of Kent and the Great Rebellion 1640–1660* (Leicester, Leicester University Press, 1966), p. 51; and see also Hasted, *The history and topographical survey*, vol. 6, p. 485.

21. Quoted by Felicity Heal, *Hospitality in early modern England* (Oxford, Clarendon Press, 1990), p. 119.

22. From the proclamation of 9 December 1615 (James F. Larkin & Paul L. Hughes, eds, *Stuart royal proclamations. Volume I, 1603–25* (Oxford, Clarendon Press, 1973), p. 357).

23. Paul L. Hughes & James F. Larkin, eds, *Tudor royal proclamations*, 3 vols (Oxford, Clarendon Press, 1964–9), vol. 3, pp. 171–2.

24. W. C. Hazlitt, ed., *Inedited tracts: illustrating the manners, opinions and occupations of Englishmen during the sixteenth and seventeenth centuries* (London, Chiswick Press, for Roxburghe Library, 1868), pp. 57–8.

25. Larkin & Hughes, *Stuart royal proclamations*, pp. 356–7. But see also for this whole argument Felicity Heal, The crown, the gentry and London: the enforcement of proclamation, 1596–1640, in *Law and government under the Tudors. Essays presented to Sir Geoffrey Elton*, eds Claire Cross *et al.* (Cambridge, Cambridge University Press, 1988), pp. 211–26.

26. As quoted from James Cleland's *The institution of a young noble man* (1607) by Malcolm Airs, The designing of five East Anglian country houses, 1505–1637, *Architectural History*, **21**, 1978, p. 56.

27. Linda Campbell, Documentary evidence for the building of Raynham Hall, *Architectural History*, **32**, 1989, pp. 52–63.

28. North, p. 76.

29. The portal predates William Kent's remodelling of 1720–30. For a date "any time between 1671 and *c.* 1700", see John Harris, Raynham Hall, *Archaeological Journal*, **118**, 1961, pp. 180–87; for *c.*1680, see Nikolaus Pevsner's account of the house (*North-West and South Norfolk*, 1962, p. 150). John Harris was the first to identify and publish the drawings of 1671 which show Raynham at the time of Charles II's visit.

30. James E. Larkin, ed., *Stuart royal proclamations. Volume II, 1625–1646* (Oxford, Clarendon Press, 1983), pp. 350–53.

31. Campbell, Documentary evidence for the building of Raynham Hall, p. 59.

32. Bülbring, *The compleat English gentleman*, pp. 122–41.

33. *Ibid.*, pp. 124–5; for the general context of Sir A. B.'s purchases, see Iain Pears, *The discovery of painting. The growth of interest in the arts in England 1680–1768* (New Haven & London, Yale University Press, 1988), ch. 2: Taste.

34. Bülbring, *The compleat English gentleman*, pp. 134–41.

35. *Ibid.*, pp. 141–2, 225; for representative plans of contemporary compact houses, see Alison Maguire & Howard Colvin, A collection of seventeenth-century architectural plans, *Architectural History*, **35**, 1992, pp. 140–69 and figs 1–41.

36. Marjorie Keniston McIntosh, *A community transformed. The manor and liberty of Havering, 1500–1620* (Cambridge, Cambridge University Press, 1991), pp. 34–42; for the very similar ratios in early seventeenth-century Cambridge, see Nigel Goose, Household size and structure in early-Stuart Cambridge, *Social History*, **5**, 1980, pp. 365–70 (household size by socio-occupational group).

37. Houlbrooke, *The English family*, p. 20 and *passim*.

38. As quoted by Alan Macfarlane in *The origins of English individualism* (Oxford, Blackwell, 1978), p. 75, and again in *Marriage and love in England* (Oxford, Blackwell, 1986), pp. 94–5.

39. For the more extreme opinions of some other Puritan divines of the Civil War period, see Christopher Durston, *The family in the English Revolution* (Oxford, Blackwell, 1989), ch. 2: The debate on the family.

40. William Whateley, *A bride-bush. Or, a direction for married persons* (London, 1623), pp. 42–4.

41. *Ibid.*, pp. 31, 216.

42. Hartley Thwaite, ed., *Abstracts of Abbotside wills 1552–1688*, Yorkshire Archaeological Society Record Series **130**, 1968, pp. 9–10.

43. Peter Smith, *Houses of the Welsh countryside* (London, HMSO, 1975), pp. 166–8; J. T. Smith, Lancashire and Cheshire houses: some problems of architectural and social history, *Archaeological Journal*, **127**, 1970, pp. 156–81; Cary Carson, Segregation in

vernacular buildings, *Vernacular Architecture*, **7**, 1976, pp. 24–9; R. Machin, *The houses of Yetminster* (Bristol, University of Bristol, 1978), pp. 117–24; and J. T. Smith, *English houses 1200–1800. The Hertfordshire evidence* (London, HMSO, 1992), pp. 106–11. Joint tenancies and divided houses are given more prominence by R. Machin, The unit system: some historical explanations, *Archaeological Journal*, **132**, 1975, pp. 187–94; while the intended permanence of at least some of those divisions is emphasized in the same issue of that journal by K. L. Sandall, The unit system in Essex, *ibid.*, pp. 195–201 and plates XIX–XX.

44. Thwaite, *Abstracts of Abbotside wills*, pp. 26–7.

45. *Ibid.*, pp. 61–2.

46. *Ibid.*, p. 80.

47. *Ibid.*, pp. 120–21.

48. Coward, *Social change and continuity in early modern England*, pp. 19–20.

49. E. A. Wrigley & R. S. Schofield, *The population history of England 1541–1871* (London, Edward Arnold, 1981), pp. 210–13.

50. Henry B. Wheatley, ed., *The diary of Samuel Pepys* (London, G. Bell & Sons, 1928), vol. 1, p. 222.

51. Joseph Hunter, ed., *The diary of Ralph Thoresby FRS* (London, Henry Colburn & Richard Bentley, 1830), vol. 1, p. 333. For the extinction of a gentry line, the Cocks of Dumbleton (Gloucestershire), see Christopher Clay, Landlords and estate management in England, 1640–1750, in *Chapters from the agrarian history of England and Wales 1500–1750. Volume 2,* ed. Christopher Clay (Cambridge, Cambridge University Press, 1990), p. 295.

52. Miriam Slater, *Family life in the seventeenth century. The Verneys of Claydon House* (London, Routledge & Kegan Paul, 1984), p. 138. But see Alan Macfarlane's critical essay on Lawrence Stone's *The family, sex and marriage in England 1500–1800* in *History and Theory*, **18**, 1979, pp. 103–26.

53. William Bray, ed., *Diary of John Evelyn Esq., F. R. S.* (London, Bickers & Son, 1879), vol. 3, pp. 219–21.

54. Evelyn, pp. 384–8, 794–803.

55. *Ibid.*, p. 797.

56. *Ibid.*, p.327; for Evelyn's garden designs at Wotton and Sayes Court, see Roy Strong, *The Renaissance garden in England* (London, Thames & Hudson, 1979), pp. 220–22 and plates 143–4.

57. Evelyn, p. 452.

58. *Ibid.*, pp. 1–3.

59. *Ibid.*, p.47; for the remains of the Evelyns' garden at Wotton, see *Surrey*, 1971, pp. 543–4.

60. Evelyn, pp. 276–7.

61. Pratt, pp. 3, 23; and for a more extended discussion of Roger Pratt and his ideas, see also Chapter 3 above.

62. *Ibid.*, pp. 4–8.

63. Evelyn, p. 316.

64. *Ibid.*, pp. 72–4, 327; and see also William Howard Adams, *The French garden 1500–1800* (London, Scolar Press, 1979), pp. 57–8.

65. K. G. Ponting, ed., *Aubrey's natural history of Wiltshire* (Newton Abbott, David & Charles, 1969), p. 83.

66. Evelyn, pp. 342–3.

67. *Ibid.*, p. 653.

68. *Ibid.*, p.757; and see above for a fuller development of this theme in Chapter 4: The Grand Tour house.

69. North, p. 71.

70. *Ibid.*, p. 68.

71. *Ibid.*, pp. 68–9.

72. *Ibid.*, p. 69.

73. *Ibid.*, pp. 69–70; for the debate about the date of Chevening – whether built in the 1650s or before Lord Dacre's death in 1630 – see Oliver Hill & John Cornforth, *English country houses. Caroline 1625–1685* (London, Country Life, 1966), pp. 25–6; Giles Worsley, in associating Chevening with Forty Hall (Middlesex) of 1629–36 and St Clere (Kent) of *c.*1633, is evidently inclined to accept both the pre-1630 date and Chevening's origins in the later Serlian manner – the astylar compact double pile – of Inigo Jones (Inigo Jones: lonely genius or practical exemplar?, *Journal of the British Archaeological Association*, **146**, 1993, pp. 110–11).

74. *West Kent and the Weald*, 1969, pp. 202–5. Nicholas Dubois (d.1735), commissioned by Stanhope's widow in 1721, was a contemporary of Colen Campbell and became one of England's leading Palladians.

75. North, p. 69.

76. Walpole, pp. 25–6.

77. Howard Colvin, *A biographical dictionary of British architects 1600–1840* (London, John Murray, 1978), pp. 337–45: Gibbs, 489–94: Kent, and 848–54: Vanbrugh.

78. Harrison, p. 114; and see above, Chapter 3: Social space, for the very similar views of Roger Ascham.

79. Lawrence Stone, *Family and fortune. Studies in aristocratic finance in the sixteenth and seventeenth centuries* (Oxford, Clarendon Press, 1973), pp. 140, 152–62; for other examples of heavy losses associated with the Civil War, see Barbara English, *The great landowners of East Yorkshire 1530–1910* (London, Harvester Press, 1990), pp. 20–21, 130–35.

80. Wrigley & Schofield, *The population history of England*, p. 212.

81. Christopher Clay, *Economic expansion and social change: England 1500–1700* (Cambridge, Cambridge University Press, 1984), vol. 1, pp. 58–64; and see also Coward, *Social change and continuity in early modern England*, pp. 46–8.

82. John Broad, The Verneys as enclosing landlords, 1600–1800, in *English rural society, 1500–1800. Essays in honour of Joan Thirsk*, eds John Chartres & David Hey (Cambridge, Cambridge University Press, 1990), pp. 34–6.

83. Clay, *Landlords and estate management in England*, pp. 317–18.

84. Evelyn, p. 585.

85. North, pp. 25–6.

86. Osmund Airy, ed., *Burnet's history of my own time* (Oxford, Clarendon Press, 1897), vol. 1, pp. 444–5.

87. *Ibid.*, vol. 1, p. 446.

88. For the ferocity of contemporary comment, see Andrew Marvell's two satirical poems, "Clarindon's House-Warming" and "Upon his House", in *The poems and letters of Andrew Marvell*, ed. H. M. Margoliouth (London, Oxford University Press, 1971), vol. 1, pp. 143–7.

89. P. J. Drury, *No other palace in the kingdom will compare with it*: The evolution of Audley End, 1605–1745, *Architectural History*, **23**, 1980, p. 3 and *passim*.

90. Bray, *Diary of John Evelyn*, vol. 3, p. 340; and see above, Chapter 3: Social space, for the full quotation and for the further comments of both Evelyn and Pepys.

# Credits

**Abbreviations**

Courtauld   The Conway Library, Courtauld Institute of Art
RCHME      Royal Commission on the Historical Monuments of England: National
           Buildings Record
RIBA       Royal Institute of British Architects: the British Architectural Library, Draw-
           ings Collection


1. House in Mermaid Street, Rye (A. F. Kersting)
2. Chimney at Grange Farm, Radwinter (Claire Donovan)
3. Farmhouse at Barrington (RCHME)
4. Gullege, East Grinstead (John Kelly)
5. North Cadbury Court (A. F. Kersting)
6. The Triangular Lodge, Rushton (A. F. Kersting)
7. Farmhouse at Glemsford (A. F. Kersting)
8. Wollaton Hall (Yale Center for British Art)
9. Farmhouse at Hornton (RCHME)
10. Euston Hall (by kind permission of the Duke of Grafton: photograph – Courtauld
    Institute of Art)
11. Hatfield House (RCHME and Society of Antiquaries, London)
12. Coleshill House (Southampton University Cartographic Unit: re-drawn from the
    plans in R. T. Gunther, ed., *The architecture of Sir Roger Pratt* (Oxford, Oxford Uni-
    versity Press, 1928)
13. Belton House (A. F. Kersting)
14. The main stair at Tyttenhanger House (RCHME)
15. The second stair at Tyttenhanger House (RCHME)
16. The State Dining Room at Chatsworth (A. F. Kersting)
17. Samuel van Hoogstraeten, *A view down a corridor*, 1662 (National Trust Photographic
    Library)
18. Bird's-eye view of Chatsworth (Courtauld)

62. Soho Square, London, in c.1725 (Guildhall Library, Corporation of London)
63. Matthias Read's prospect of Whitehaven (Yale Center for British Art)
64. Merchant houses in Howgill Street, Whitehaven (RCHME)
65. Staircase at Gaytons, Much Hadham (RCHME)
66. Upper Calderdale in 1845 (Central Library, Halifax)
67. High Bentley Farmhouse, Calderdale (Southampton University Cartographic Unit: (c) RCHME Crown Copyright)
68. Sarsden House in the 1690s (Mervyn Macartney, *English houses and gardens in the 17th and 18th centuries. A series of bird's-eye views* (London, Batsford, 1908), plate XX)
69. Broome Park, Barham, in c.1720 (*ibid.*, plate XVII)
70. The south range at Lees Court (RCHME)
71. Plans of the Duke of Beaufort's London lodgings (Bodleian Library, Oxford, MS Rawl. D.710, fol. 88r)
72. The west (entrance) front of Raynham Hall in 1671 (RIBA)
73. The east front of Raynham Hall (A. F. Kersting)
74. Bird's-eye view of Sir Robert Atkyns's seat at Swell (Courtauld)
75. Samuel Pepys's library in c.1690 (the Master and Fellows, Magdalene College, Cambridge)
76. Dairy Farmhouse, Tacolneston (RCHME)
77. Chevening, from an estate map of 1679 (Courtauld)
78. William Kent's arcaded terrace at Rousham (A. F. Kersting)

## Permissions

I acknowledge with gratitude the permission of the National Buildings Record (RCHME) to publish a redrawing of the plans of High Bentley from *Rural houses of West Yorkshire 1400–1830* (1986), figs 52 and 143; also of Oxford University Press to use extracts from E. S. de Beer, ed., *The diary of John Evelyn* (1959), and Howard Colvin & John Newman, eds, *Of building. Roger North's writings on architecture* (1981). I owe the Rawlinson plans of Beaufort's London lodgings (71) to Alison Maguire who first published them (with Howard Colvin) in *Architectural History*, **35**, 1992, fig. 15.

# Index